PRAISE FOR *HOW T[*

"*How to Buy a Gorilla* can change the relationship between those who buy and those who sell marketing services ... if you let it. Insightful, practical and readable, it's a highly recommended handbook for one of marketing's toughest challenges."
Mark Earls, aka HERDmeister, author of *HERD*,
I'll Have What She's Having and *Copy, Copy, Copy*

"The greatest challenge of any marketing leader is getting and motivating the right agency talent to work on their briefs. I've benefitted from David's expertise first hand and I know it works. Now that it's written down in *How to Buy a Gorilla* this toughest of challenges just got a lot easier."
Stewart Fox Mills, Commercial Director, Abellio UK

"The marketers who win are those who are brave. Thought-provoking and insightful, David's book is packed with practical tools to help you develop bold marketing ideas and build the business case for bravery. An indispensable guide."
Gemma Greaves, Chief Executive, The Marketing Society, and Founder, Cabal

"For agencies and marketers looking to build higher trust and improve mutual performance, *How to Buy a Gorilla* builds a convincing case for the interdependent roles of trust and control, incentives and behaviour, and risk and reward. Most importantly, David Meikle unpeels the true nature of knowledge work, showing how buyers of marketing services can avoid paying the same price for 'eureka moments' and 'busy fools'."
Tim Williams, Founding Partner, Ignition Group

"With a humour and humanity so often missing from 'how to' business books, David Meikle applies wisdom and clarity of thought to the vexing subject of procuring creativity. A timely and much needed contribution to a debate that directly concerns all marketers and their agencies."
Tom Knox, President, Institute of Practitioners in Advertising,
and Chairman, MullenLowe London

"The 'Mexican standoff' so commonly keeping marketing, procurement and agencies in a state of mutual mistrust hitherto seemed irreconcilable. Unlike most standoffs which end with winners and losers, in *How to Buy a Gorilla* David cleverly shows how marketing, procurement and agencies can collaborate in more trusting, more productive and more effective ways in order to mutually prosper. This is the book marketers and agencies didn't know they were waiting for!"
Antonis Kocheilas, Managing Partner, Global Client Strategy, Ogilvy

"David Meikle has written the ultimate book on how to strategically source agency services. *How to Buy a Gorilla* should be on the shelf of every marketing procurement manager – and it should be dog-eared from constant use!"
Gerry Preece, External View Consulting and former
Director of Marketing Procurement, Procter & Gamble

"*How to Buy a Gorilla* is one of the few books I have read that really grasps the complexity of agency selection in today's world. David captures the essence of not just buying, but also building relationships with, external talent. Of course, there are a few tips there for agencies, too, as I believe it's invaluable for agencies to view the issues from the advertiser's perspective. A book that will change the way you think about the agency/client relationship."
Jenny Biggam, Founder, the7stars

"Getting great work is hard and usually only happens when the various stars align. *How to Buy a Gorilla* offers an unusually perceptive assessment of the client/agency dynamic, and correctly identifies the need to align on ambition and appetite for risk as the foundation of any high performing relationship. It then backs this up with some great tools and advice to help create the ecosystem required for creativity to flourish."
Phil Rumbol, buyer of the original Cadbury's Gorilla

"As much as great market intelligence and research are vital, they still require great agency talent to turn them into an effective strategy and a powerful creative idea. *How to Buy a Gorilla* is one of the most comprehensive approaches not only to find the right agency, but how to identify, motivate and work with the right talent. Essential reading for all marketers."
Debrah Harding, Managing Director, Market Research Society

"We have more evidence than ever of creativity's contribution to business growth. There's nothing for a marketer to fear – unless their competitors have this book and they themselves don't."
John Kearon, CEO, System1 Group

"The most comprehensive and convincing explanation for why clients so rarely get the advertising they want. Bravo!"
Blair Enns, author of *The Win Without Pitching Manifesto*

"In an area that's too often full of sound, fury, bitterness and recrimination, David Meikle applies science and sense to the great advertising conundrum: how to produce an idea that will stop people in their tracks and that they'll remember forever? You would expect D&AD to heartily approve of this, and we do. It will provide invaluable insight, tools and processes to those with the good sense to read it."
Tim Lindsay, CEO, D&AD

"David Meikle argues persuasively that a brand's ambitiousness and risk profile are strategic considerations, which can also help to refine the alignment of client and agency interests and so improve outcomes for all. It's about horses for courses – except they're monkeys."
David Abrahams, Director, Brand Mediation, and author of *Brand Risk – Adding Risk Literacy to Brand Management*

"With his unique three-way perspective, David Meikle explains why the historic standoff between advertising agencies, marketing and procurement is serving no one's interests satisfactorily and what needs to change on all sides. This is essential reading for anyone involved in the buying, managing or creation of advertising."
Tom Lewis, Finance Director, Institute of Practitioners in Advertising

"David Meikle's *How to Buy a Gorilla* is a refreshingly thoughtful, well informed and entertaining treatise on the eternal triangle of marketing, agency and procurement. In this, it is altogether rarer than gorillas themselves! Moreover, it provides a clear and actionable framework for all three protagonists to end their 'Mexican standoff' to the ultimate benefit of the brands they serve."
Nick Ford, Director Global Client Operations, WPP

Published by
LID Publishing Limited
The Record Hall, Studio 204,
16-16a Baldwins Gardens,
London EC1N 7RJ, UK

524 Broadway, 11th Floor, Suite 08-120,
New York, NY 10012, US

info@lidpublishing.com
www.lidpublishing.com

A member of:

BPR Business Publishers Roundtable

www.businesspublishersroundtable.com

All reasonable efforts have been made to obtain necessary copyright permissions. Any omissions or errors are unintentional and will, if brought to the attention of the author david@htbag.co.uk, be corrected in future printings.

Printed in Great Britain by TJ International
ISBN: 978-1-912555-31-4

Cover and page design: Matthew Renaudin and Caroline Li

DAVID MEIKLE

HOW TO BUY A GORILLA

THE ULTIMATE GUIDE TO SELECTING, PAYING AND WORKING WITH AGENCIES FOR MORE POWERFUL ADVERTISING

LONDON   NEW YORK   SHANGHAI
MADRID   BARCELONA   BOGOTA
MEXICO CITY   MONTERREY   BUENOS AIRES

CONTENTS

PART TWO

PART THREE

To James,

With best wishes,

Daniel.

For Olga and Daniel.

INTRODUCTION

On 31 August 2007, during the finale of *Big Brother*, several million people sat in a sort of transfixed bewilderment watching their televisions – during the commercial break. When the ad they were watching opened, the camera tracked across a purple screen subtly announcing that viewers were watching *A Glass and a Half Full Production*, until the tracking shot stopped on a close-up – literally a nostril shot – of what appeared to be a real gorilla. In the background, the strangely familiar introduction to Phil Collins' "In the Air Tonight" was playing, building anticipation for heaven only knew what. Viewers were gripped. Many were saying to themselves, "I love this song," others were saying, "I secretly love this song," but they were all asking themselves, "What the hell is going on?"

The gorilla was breathing slowly and heavily as the musical introduction continued; he was clearly focusing on the music. At one point, the camera seemed to get too close to his face for comfort – he flashed a gold tooth in a quick grimace to the camera as if to say, "Let me concentrate." (It can't be a real gorilla, can it?) Nonetheless, the camera slowly pulled back – out of fear or respect or both – as the music continued ...

Finally, the camera pulled right back and viewers could see that the gorilla was sitting behind a drum kit in a recording studio. Just then, he sprang to life, playing the opening drum break of "In the Air Tonight" with total concentration and commitment, combined with the strength that only a gorilla possesses.

Pack shot (Cadbury's Dairy Milk chocolate bar) and caption: "A glass and a half full of joy."

Across the nation hairs stood on end on the backs of the necks of millions. In addition to the reaction of the *Big Brother* viewers was the reaction of the advertising industry in immediate and profound admiration and envy at the same time. "How on earth did they get to make that?" And in the marketing community: "Why can't I get ads like that for my brand?" For the next two years, brands in the market for new agencies kept saying, "We want a gorilla."

For a while, 'Gorilla' became shorthand for high-impact, original, transformative creative work, and this is the shorthand I'm re-establishing.

Not because I would ever suggest a marketer should brief their agency by referencing somebody else's creative work – that would be exactly the wrong thing to do – but because gorillas are both almost hypnotic in the attention they demand, and (I use the word advisedly) awesome – they fill you with awe. If you ever happened across a gorilla in the wild, you would stop in your tracks with an overwhelming feeling of excitement and terror at the same time. So, I think it makes a suitable mnemonic for that kind of advertising – the kind of advertising that changes things. It doesn't mean any more than that for our purposes; it doesn't necessarily mean dramatic, or funny or something that goes viral or that it even needs to be long or short – it means transformative, engaging and effective, the stuff that stops viewers in their tracks.

Most big brands have the kind of business problem that would benefit from advertising that has this kind of effect – advertising that could achieve sales growth and make potential customers and consumers feel great about the brand being advertised. But the advertising and marketing industries seem to harbour a belief that developing these kinds of ideas is something serendipitous, that once in a blue moon the stars are aligned such that a great piece of advertising is born and that perhaps you were lucky enough to have had it born for your brand. The scarcity with which such transformative ideas come along would certainly support this fatalistic belief. However, if you were to ask copywriters and art directors in ad agencies if there is such a scarcity, they would agree that few have been made, but many have been written. Many Gorillas have been presented, but few have been bought. And of those Gorilla ideas that have been bought, few have gone into production uncompromised, retaining the same impact as had been originally intended and scripted. So, a large part of the reason such transformative ads are so rare is because the circumstances that allow such work to be made are so rarely created between a client and its agency.

How to Buy a Gorilla (or HTBAG) is a book that will help marketers take the fate of their advertising – i.e., whether or not they'll get a Gorilla – out of the lap of the gods and back under their control. It would be absolutely true to say that not all business problems require a Gorilla, so we will also look at how marketers can create the circumstances conducive to other kinds of advertising for other kinds of business problems. These will be characterized by two other primates: 'Spider Monkeys' and 'Orangutans'.

But the kind of problem a Gorilla can help solve is probably the most common. It is one where a market leader has an opportunity to grow its market share and, at the same time, fight off its competitors, large and small. So, we'll spend more of our time on Gorillas.

The central challenge for marketers is to better manage the irrefutable truth that is at the centre of the issue: a great brief doesn't guarantee a great campaign. The reason is that it is not just the brief but the environment in which it is being developed – the client/agency relationship – that influences its outcome.

NATURE VERSUS NURTURE

One of the oldest debates in the scientific community is over what determines human intelligence. Many psychologists and geneticists seem to have finally settled on a 50:50 attribution between 'nature' – the genetic make-up of an individual – and 'nurture' – the environment in which they grow up and from which they learn. Similarly, to think that a great brief is enough to get great, transformative advertising is not unlike a farmer believing his crops will succeed as long as he buys the right seed, regardless of the fertility of the soil, or the subsequent weather conditions it might experience, or the pesticides he might need to protect it as it grows, or when he might need to leave well enough alone. A farmer doesn't leave it to fate when his interventions can deliver a greater yield. Likewise, when great campaigns have been created, it hasn't been just luck that saw them to fruition, but the management of many variables in the client/agency relationship. As we will see, one of the greatest of these variables is access to the right agency talent. When Steve Jobs returned to Apple in 1997, he abandoned a pitch process they were running and appointed Chiat Day because he knew the talent that he needed was there – the result was the famous 'Think Different' campaign.

I believe that the marketing communications business – brands and agencies – can draw a useful parallel between how the scientific community has approached what determines intelligence and how clients and their agencies develop and produce their ideas. Therefore, when I refer to 'nurture' I am referring to all aspects of the client/agency relationship: the way clients pay their agencies, how much they pay them, the clients' processes and their behaviours. Because nurture is what affects the agency talent – and the better the nurture, the higher the calibre of talent a client brief will attract, and the more motivated the agency talent will be to deliver a Gorilla for them. But nurture can also be changed and the relationship altered so marketers can get the right kind of talent for the specific kind of advertising monkey they need. Some brands may need to play it safe (perhaps because there's no need *not* to play it safe, or perhaps because they don't want to cannibalize other parts of their own business); we'll call this the need for an Orangutan. On the other hand, some brands need to punch well above their weight because they can't afford to compete with the market leaders' media investments. We'll characterize this kind of advertising as a Spider Monkey. Accessing them all requires going through 'The Monkey House'.

So, starting with the business needs of the brands, The Monkey House will show you how to identify the monkey your brand needs and get the agency talent that can deliver it.

In addition, The Monkey House will show you how you can source and select the right kind of agency for your needs, how to manage the agency and keep its people motivated. It can also show you how to fix things if you're not happy with your agency's output/service.

———————

There's a straightforward logic to how The Monkey House works (see *figure 1*).

Figure 1

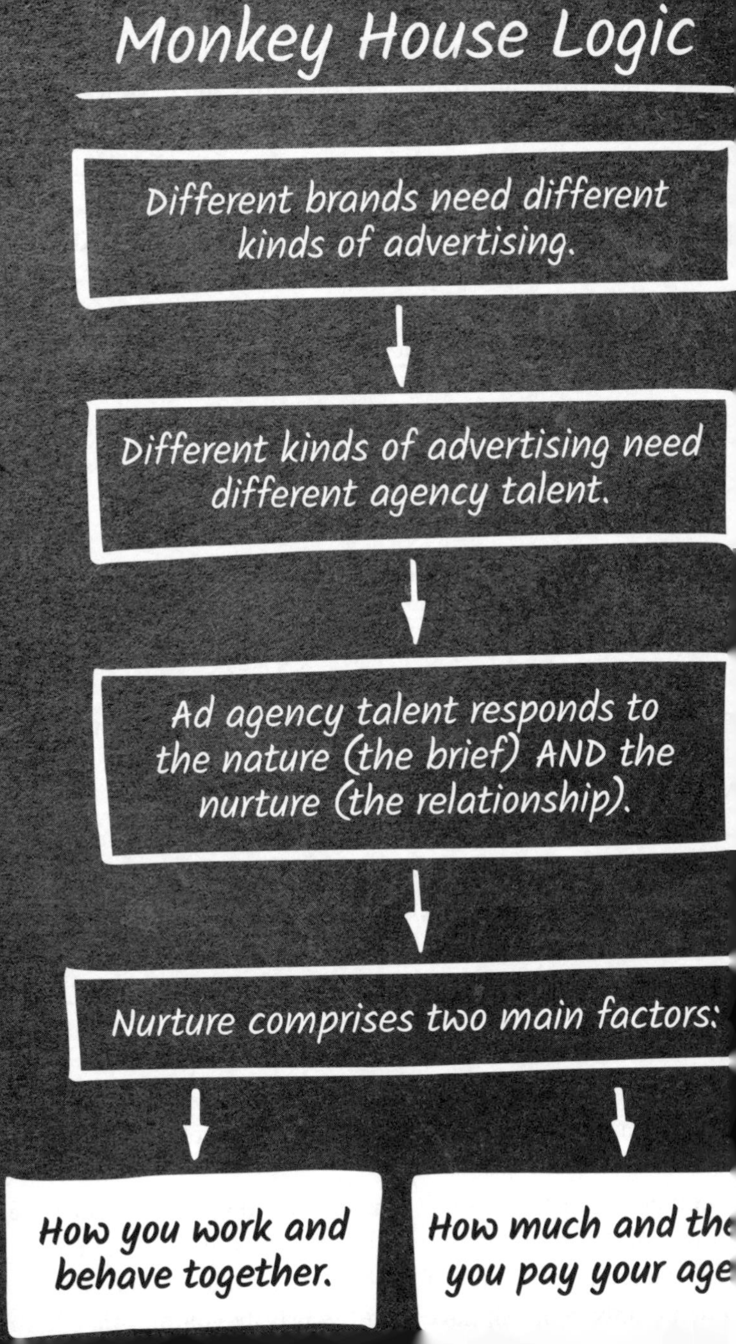

Monkey House Logic

Different brands need different kinds of advertising.

↓

Different kinds of advertising need different agency talent.

↓

Ad agency talent responds to the nature (the brief) AND the nurture (the relationship).

↓

Nurture comprises two main factors:

↓   ↓

How you work and behave together.

How much and the[...] you pay your age[...]

We'll start by characterizing three different kinds of brands' advertising needs – monkeys – as three different primates:

- The 'Gorilla' – usually higher media investment in a ubiquitous, breakthrough, transformative idea that stops you in your tracks.
- The 'Spider Monkey' – lower available media investment; therefore it must work that much harder to be noticed – distinctive, extraordinary.
- The 'Orangutan' – higher media investment for a more predictable return from a slower, steadier but powerful campaign.

And we'll use these characterizations as reminders of the kinds of nurture they each require; we'll extend my metaphor so that 'food' is symbolic of agency remuneration and 'training' symbolic of the client/ agency relationship:

Gorilla –
Good for: Growing market share and defending it from other Gorillas and Spider Monkeys.
Food: Feed it well; nobody wants a hungry Gorilla. Responds to significant rewards.
Training: Be respectful, listen and give it the freedom it needs to perform.

Spider Monkey –
Good for: Growing market share from a small base – stealing from Gorillas.
Food: Doesn't need a lot of food – but likes rewards.
Training: Needs much more stimulation, love, kindness and freedom to perform.

Orangutan –
Good for: Defending market share against other Orangutans.
Food: Feed it well, but just enough to keep it effective. Reward success.
Training: Give it clear objectives and exercise firm discipline as necessary.

When it comes to nurture, many (particularly big) advertisers have their own way of doing things. Anybody who has worked as a marketer or in an agency for the likes of Procter & Gamble or GlaxoSmithKline, to name only two, will have seen the private volumes they have published on their advertising campaign development and creative processes. These volumes include how to work with their agencies, find new agencies, pay them and so forth. The irony of 'their own way' is that the more I have experienced different clients in different countries and categories over the years, the more similar they appear to be in the way they shortlist, select and appoint agencies, manage agency relationships, employ development processes, pay and incentivize agencies – regardless of their differing needs and objectives on either a corporate or a brand level.

For companies with portfolios of different brands, there appears to be the same development processes, remuneration and incentives for their agencies, regardless of the differing needs of an individual brand. In much the same way, pressing all children to conform by enforcing the same methods and teachings, regardless of their individual talents, will not get the best from them; brand owners having their own way inhibits the potential of each brand if it doesn't suit that particular established procedure or set of rules.

Each monkey[1] needs to be nurtured differently. The challenge for today's marketer is to do some things differently in order to nurture the outcome they desire.

But marketers are not alone in creating the nurturing environment. The introduction of procurement into the mix has added a third dimension to this relationship. What used to be an agency/marketing two-way relationship is now an agency/marketing/procurement triangle. More challenging still, each corner of the triangle often has a different agenda from the other two.

To elaborate: agencies need to make a reasonable margin (that's the point of being in business), produce good advertising and attract/retain clients and talent. Marketers often believe agencies are wilfully inefficient (because they charge by the hour) and only want great creative work to demonstrate their own prowess, and not for the benefit of the client's brand. Procurement people often think that agencies are profligate rip-off merchants and that marketers are flaky. Plus, procurement is commonly incentivized to take as much money from both marketing and agencies as they can justify or achieve.

Yet, together, these three parties are responsible for producing advertising in which the brands invest millions, or tens of millions, while the three don't have a clear, shared interest behind which they are all aligned and motivated. Furthermore, they are not aligned according to their specific circumstances and business objectives: they mostly do what they've always done – just a little bit harder or cheaper or faster.

The one thing that should be uniting marketing, procurement and agencies is the positive effect of marketing campaigns on the client's business. And much of the effort expended between these three groups is wasted because they have spent their time in conflict over how they do things instead of cooperating effectively and actually doing them.

But by characterizing the kind of advertising that brands need based on their market circumstances, we can use a framework to determine how best to nurture the relationship appropriately.

WELCOME TO THE MONKEY HOUSE

The Monkey House is a straightforward framework to help marketers, procurement and agencies design their relationship so they can best produce the advertising they need, according to the client's business problem. The Monkey House includes a selection of tools that can be used to diagnose a brand's current nurture practices and prescribe how to change them to suit the kind of advertising monkey the brand needs. The Monkey House can help that brand understand and navigate the appropriate selection, appointment, remuneration, management and motivation of their agencies. But each monkey has a different level of risk attached to it, which is part of the nature of any investment.

Risk is a crucial four-letter word here. Over the last couple of decades, and not least with the rise of procurement in the marketing category (whose profession has a primary role in risk management), agencies' fees have been in significant decline, and not without consequence. As brands' investments in their agencies have diminished (reduced fees), so therefore their returns must have diminished in a manner consistent with every principle of economics, unless they have somehow increased their risk. The Monkey House also helps brands identify where their risk might be. While marketers and their procurement counterparts might think that they have successfully negotiated the same value or even more value for less, in almost every circumstance they have (perhaps unwittingly) increased their risk instead, though it may not always be apparent how they have done it.

In most instances, I've set out three parallel tracks in this book of how clients work with, pay and motivate agencies, and how agencies respond to these stimuli. Each of these tracks matches a monkey, i.e., whether the client needs a Spider Monkey, a Gorilla or an Orangutan. But this is not to suggest that there is an equal need for these three tracks; advertised brands are not evenly distributed across these three sets of circumstances – far from it.

By setting out these three tracks in parallel, we can compare practices and strategies for client/agency relationships that will:

a) Serve as a broader range of comparison than our currently narrowing field of 'best-practice' offers.
b) Illustrate how the needs of these different circumstances require different kinds of relationships.
c) Most importantly, make explicitly clear that brands that need Gorillas or Spider Monkeys cannot avoid a greater degree of risk if they want to grow. They can spend money to mitigate it, they can move risk or hide it, but they cannot escape it.

So, most of our time will be spent on Gorillas, although looking at Spider Monkeys and Orangutans will be useful in order to illustrate their differences.

All of this might sound a little complex, but it will become much clearer. From my own experience, having spent most of my career managing integrated campaigns for different products – with different propositions, based on different consumer insights, expressed in all sorts of creative ways, through combinations of media channels for different audiences, with budgets ranging from the meagre to the king's ransom – I know that using The Monkey House framework is far less complex.

A NOTE TO READERS

Most business books are by authors with at least one or two heavyweight academic qualifications. I'm not one of them. Although I'm from an academic family, I enjoyed working for a living so much that my one gap year turned into two, and then somehow it turned into a career in advertising.

HTBAG and The Monkey House are not the result of a single piece of extensive research, but of multiple observations throughout my career. They are a selection of my own case studies and those of others. I believe the conclusions I have drawn to be self-evidently true, as do the many industry leaders with whom I have already shared this thinking. The arguments I make are pretty fundamental, so I have found that analogies and comparisons to our broader life experiences (beyond visiting the zoo) are often useful to illustrate my contentions, sometimes more useful than the case studies.

It is also important to note that case studies (most are located in chapter six) will illustrate how some or all of The Monkey House has been applied to the specific circumstances and needs of each case. The practices adopted in the case studies are not intended to be perfectly replicated by others, because the straight replication of one advertiser's practice to another's is exactly what HTBAG seeks to avoid. It will likely come as no surprise that the detailed financial aspects of the case studies are confidential and hence necessarily kept vague.

You will also notice that I'm not shy about using a number of generalizations. These have been necessary to create a useful framework broad enough to accommodate any client business problem while, somewhat paradoxically perhaps, specific enough to be useful. They are mostly generalizations about the state of the advertising and marketing industry – but a key principle of The Monkey House is that as much as I might generalize about the problems, we cannot generalize about the solutions. And although there will always be exceptions to these generalizations, that does not invalidate them per se.

My experience has predominantly been in creative advertising agencies and integrated agencies. Although I generally refer to these kinds of agencies, the insights I have discovered are applicable to other marketing services disciplines. However, the subtler differences between agency disciplines are too many to effectively nuance while staying sufficiently focused on the greater benefit of the generalization, so I make only occasional references to other marketing communications disciplines.

Also, all big creative agencies are not entirely alike, despite their surface appearance, such as geographical reach. For the purposes of The Monkey House, the agencies I refer to are the largest national and international creative agencies and agency networks – the big agencies that handle the big brands.

So, please don't be offended if you are an exception to my generalizations – I hope you are – but I sincerely doubt that a reader couldn't improve their situation by using The Monkey House, at least to some degree, by applying some of the ideas laid out in HTBAG. Likewise, The Monkey House will make you more acutely aware of how the others in the triangle are affecting your advertising outcomes.

The book is divided into three parts. Part one is mostly my analysis of the problems or shortfalls of the common agency/marketing/procurement business paradigm – it introduces The Monkey House framework. Part two provides the more practical improvements that The Monkey House can make to the current pitching, paying and working with agencies paradigms. Finally, part three looks at the broader challenges – the implications of change to agencies, marketing and procurement. I would strongly recommend that readers start at the beginning, but – in case you're already familiar with The Monkey House framework or don't have the time – you can refer to the practical guide. Useful parallels or examples are mostly in tinted boxes, so you can either skip them if you understand the concept or find them again easily if they prove useful. I would recommend that you read all of part three, regardless of your role, so that you understand the implications not only for your own discipline but also for the disciplines upon which you depend.

I begin each chapter with an abstract of the existing industry paradigm – i.e., the problem – and then present The Monkey House's alternative model. However, The Monkey House paradigm will only be able to offer direction about what could actually be done differently; the specifics will depend on the unique set of advertiser and agency circumstances.

It has been a long and, at times, difficult journey to develop this thinking; I hope you find it as valuable as I have enjoyed baking, honing, refining and writing it.[2]

WHY ME?

There are two main factors that led me to write HTBAG. The first was the general path my career in advertising took, and the second was what I can best describe as the nearest I have come to a heart attack.

First, I need to tell you a little about how I got to this point in my career. After a few years in small-time UK advertising and marketing roles, in 1995 I landed what I would describe as my first 'proper' job in advertising. I became an account manager for Grey Advertising in London. Through a combination of excitement, the daily adrenalin of an ad agency, hard work, luck and the mentorship of the likes of Neil Jenner – a stalwart adman since the 70s – my career followed the path that a good account man's ought to. And, at the age of 30, I made it on to the board of directors. This was the 'you know you're making it' criterion, which I scraped about two months before my 31st birthday. Then what?

As I reached this level of responsibility in a significant-sized agency, I often fell into the seemingly interminable pub conversations that revolved around "why can't things be better/easier/more creative/more fun?" Ad folk of all disciplines and in varying states of insobriety regularly gather in pubs, bars and restaurants and moan about their clients, like the husband who says his wife doesn't understand him and vice versa. At first they were interesting to the uninitiated – so you learned stuff – but more to the point, perhaps, there was plenty of drinking, socializing and fun to be had. It was like a rite of passage for a maturing ad man

But these conversations always concluded at a point of hopelessness: "The client would never buy it"; "They don't trust us"; "They don't have the authority to be that brave"; "It'll never fly", etc. These conversations and thoughts stayed with me as my career continued. In 2000, I joined Ogilvy & Mather as a business director for the BP retail account across Europe. Later, after spells on GSK, Nestlé and what was then the Central Office of Information, I left O&M London to become the managing director of Ogilvy Moscow.

Up to this point, my career had largely comprised troubleshooting difficult accounts. I was often the guy to take on the account that was wobbling or that represented a monumental challenge of some sort. When John Seifert, a senior executive at O&M New York at that time, now their Global President and CEO, interviewed me for the BP role, he warned me: "Working on this business is like drinking from a fire hose."

And it was. But even that part of my troubleshooting career turned out to have been a walk in the park compared to advertising life in Moscow.

When I arrived in what was then Propaganda Ogilvy (an affiliate of the O&M network proper), I quickly discovered that of the approximately 20 clients the agency had, about 18 of them wanted to fire the agency. They were all tightly strapped to Ogilvy by virtue of their global agreements to work with the Ogilvy network, but the market was booming and the agency wasn't delivering. The contract prevented most of them from leaving, but it's never easy to have to share a sandpit with a child who hates you with every fibre of their being, and that's what it felt like.

This would require a new level of pub conversation.

Four years of tireless hard work and the agency had grown more than 500% in top-line revenue. WPP began and completed their acquisition of the company. Ogilvy Russia evolved into five different business entities in varying disciplines of marketing communication and, most importantly, Ogilvy Russia held the highest spot on almost every client's roster – for some we were achieving some of the highest satisfaction scores in Russia of any Ogilvy office in the world. I had developed my troubleshooting credentials further and had gained broader and deeper insights into the advertising business and many more client business categories.

As for the near heart attack – the second factor that led me to write this book – that happened when I was drinking from the BP fire hose. About a year after starting at Ogilvy, we had assembled a proper BP team in Ogilvy London, and had launched a new corporate identity and brand mission for BP globally. In spring 2001 we were asked to launch a new BP retail offer called BP Connect in the US and the UK, which were the first markets to adopt the new retail strategy. (BP's global retail account was being run from Ogilvy Chicago, due to its proximity to BP's global lead office for retail.)

The launch of BP Connect would require three different TV ads, which were being developed by our Chicago team. Given the sensitivity of the BP brand heritage (i.e., BP once stood for British Petroleum and was still perceived as a British institution by the UK), it was decided that I should lead a small team from the London office to be involved in the shoot. This would help to make sure that the advertising would be adaptable to run in the UK and that it didn't look too American. I duly went to LA for the shoot in February with a copywriter called Mark Copper, a TV producer and an account coordinator. None of us had seen a script from our Chicago office.

Soon after we arrived, we went to a meeting with a seasoned, highly skilled and oft-decorated commercials director called Leslie Dektor. The creative work developed by my Chicago colleagues was presented to Leslie and us at the same time – and our worst fears were confirmed. For a brand formerly known as British Petroleum, the style and the substance of the advertising would not be well received in the UK. Mark and I were told that the pictures were fixed and that we needed to rewrite the scripts so that new voiceovers for them would work in the UK. This was our challenge. After a long day, we retired to our hotel and proceeded to rewrite the first script as best we could. In the early hours of the morning, we felt we had done enough to make something that wouldn't be embarrassing, but it would hardly trouble the judges.

The following day, tired and bleary-eyed, we shared our reworked ad with the assembled group. It turned out that sleep-deprivation and more than a few bottles of Sierra Nevada Pale Ale had done the trick. Leslie loved the rework. He was visibly enthused about the way we had developed the idea from our colleagues' existing visual treatment – and he said as much. Indeed, Leslie asked our Chicago colleagues if perhaps they could do something a little more like our treatment.

The next day the Chicago team's new treatment sent us straight back to the drawing board. They had departed entirely from their original script, the visual treatment they had first presented, and our improvements on it. They had something to shoot and once again we had nothing. So, Mark and I had to work through the night again. The clock was ticking down to the start of the shoot, casting was going ahead, locations and sets were being approved. We were trying hard to hang on to a process that was clearly running away from us, while at the same time being responsible for bringing something home in the can that wouldn't upset the consumer or embarrass BP or indeed the agency.

By the end of that week it felt like I had a ten-pound weight pressing on my sternum all day. I honestly thought I would have a heart attack. My UK boss, Glen Fraser, had threatened to bring us home and leave it to my Chicago colleagues to face the music without us, but unfortunately we stayed. The weight was there when I woke in the morning and stayed until I fell asleep at night. When I returned to London after ten weeks in and out of the States, it was still there. I gave up alcohol and I even gave up caffeine – no change. Ogilvy London provided me with a stress counsellor. I listened to her tapes and went to her sessions and still there was no improvement. Finally, I asked to see a doctor and, after a little negotiation, Ogilvy provided me with an appointment to see a private GP.

He was a young doctor, probably only in his mid-thirties, so only a few years older than me at that time. He had a very calm and gentle demeanour, and invited me into his treatment room and asked me to sit. "Now, what seems to be the problem?" he asked soothingly, so I began by describing the weight on my chest. Then he asked me about my job and, for the next three quarters of an hour, I described my role to this very attentive doctor. He asked very few further questions; he just patiently listened to my ordeals of the last six months: the LA story, in and out of Chicago every other week, pulling together a team, etc. Finally, when I had finished, he sat back. He paused. Calmly, and with a gentle, sympathetic smile, which only doctors seem to be able to do (do they teach this stuff in medical school?), he calmly said, "I think I know what your problem is."

The cynical ad-man voice inside me immediately had two thoughts:

1) "Yeah, right ..."
2) "If he does know, did I give up alcohol and caffeine for nothing?"

Silencing the cynic in my head, I raised my eyebrows in an expectant "Go on then..." type of gesture. The doctor said, simply, "You've got responsibility without control."

It was the closest I have ever come to an epiphany. No clouds parted in the skies, no scales fell from my eyes, but it really felt like they should have. In fact, a chorus of angels singing hallelujah would not have gone amiss, because with almost immediate effect, the weight lifted from my chest. My understanding of the simple relationship between responsibility and control changed the way I have worked ever since.

The relationship between responsibility and control cascades down hierarchies and supply chains. My Chicago colleagues were under pressure; their client was under pressure to deliver the campaign for his boss, so everybody down the line was stressed because they didn't have control over the means to properly fulfil what was being demanded of them.

The relationship of responsibility and control has not only informed every working relationship I have had since, but it has also developed into the 'Meikle Matrix', which is a central pillar of The Monkey House.

By the time I had done four years in Russia, I had met and married my wife, Olga, and we had decided that there was life beyond Moscow. But I had learned even more about client/agency relationships than before – though perhaps at a darker end of the spectrum. And, more importantly for the development of The Monkey House, I learned a lot about running an advertising agency as a business in terms of people, clients and money. Returning to London towards the end of 2007, I took some time out and finally resolved to get back on the advertising horse just as Lehman Bros collapsed. Great.

Appetites for relatively expensive ad agency senior management went from 'healthy' to 'starvation diet'. And, as we know, necessity is the mother of invention, so in due course I started a business called Salt Partners with two friends whose circumstances were similar to mine.

With Salt as our symbol of value, our idea was to help advertisers get better performance from their agencies. My partners, Simon Steel and Steve Pollack, were specialists in production and media, respectively, so between us we felt like we had it covered. When more stable opportunities presented themselves to Simon and then Steve, understandably, each took his own course and left me with the company.

Nonetheless, pressing on with a useful combination of limited options, bloody-minded determination, and perhaps a little cognitive dissonance, I started to develop the work that would become The Monkey House. With the help of Phil Massey, a procurement specialist, and Jonathan Stirling, a media guru, I pitched and won a relationship assessment assignment for the Post Office in January 2012. As it turned out, the Post Office would become my first Monkey House case study.

So why did I write HTBAG? Partly because I've spent a long time fixing broken advertising relationships with a reasonable degree of success; partly because I nearly had a heart attack in LA; partly because Lehman Bros collapsed; partly because I'd like to have something to show for all this effort; and party because books make effective new business tools for consultants. But mostly because I genuinely believe that there are a lot of advertisers and their agencies that could be doing better than they are currently, and to their mutual benefit.

The Monkey House is not something that I could have developed while occupying a corner of the marketing, procurement and agency triangle, where I was very effectively blinkered by my own agenda. Likewise, marketers and procurement agencies can't see each others' nor their agencies' agendas and challenges. When I left the advertising business, I became much more indifferent to the advertising agency agenda and I could examine the causes and effects of relationship problems with much greater objectivity. With this newly discovered objectivity, The Monkey House began to germinate as an idea.

WHAT IS THE MONKEY HOUSE?

The Monkey House started as an analysis of a problem. Then it morphed into a structure from which companies can find their own most appropriate solution. It is a strategic framework inasmuch as it doesn't use a single business model designed for a single purpose. It might sound like MBA jargon, but it is the best way I have found so far to describe it briefly. The Monkey House comprises multiple models. Put together into a framework, it allows you to do a number of things more easily, including:

a) Define your business problem, your marketing problem and how to make the latter contribute to the solution of the former.

b) Analyse your existing client/agency relationships and assess their suitability for the task at hand.

c) Design new or different client/agency working relationships and processes to create the optimal environment within which the best possible solution to the marketing problem is more likely to be created.

d) Design your agency's remuneration, incentives and deterrents to keep everybody's eyes on the same prize.

In the same way that every marketing problem or objective is unique, so too must be the relationships that are designed to solve them. The Monkey House doesn't provide prescriptive outputs. The complexities of each client/agency relationship across all marketing categories, from pharmaceutical to automotive, in any marketing discipline, in any country in the world, would make it impossible. But The Monkey House provides a framework within which agencies and their marketing and procurement clients can design and build better, healthier, more efficient, more productive and more appropriate relationships, processes and remuneration. The Monkey House produces three sets of 'best principles' instead of 'best practices', and each set of principles is specific to the kind of advertising monkey the brand needs.

WHAT'S IN IT FOR YOU?

In 1986 the late, great Frank Budgen and his partner John Webster worked at Boase Massimi Pollitt (BMP) and together they made an exquisite ad for *The Guardian* newspaper. In it we witnessed an event from three different perspectives. In the first it looks like a skinhead is running down a pavement on a terraced street away from two men in a car who appear to be pointing at him and chasing after him. In the second, from the point of view of the car, the skinhead appears to be attacking a businessman who was walking along minding his own business – the pointing from the car was to warn him of the attack. But, from the third perspective we see that we have all misunderstood the skinhead, who is actually trying to save the businessman from a pallet of bricks that was about to fall on him, at which the guys in the car had actually been pointing. The skinhead saves the businessman and *The Guardian* voice-over explains that it is only when you get the whole picture that you can really understand what is going on.

This commercial is a great analogy for The Monkey House insofar as each of the three key players – agencies, marketing and procurement – will benefit from understanding each other's points of view better. When each party can see from two other perspectives, and also understand the whole picture, they can all benefit from more trusting, more productive and more efficient relationships. Interestingly, when I have used this ad as an analogy for The Monkey House, everybody – whether marketing, procurement or agencies – has identified themselves with the role of the misunderstood skinhead, selflessly trying to do the right thing but being misjudged.

The Monkey House is neutral to the individual wishes and interests of each of these parties; it is only on the side of the business problem that the three need to solve. By starting with the definition of the problem as the shared interest, The Monkey House then helps to create the 'nurture' that is appropriate to the advertising monkey the brand needs and on which the teams from each corner of the triangle can work.

The Monkey House can be used to inform and shape a number of different activities to ensure that they are appropriate to achieving the ultimate goal, including:

- Sourcing agencies
- Running tenders and pitches
- Remunerating and incentivizing agencies
- Designing processes and ways of working
- Managing and improving client/agency relationships.

We will examine these in more detail in part two. Additionally, The Monkey House provides a very effective diagnostic process to assess what is and what isn't right about the relationships in the triangle between marketing, procurement and agencies.

First we need to fully understand the limitations of our current models and the problems they can create. This is the primary purpose of part one.

---

[1] I know this is biologically inaccurate (monkeys have tails, apes do not), but this is a marketing book, not a biology book.

[2] I've also included occasional footnotes at the end of each chapter to which they relate. Consistent with convention, they're not essential but I've tried to keep them interesting.

PART

ONE

WHAT PROBLEM IS THE MONKEY HOUSE TRYING TO SOLVE?

"Above all, success in business requires two things: a winning competitive strategy, and superb organizational execution. Distrust is the enemy of both. I submit that while high trust won't necessarily rescue a poor strategy, low trust will almost always derail a good one."

Stephen MR Covey
Author, *The Speed of Trust*

THE INDUSTRY PARADIGM

Marketing, procurement and agencies have little shared interest. Marketers are often frustrated by agencies, who are perceived to be in pursuit of their own agendas – usually creative and financial.

Creative advertising agencies struggle for growth and margin. To survive, they have to improve their financial performance and attract and retain both clients and talent.

Procurement is incentivized to cut marketing expenditure with little or no accountability for the consequences to the ultimate return on investment.

The relationship triangle created between these three parties is dysfunctional because each one's interests are, at best, divergent and – at worst – mutually exclusive of the other two.

Conflicting or unaligned interests engender distrust. Hence, mutual distrust is almost the industry norm. Nonetheless, these three parties are charged with cooperating to solve complex, open-ended marketing and communications problems involving huge financial investment.

Remuneration practices and marketing's ways of working have become almost standardized, irrespective of the brand problem trying to be solved.

THE MONKEY HOUSE PARADIGM

The Monkey House's first task is to identify the shared goal for marketing, procurement and agencies: What business or marketing problem are we trying to solve? What kind of advertising monkey do we need?

Depending upon the nature of this problem – such as the client's market position, available investment in marketing, competitive threat, category conditions and their appetite for risk – The Monkey House determines how to create relationships, processes, remuneration and agency incentives that are equally unique to that objective. This will attract and motivate agency talent appropriately to create the optimal available solution (i.e., the right monkey).

Better-defined roles and responsibilities for marketing, procurement and agencies, and a mutual accountability for each other's performance, will engender higher trust and more productive relationships between them – all in pursuit of the same goal.

An analogy of the problem might be found in one of the final scenes of Sergio Leone's 1966 *The Good, the Bad and the Ugly*. After a long search for a grave in which a fortune has been hidden, Clint Eastwood, Lee Van Cleef and Eli Wallach find themselves in a classic Mexican standoff. Each man has a gun or two and needs to defend himself against the other two; hence nobody trusts anybody else. Each of the three is exclusively in pursuit of his own interest and is prepared to kill the others to fulfil it. So the three of them stand there in a large triangle, fingers ready to draw their weapons, in tense silence, moving only their eyes, and for a long, long, long time, nothing happens …

Too often marketing, procurement and agencies find themselves in similar standoffs, each occupying one corner of a triangle of mutual distrust (though thankfully, usually not armed). However, whereas the heroes and anti-heroes of Leone's classic each want the prize for themselves, marketing, procurement and agencies have to work together to solve complex and open-ended marketing problems for the brand.

And Mexican standoffs are not easy circumstances from which to escape. With guns pointed at each other, initiatives offered by any individual to get them all out of the fix are universally met with cynicism. Nobody believes that the other person is being honest or cooperative or altruistic.

Similarly, in the triangle of marketing, procurement and agencies, the three are chained together out of an obligation to create marketing campaigns – and not out of any clear shared interest. A summary of the typical perspectives we find in each corner of the triangle might, with varying degrees of intensity, look like this (see *figure 2*).

Marketers:

Agencies are generally slower than they should be, dragging their feet and taking more time so they can charge more in fees. They often try to sell us work that we don't want just to enhance their creative reputation. We've got to keep our eyes on them to keep them on budget and on track so that the ads they make suit our needs more than theirs.

Procurement doesn't understand marketing. They keep trying to reduce our marketing budgets too much. While sometimes we appreciate their help so that our agency doesn't rip us off, if we don't have complete control of our money, then we can't respond to the changing market and the changing needs of our brands. They don't understand agencies as well as we do and there has to be some give and take in the agency relationship for us to get what we need, when we need it.

Procurement:

Agencies are generally profligate and greedy. They are unnecessarily and deliberately inefficient and more profitable than they admit they are. We have access to good data and when we lean on them, we can get good data from them (time-sheets, overheads, etc.) to make sure we're not getting ripped off.

Marketing people just don't get it. They waste money here, there and everywhere, often without any idea of the return. Thankfully we're here to look after the financial interests of our company – they can look after the creative and other stuff. Their approach to supplier management is woefully poor. They don't understand enough about sourcing strategy and supplier relationship management to be left to manage their marketing services roster unchecked by us.

Agencies:
If marketers knew what they were doing, we wouldn't waste nearly as much time developing strategies and creative ideas over and over again – but there's no telling them. We have no choice but to continue doing our best, inefficient as it is. But our clients should really be buying much more exciting creative ideas from us; we can do so much better than they're currently getting. Yes, it would be better for us, but it would be much better for them, too.

Procurement doesn't know a thing about advertising. Most of them are just bullies. Most agencies aren't making anything like the kind of profit we should be and they're so aggressive that unless we keep doing their silly deals they'll take the business away. We're damned if we take their business and we're damned if we don't – but in any event, the current situation is not sustainable.

While these are obviously extreme positions to make my point, I'm sure at least some of this rings true, and most likely a lot of it does – and for many to an uncomfortable degree. The three are pulling apart, not together. I have deliberately used emotive language because this is often the actual language they use, albeit usually behind closed doors. And in many instances their dealings become personal.

Figure 2

The Agency, Marketing Procurement Triangle

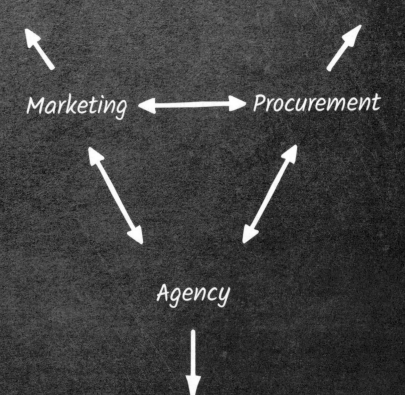

So, as I've already said, the interests of these three are often divergent and, at worst, mutually exclusive. But together they are responsible for developing complicated, integrated advertising campaigns into which the advertiser is going to pour millions of pounds, dollars or euros, in exchange for an even greater return on the total investment.

Stephen MR Covey, (son of the Stephen Covey of 7 Habits fame) wrote a weighty tome called *The Speed of Trust*. One of the most profound insights that came from this book was brilliant and concise: low trust demands low speed and creates high cost, and conversely, high trust allows high speed and can lower cost.

By way of example, I heard the story of a coffee seller working from a street stand in New York. He found that he spent about a third of his time making change for his customers instead of making coffee. Such was the reputation of his coffee that he would have a line of customers waiting for him while he scrabbled around for nickels and dimes to give change to the ones he had served. The coffee seller's high-trust solution was to ask customers to make their own change – what Americans often refer to as an 'honor system'.[3] Customers were happy to do it and the numbers in the queue went down as revenue and customer satisfaction went up. In the UK, the stationer WHSmith has a similar scheme, whereby customers are trusted to help themselves to their newspaper and drop the right change into a box next to the newsstand. If the coffee seller or WHSmith wanted to achieve that level of sales otherwise, they would have to hire more staff, at greater cost. High trust equals high speed equals low cost.

An example of a low-trust situation would be internet banking security. As hackers have become more sophisticated, the investment in online security has had to increase. When I started banking online, all I needed was a couple of passwords, whereas to access my accounts now I must use two different devices and enter payee account number details more than once because the banks cannot afford to trust that I am me anymore. Low trust equals low speed equals high cost.

"Without trust we don't truly collaborate; we merely coordinate or, at best, cooperate. It is trust that transforms a group of people into a team."

Steven MR Covey
Author, *The Speed of Trust*

Let's apply this simple principle to the client/agency relationship. How much time is spent on creative, constructive, innovative, collaborative behaviour and how much on aggressive, protective, defensive, argumentative behaviour? Worse still, these defensive/aggressive behaviours don't actually produce anything except usually redundant arse-covering insurance policies in the form of documents or emails to which they can refer if things go wrong. (I should add that I am not against argument and confrontation in the development of ad campaigns; sometimes it's only through argument that we can determine what we really think about something, but clients and agencies should be having these arguments over the 'nature' not the 'nurture'.)

Agencies spend hours and hours doing this thing we call 'arse-covering'. Arse-covering consists of over-communicating (internally to agency stakeholders and externally to clients), to make sure the agency cannot be blamed or can legitimately explain why something didn't or won't happen as agreed. Arse-covering also confirms client decisions in writing in case something goes wrong.

But such activity is hardly for the purpose of providing the best service to clients, and in some cases it could account for as much as 20% of an agency's time. Marketers are equally culpable for the time they expend on these negative behaviours. Agencies have to prove or justify their recommendations more than ever before. There is little faith that creatively innovative or 'breakthrough' ideas have actually been created for the client's benefit rather than to illustrate the agency's creative prowess.

The excellent Institute of Practitioners in Advertising (IPA)[4] paper, *The Long and the Short of It*, by Les Binet and Peter Field, even asserted that:

> *"Emotional campaigns, and in particular those that are highly creative and generate powerful fame/buzz effects, produce considerably more powerful long-term business effects than rational persuasion campaigns."*

The win-win of great creative work has empirical evidence, but still the cynicism of the creative agency's agenda persists.

Equally, though, marketers are often not sufficiently trusted by their own stakeholders. Frequently the hoops of research that agencies' work has to jump through are there just to show that the investment in a campaign can be justified to the client's executive board. "We 'know' it will work because [insert research agency name here] tells us it will."

The key to solving all these problems is to establish a common interest between marketing, procurement and agencies, so that each can begin to dispense with their unproductive defensive/protective/aggressive behaviours and processes in favour of the creative/productive/value-building ones.

Trust has complex and tricky properties, though – it is not as straightforward as to simply decide that one day we'll all have a shared interest, be accountable to one another and start operating efficiently like a trusting team. We have to be aware of these facets and create a trusting, 'nurturing' environment, which is enabled by policy and process, supported by symbols of our break from our previous ways of working, and encouraged and reinforced every day until it becomes the norm (see chapter nine and the Avis Advertising Philosophy as an early and effective example).

All agencies and all advertisers are different, so there isn't one simple formula to create a more trusting relationship. But, in building trust, we need to consider at least five related qualities of trust:

1) Mutuality:
   How will we define our shared set of values and behaviours? How can we bring them alive and live them every day? What are the symbols and the language we will use to protect our shared philosophy? How can we ensure that we use only open and honest communications?

2) Consistency:
   How can we ensure a lasting solution so that the performance of our relationship is consistent over time?

3) Clarity:
   What is the shared interest that will benefit both organizations? How should we define it as specifically as we can? How can we ensure that both organizations are sufficiently motivated by it?

4) Congruity:
   Walking the talk. How can we make sure that we do what we say we'll do? How can we be accountable to each other for this?

5) Authenticity:
   How can we ensure that everything we are doing is uncompromisingly authentic? From the development of the brief to the analysis of the results, if any aspect is not the real deal, then cracks will quickly show in the relationship. Client and agency must celebrate successes

and acknowledge and even commiserate their failures together – as a single and authentic team.

> # We cannot establish trust without a common interest.

Such is the complexity of effective relationships between client and agency that they cannot be taken for granted and even the good ones need to be actively managed. Creating new client/agency relationships also takes a great deal of thought, skill and experience – the pitching process and contract negotiations currently used in the advertising industry are frequently, regrettably not up to the task. Most importantly, given the diversity of brands' needs, we must dispense with ideas of best practice.

SUMMARY

- Marketing, procurement and agencies are often in a Mexican standoff of mutual distrust.
- Standoffs are time-consuming and expensive. Low trust = low speed = high cost.
- A common goal to which all parties are collectively and mutually accountable will dissolve such standoffs.
- With a common goal and a shared interest, marketing, procurement and agencies will pull together instead of apart, forming more effective, productive teams.
- The mutual distrust of these three parties may be ingrained, but this does not mean that a new relationship with a different agency is needed. To create trusting relationships, a trusting environment is required, enabled by policy and process, and supported by symbols of change that encourage and reinforce the change every day.

---

[3] Which is like 'honour', just misspelled.

[4] Institute of Practitioners in Advertising in association with Thinkbox.

CHAPTER TWO

WELCOME TO THE MONKEY HOUSE

"The biggest risk is not taking any risk ... In a world that's changing really quickly, the only strategy that is guaranteed to fail is not taking risks."

Mark Zuckerberg
Chairman and Chief Executive, Facebook

THE RISK PARADIGM

The roles of risk (strategy and creative) in the development of an ad campaign, and both the procedural and financial relationships between client and agency, have been changing over time.

In the wake of numerous recessions and a global financial crisis, marketing departments – and in turn, their agencies – have often been required to mitigate risk in order to justify campaign investment per se.

While mitigating brand risk during times of economic recession might make sense in favour of greater certainty of a lower return, these risk-avoidance strategies and procedures have been maintained during times of market growth or when growth of market share has been achievable.

Likewise, a brand's particular market circumstances, its share of that market and its competitive threat determine the role of risk in that brand's success.

Brand management and agency remuneration principles of best practice are mostly consistent with risk aversion. They fail to identify how these best practices should alter according to the needs of the brands and the strategic appetites for risk that they should have.

In most instances, the measures clients take to mitigate risk only make their marketing objectives less achievable.

THE MONKEY HOUSE RISK PARADIGM

Differing business and market circumstances require differing attitudes to risk. Brands in static or declining markets are probably at less risk of new entrants than those in growing markets, or markets where growth is realistic or attainable.

Growth markets are riskier markets – they see more new competitor entrants, greater marketing investment and more product and brand innovation than flat or declining markets.

Brands in growth markets therefore need high-performing monkeys: Gorillas and Spider Monkeys. Brands in static, declining or non-competitive markets are at less risk and may prefer more predictable advertising: Orangutans.

These differing advertising needs require different approaches to risk in both strategy and creativity.

The Monkey House paradigm provides a framework within which the roles of risk are clear and the working and financial relationships with agencies are designed to develop the most appropriate and more effective campaigns.

Implicit in the development of advertising campaigns designed to create change is a role for risk insofar as we cannot be certain of the effectiveness of any campaign until after the investment has been made. This is the inescapable nature of any investment: money is exchanged in the hope that it will transform back into a sum of money greater than the principal.

Over the course of the last 20 years or so, I have witnessed numerous national recessions and one global financial crisis. These can be tricky times in the world of marketing communications. The marketer's investment fund is often the first to go from the corporate balance sheet in the belief that either:

a) They won't be able to generate a sufficient return in a depressed economic climate.
b) It won't make any difference to the brand in the long run so why not cut it?
c) There's no better part of the balance sheet to fill the gap in the bottom line.

And often all three are the reasons given.

Consequently, agencies are usually the first to suffer in the brand's supplier base as campaigns and budgets are cut. Agencies are also one of the last to recover, because as their finances begin to improve, the client will have other priorities to address before reinstating marketing budgets.

Through the recessions, I have witnessed two significant trends develop in client/agency relationships:

1) The burden of proof behind the advertising strategy and the creative work has increased. For example, whereas the qualitative and quantitative research of creative ideas was once applied according to a need for them, now the two are often mandatory parts of the campaign development process. They are often used repeatedly until an idea 'passes', rather than as a means of optimizing something the client and agency already agree is good.

2) The transparency of agency costs (salary and overhead) and the accountability of the agency's campaigns' performance have both increased. For example, in the 1980s and early 1990s, when marketing procurement was still in its infancy, most clients showed little interest in the hours their agency worked. Through a series of recessions and 'cost cutting', agency revenues have fallen, and they are expected to be transparent about their costs (overhead, etc.), and performance-related bonuses or PRB (contingent on the brand's sales or the effectiveness of their advertising), which have trebled from 1997 to 2012 according to ISBA's data.[5]

As we saw in *figure 1*, the client/agency relationship – nurture – can be divided into two main facets. The first is their working relationship – this includes the processes they adopt in the development of strategies and ad campaigns, their behaviours and attitudes to one another, and even less tangible aspects such as the reputational impact they might enjoy or suffer from each other. The second is the commercial relationship – this includes the scale of the revenue the client represents within the agency, their contractual terms, incentives and disincentives related to agency performance/campaign effectiveness, client profitability and client contribution to agency overheads.

These two different aspects of nurture evolved, but the evolutionary jumps, which have led to 'normal' modi operandi, have often been made during times of financial downturn, and have established more risk-averse ways of working with and paying agencies. Once economies have recovered and opportunities for growth have been restored, our processes and payments have *remained* in a cynical and risk-averse mode rather than reverting to a more speculative and more risk-savvy mode, which would be appropriate to growth opportunities in more prosperous times.

In some circumstances, it could be argued that this is fair enough. For some brands and business problems, finer-tuned and precise campaigns are essential. For example, when a client has multiple brands in the same category and wants to avoid cannibalization of one in favour of another. But my observation is that these high-control measures are applied almost universally by all clients, irrespective of the marketing objective. This is stifling the performance of the agency and, in turn, its advertising, and consequently, the return on marketing investment (ROI) of the brands. Essentially, the actions of clients are moving them further from their objectives, not closer to them.

As I warned earlier, this is a broad generalization. It does not pass by without recognition of the highly variable needs of brands and businesses depending upon their market circumstances, strategies, investment coffers, etc., each of which would demand different degrees and types of risk. Although each brand's circumstances are different, in order to start compartmentalizing the different ways by which clients can manage their agencies into workable chunks, let's characterize these circumstances by two main factors: 1) The market's growth or capacity to grow their market share (i.e., its responsiveness to advertising, see *figure 3*) and 2) Their market share.

Figure 3

Market Conditions and Ambitions

Capacity to grow   Large market share

By overlaying these two factors, we have created three different circumstances. In the left-hand section, the brand has capacity to grow, but limited market share. In these circumstances, assuming the brand owner
is committing to the brand's future, the brand needs to increase its risk
because its marketing investment is likely to be much lower than the
market leaders. In short, it needs to punch above its weight. This brand
needs to grow massively in comparison to its base.

In the middle section, the brand has a high market share in a market
with a capacity to grow. This means other brands have the capacity to
grow too, at the expense of the market leaders' share. In order to defend
its market share and to grow, the brand must be risk-savvy – investing
in new product development (NPD) and arresting marketing communications – innovating on both fronts to keep their existing users
interested and loyal, and to attract new customers. This brand needs
to grow, but not as much compared to its base share. It should also be
confident enough to innovate and take risks with innovation because it
has already achieved a loyal base.

In the right-hand section, the brand has a high market share, but
there is limited or no capacity for growth. If the brand is in a flat or
declining market, there is limited risk of new entrants, so a brand's
activity need only be as much as is necessary to defend its position or
perhaps steal a little market share from another market leader. This
brand needs to hold on to the market share it has and limit its decline
if the market is declining. (Or, it might be that the brand owners have
other brands in the same category and therefore they deliberately limit
the brand's opportunity to grow.)

Let's characterize these three brand needs by the advertising from
which they would most benefit:

Figure 4

The Monkey House

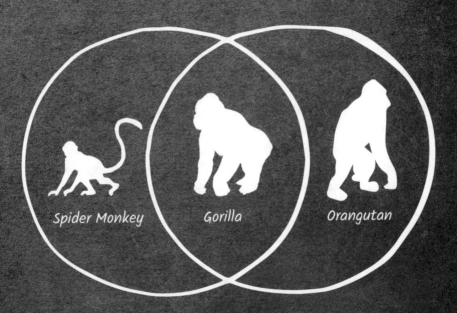

Capacity to grow   Large market share

We will refer to the market situations and the kind of advertising best suited to them as Spider Monkeys, Gorillas and Orangutans.

THE MONKEY HOUSE AND RISK

In all walks of life, risk is where the higher returns may be found and there is no way around it. Whether it's returns on financial investments, adrenalin levels from extreme sports or even good, old-fashioned gambling in a casino, the higher the risk, the higher the potential return. Likewise, however, high returns don't come without equal prospects of either high investment at low risk or low investments at high risk – and there doesn't seem to be any way around this either.

Risk in a marketing context means the unpredictability of return, or the variability of the performance of any component in a marketing campaign. Risk could be found in the innovative nature of the proposition, the creative expression of it, the choice of media channel and so on.[6] But the key point here is the connection between innovation and risk. Implicit in innovation is newness, and with newness there must be some degree of risk, i.e., an amount of wisely judged unpredictability of how the innovation ultimately will be received, the truth of which can never be known with certainty before the innovation is exposed to its intended audience. You'll never know until you try.

When we consider risk in the context of business problems or brand objectives, in growth markets (Spider Monkeys and Gorillas), innovation is an essential ingredient to attract new customers, stimulate loyal ones, or make lapsed customers reappraise and potentially return to the brand.

Gorilla brands have a degree of critical mass or momentum that can mitigate a loss if the risk of their innovation doesn't pay off. They are established in a growth market with a high market share. The key implication of their high share in a growth market is that they should enjoy a good degree of success anyway, thanks to an existing customer base, brand salience and established distribution. Unless their marketing efforts might actively dissuade potential customers from buying from them, they can be confident that the upside of the gamble is not only necessary, but also worth it.

Spider Monkey brands are more vulnerable. They will have a smaller market share in a growth market and probably a smaller share of voice in the melee of all their competitors' ad campaigns. If they cannot compete in investment levels, then they have to stand out with the resources they have available and shout that much louder and more effectively in order to achieve growth; or they must deploy their limited resources more selectively and differently to their competitive pack. If their investments are comparable to Gorilla brands, they must still innovate in a competitive market to keep abreast of Gorilla brands. (There's nothing to stop you prescribing a Gorilla for a Spider Monkey problem if you have the cash.) Spider Monkeys must over-commit to their cause. They must embrace risk to survive, even if a miscalculated risk might mean failure.

Orangutan brands mitigate risk in favour of a more predictable return on which their company's other businesses or their bottom line relies. In flat, declining or largely inert categories where new challengers are unlikely to appear, such levels of risk are both unnecessary and probably unwise. Why would you risk anything beyond what your business relies on? For this reason, we'll see simple, unthreatening improvements to existing products, offering enough differentiation from their previous version to make their customers feel loyal, and just enough for lapsing users to reappraise, but not enough to polarize a base or threaten any real part of the critical mass from which the brand owner is harvesting profit.

This is not to suggest that brands with a high market share in flat or declining markets cannot act like Gorillas and attack their competitors' shares of the market. By all means, they can decide to be a challenger at any time. Orangutans are only for brands that want safer and more predictable returns.

None of this is to suggest that brands should take risks unnecessarily. Many will use qualitative or quantitative research groups to test their ideas before going to market and sometimes that will yield Gorillas. But often research encourages brands to gravitate to the mean, to do what they've done before or to do what others do. As much as this will mitigate risk, it is also likely to diminish returns as the brand becomes more ordinary. For Spider Monkey brands, playing safe could be the very cause of their downfall, while for Gorilla brands, playing safe can mean that the distinctiveness of their campaign, the very thing they need, is tempered and the ROI compromised – essentially too much interference makes Gorillas become Orangutans.

By way of example, I was once interviewing candidates for an account director role when I encountered one applicant for the job who had recently been working on Nike at Wieden+Kennedy. I asked him what Nike was like as a client and he replied, something along the lines of: "They are a truly great client. It took me a while to get used to their culture and their approach, which was embarrassing at times. I remember once being in a meeting at the agency with the client and we were reviewing creative work. All the senior clients were there, marketing director, brand manager, head of this, head of that, and when we decided which routes we all liked, I asked what their research procedures were. The room fell quiet and the marketing director turned to me and politely said, 'Look around the table; if the people collected here don't know what we should be doing with our creative work, then they shouldn't be sat at this table. We're happy, let's move on.'"

It is critically important to consider the role of agency talent when there is a need for creative innovation and its implicit risk. Using 'edgy' creative work as an example, the magnitude of the risk is likely perceived very differently by the client than by the agency, in much the same way as the risk of open-heart surgery is perceived to be much greater by the patient than by the accomplished surgeon. The difference is that nervous patients rarely instruct surgeons to do things differently or operate on them 'their way' – being quiet is what patients do well and clients do less well. But similarly, surgeons can usually reassure patients that their exposure to risk is minimal and remind them of their qualifications and experience – this is what surgeons do well and agencies do less well.

Sometimes we will find that exceptional agency talent is able to persuade the most risk-averse client to buy what they perceive is a risky idea. However, this should be considered a false positive rather than the only paradigm by which we can improve the calibre of advertising creativity. The business problem must determine the role for creativity; it cannot rely on whether the agency is able to front exceptionally charismatic and persuasive people on a client's account. In summary, the approach to risk from our collection of primates looks like this (see *figure 5*):

Figure 5

The Monkey House
and Risk in Summary

Name	Brand/Business circumstances	Role of risk °
Spider Monkey	Low share of voice vs. competitors, new market entrants, continued innovation on product and brand levels.	Essential. Advertisers must be ready to embrace risk and recognize their potential loss as much as their potential gain.
Gorilla	Leading in the market, fighting off challengers and other market leaders – both likely innovators of product and brand.	Essential. The relative downside of a failed gamble is, however, likely to be mitigated by the brand's existing momentum in a buoyant market.
Orangutan	Little competitive activity due to static or declining market. Innovation and investment less necessary.	Mitigated. Although there is some risk in activities like product restaging, risk is minimized in favour of predictability of return.

As an aside, when considering ROI, we must be careful not to consign it exclusively to the achievement of growth in sales. There are many different measures for what might constitute a return on advertising investment. In many categories, market share would collapse without the continued support of broadcast advertising.

Categories like insurance consist of 'always-on' advertisers, relying on both salience and recency to be effective, because the need to buy most insurance comes around only once a year, and the rest of the time we're not that interested. In some consumer goods categories, a brand's sales might be sustainable for a period without advertising by virtue of its strong distribution. However, such brands regularly advertise anyway, because if their market share starts to ebb, the cost of recovering that share can sometimes be greater than it would have been to maintain it (and they may rely on the push of advertising to retain their distribution levels). Consider also advertising that achieves a diminished decline in the face of a powerful competitor who has a better product; this could represent a good return on investment. If an ad campaign managed to limit the loss of market share to a competitor where other competitors have lost more, then that ad campaign has limited losses and done a good job while the client can try to fix their product.

Even if ROI isn't credited with the maintenance of a brand's market share but only for its growth, we must also consider the profitability of incremental sales. The risk of recovering a brand's marketing investment is vastly reduced if it is highly profitable, and even more so if it is both profitable and the increased sales level is sustainable. This point is perfectly illustrated in the following scenario from the excellent book *Buying Less for Less:*[7]

"Let's say you have a business with $10 million in revenue and a 10% profit margin. So you make $1 million/yr. Let's also say you're the marketing procurement person and you're in the process of hiring a general market creative/ad agency to help lead the marketing work. You work with your marketing team to write an excellent Statement of Work, and two agencies bid on it. Orange Agency quotes a fee of $40K and Apple Agency offers a fee of $100K. Apple is more than double the cost of Orange. They're both 'in-spec'. They're both on your qualified vendor list. Which do you buy?

What if one year later Apple Agency drove a 15% lift in your business? Great marketing can do that, and it's not uncommon. Also assume that you have a profit margin of 40% on incremental sales (fixed costs like overhead and facilities have already been covered). That 15% lift translates to $600K in incremental profit. By contrast, what if one year later Orange Agency's marketing solutions resulted in a 3% decline in your business? Poor marketing can do this, and it's not uncommon. This scenario means a $120k decline in profits. The difference is $720K. Which agency do you wish you had signed up with?"

If we consider risk in marketing communication, it can manifest itself in a number of different ways: unproven advertising strategies, propositions, ideas or even executional styles and – as Preece and Wohlwerth illustrated in the excerpt above – going for the cheaper option can be a risk. There is unlimited variability in the creative component of an advertising campaign and with that unlimited variability is unlimited possible risk. If an ad is too boring, it risks not being noticed and not registering in the minds of the audience it seeks to persuade. Conversely, if the ad is too creatively crazy, it risks confusing the audience or upstaging the brand so the ad is remembered but the brand is forgotten.

The safer and more conventional the ad – its idea, its format, its style, its proposition – the less the risk of being misunderstood, but the risk of being unnoticed is greater. This can only be compensated for with a high investment in its exposure through bought media, i.e., a dull message needs to be seen more often to register and then persuade. But an effective, innovative, engaging ad – which is higher risk insofar as it is new and different – needs less exposure to persuade. We can consider this principle in a simple equation that demonstrates the impact of a conventional advertising campaign (see *figure 6*).

Figure 6

Share of Mind

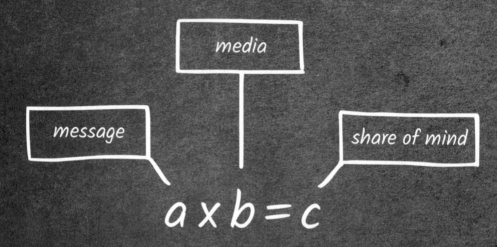

a = message – originality, cut-through, engagement with an advertising message.

b = paid media – media exposure, coverage, frequency.

c = share of mind – the degree to which the advertising has engaged a consumer consciously or subconsciously, and its salience.

"Before you can have a share of market, you must have a share of mind."

Leo Burnett 1891–1971
Founder, Leo Burnett

Of the two variables, a represents the greater variability of risk versus the better-known and more measurable exposure of the message in b through paid-for media channels.[8] Of course, brands can adopt riskier media strategies and channel selections according to their appetite for them and their budgets. However, in most instances, if reliable media are affordable and will achieve your goal, why wouldn't you use them, at least for most of your media mix?

If a has a high value and b has a high value, then it stands to reason that c – share of mind – will be greater by whatever measure you might want, and the campaign will be most effective. High values for a and b are not only necessary for Gorilla brands, but also expected by consumers; they're what make market leaders famous.

Spider Monkey brands and, in particular, new brands, are less likely to have the capital to afford a high value for b, so they are dependent upon achieving the highest possible value for a in order to achieve their best achievable value for c.

Orangutan brands, which by their nature require stable, predictable returns, will therefore more happily adopt a lower value for a. Because they know that their track record of buying their exposure in b delivers a largely predictable return, they need to maintain their market share with c.

Probably the advertising hall-of-fame classic example of this principle would be Steve Hayden's legendary launch ad for Apple in 1984. Directed by Ridley Scott, the ad only received one significant airing in January 1984 during a break in the Super Bowl. A very high value for a, and very low frequency value for b, equalled a high share of mind.

Again, I must stress that this is illustrative of an approach to risk; there are other ways these principles and a marketer's attitude to risk can achieve great returns.

In another IPA paper,[9] it was suggested that: "For an average campaign for an average brand, expect market share growth of 0.5 percentage points for each 10 points of excess share of voice." For example, if your brand has a 20% market share and a 30% share of voice, all other things being equal, it can expect to grow by 0.5% share points. If brands want to and they have the investment, they can simply buy market share at relatively low risk.

If we think of the way online video content has developed, it often has a very high value for a and a low cost for b. So, its success at generating share of mind is entirely contingent on a and the effect of social media. The cost of a is also usually comparably lower than conventional advertising – and content can be more hit-and-miss. But, to the brand community, this often represents an acceptable risk as part of a greater media mix; i.e., there's a good potential upside for a relative low ante of the content's production cost. For other campaigns, an increased stake in the cost of a is a calculated risk that diminishes the likelihood of failure to gain the viral exposure effect of social media, which it depends on for a greater share of mind. Sainsbury's, a leading UK retailer, makes a great example of this principle in action with their Christmas campaign in 2015 (see Sainsbury's case study in chapter six).

The point of this somewhat in-depth examination into risk is this: if conservative and risk-averse ideas of 'best practice' (for agency ways of working and remuneration) reduce the engagement of a, then effectiveness becomes reliant on the more expensive value of media in b to achieve campaign success. For some brands, in some market conditions, this might be the right or necessary thing to do, but for many their risk aversion and conservatism are by default, not design, and it is not what their brand needs – in fact, it's the very opposite.

COPYING BEST PRACTICE – MONKEY SEE, MONKEY DO

The problem with copying another company's idea of best practice is that their circumstances may have a different relationship to creative risk from your own.

For example, the media agency for a client of mine proposed to them that they split their media expenditure by a ratio of 70:20:10, whereby each portion of their overall media investment would be treated differently: 70% of the expenditure would be invested in reliable media that provide a proven and predictable return on investment; 20% would be invested in media that were established and likely to provide a reliable return, but with less empirical proof; and 10% would be spent on media that were new, innovative and unproven. The idea appealed to my client; it seemed to them like a sensible media risk strategy. Except, I pointed out, that their specific business problems were different from (and not even remotely comparable to) the business problems of the client who originally adopted this approach – which I had been told was Coca-Cola. My client was struggling with low market share for most of their products, and as such they had insufficient media funds to compete with the market leaders. Compounding this challenge was the fact that they had a risk-averse corporate culture. So logically, why wouldn't they adopt a 99:1 ratio? In this way, they would only invest in media that provided a reliable marketing return on investment, accommodating their low-risk culture and paying for it. Or they could challenge the culture of the company and decide to adopt a new risk strategy and buy a 20:80 ratio, where only 20% is invested in media with a predictable return and 80% in high-risk media with a higher risk of a higher return. Adopting the strategy of another company, a market leader in a different category, with saturated distribution and 100% brand awareness, presented no logical thinking at all – it was arbitrary. It was also based on the assumption, even if their business problems were comparable, that the strategy attributed to Coca-Cola was right in the first instance.

It is for this reason that The Monkey House starts with the client's specific business problem, category, culture and circumstances, so that the advertiser can make informed value judgements specific to their brand's needs and their appetite for risk. In the same way, I wouldn't expect my doctor to prescribe arbitrarily the same treatment for me and another patient. So we cannot blindly adopt other marketers' processes, or strategies, or media mixes, or timings, or pitch processes unless we're sure they will be consistent with our business needs and our appetite or need for risk.

> *Ideas of best practice are*
> *misnomers; often they're*
> *not appropriate to the business*
> *problems we need to solve.*

What I'm directly challenging here is the idea that there is a 'best practice' for marketers to source, select, appoint, remunerate and work with
their agencies. What The Monkey House provides is a means to assess a
brand's need and establish a set of 'best principles' according to that need
and in the context of the business problem.

WORKING VERSUS NONWORKING MARKETING INVESTMENT

While we consider risk and the equation to achieve a high share of mind
(see *figure 6*, above), one of the most troubling marketing concepts is
that of 'working' versus 'nonworking' marketing spend.

The idea behind these terms is that marketing expenditure is differentiated between two buckets. In bucket one, working marketing spend
is capital invested that directly increases brand exposure to the audience,
such as paid media, in-store activity, sponsorship. Whereas, in the second
bucket, nonworking marketing spend is that which is invested in the creation of advertising to fill the media, such as agency fees, original production costs (TV production companies, talent fees, etc.), and 'downstream'
production costs (duplication and distribution of advertising assets).

Considering the equation in *figure 6*, this essentially means reducing
the investment in a and, in most instances, investing those savings in b.
The assumption is that b represents a lower-risk, more predictable return
on investment, so it is logical and understandable to want to increase
spend on b. But to increase spend on b at the expense of a would only
suit some very specific marketing objectives – like buying market share,
as I mentioned above. The thing that is most bewildering is that this is a
strategic approach to marketing investment adopted by many companies
with portfolios of brands. In such companies, each brand has different
competitor sets, different market circumstances and different sizes of

marketing war chests. Some of their brands need Spider Monkeys, some need Gorillas and some need Orangutans, but for the big-multinational portfolio companies, most need Gorillas. Therefore, to reduce the investment in *a* is to reduce investment in the thing that will differentiate the brands. To reduce that investment is to risk mediocrity, which would require a far greater investment in *b* to compensate for it. Some brands may argue that their rational point of difference – the unique features, greater benefits, improved efficacy and so forth of their product – does the job of differentiation. But again, we know that emotional persuasion sells more effectively from *The Long and the Short of It*.

And this whole argument for the role of creativity is before we consider the rise of content marketing, where *a* is the primary investment (as we will see in the Sainsbury's case study in chapter six), or even the sole investment in content.

OVERPLAYING YOUR PROCUREMENT HAND

Putting the flaws of the nonworking spend reduction strategy to one side for a moment, there are other consequences of this kind of practice. It can lead to very heavy-handed negotiation of terms when buying agency services and, unfortunately, many agencies are susceptible to doing silly deals with big clients.

This will be news to many in the client world – particularly those in marketing procurement. Many in marketing procurement (and indeed some in marketing) believe that there's still plenty of fat to be cut when they reduce their agencies' fees by that extra few per cent each year. And that if there wasn't, then agencies wouldn't accept these significantly lower fee proposals. In negotiations, you might want to keep pushing until the other party refuses, and then – knowing you have gone as far as you can – you could revert to the previous lowest offer and you have a deal. But to do so is to risk how the seller responds when they resent a deal into which they've been forced. You haven't reduced investment and maintained the value return, you've just increased risk somewhere else – talent priorities in supplier preference. (See the next chapter.)

In fairness to clients, most folks believe that it must be a lie if an agency claims they won't make a profit from a deal to which they agree. Why would anybody agree to such a deal? We will explore this problem in much more detail in chapter eight, but for now: large, portfolio businesses with large shares of agency revenues can squeeze their agencies so that their accounts are not profitable. However, these clients make such large contributions to their agencies' overhead that they are too big to resign. The result is that the agencies bearing this burden become more and more financially unstable and could be in significant trouble if they lost another piece of business or if another client decided to follow suit and do equally nasty deals. The whole situation is unsustainable. Agencies have an obligation to their own shareholders and to all their clients to make each client pay its own way. If one or two clients attempt to devolve responsibility for the agency's profitability to the other clients, they could literally ruin it for all of them, but the agencies don't have (or don't feel they have) sufficient selling power to stop them.

In order to get the monkey that you need, the agency needs to match its talent to the client's task. The talent that is most difficult to access comprises those that can better develop Gorillas and Spider Monkeys. Having said that, it is much easier to access those who can develop ordinary Orangutan ideas, because the process is so much more prescriptive. (Though really good Orangutans still need great agency talent.) And talent has an important say in who does what in your agency. In the next chapter we'll look at agencies, how they work and how talent works within them.

SUMMARY

- Risk is unavoidable and needs to be employed strategically according to a brand's circumstances.
- A calculated and strategic approach to risk is implicit in innovation.
- Increasingly challenging conditions in the client/agency relationship, established in times of recession, stifle agency value in the long term and their ability to develop Gorillas and Spider Monkeys.
- Risk-averse ways of working with agencies have become commonplace and are not usually conducive to achieving optimal ROI for Spider Monkey and Gorilla brands.
- Different brands have different needs and market circumstances that can be usefully categorized by The Monkey House.
- Spider Monkeys and Gorillas – i.e., brands in growth markets or markets that are responsive to advertising and innovation – must be innovative to stave off new and existing competitors.
- Marketing strategies that focus on transferring spend from 'non-working' to 'working' dollars believe they are risk-averse, but their divestment from brand innovation can be a risk in itself.

[5] Incorporated Society of British Advertisers. *Paying for Advertising VI*, Advertising Research Centre, ISBA 2013.

[6] This assumes of course that the product or service itself is proven relevant and of value to the consumer and therefore relatively risk-free, because, as Bill Bernbach succinctly put it in 1965 in an interview with *The Wall Street Journal*, "A great ad campaign will make a bad product fail faster."

[7] Gerry Preece and Russel Wohlwerth, *Buying Less for Less* (Buckdale Publishing, 2014).

[8] Media have huge variables, too. This model assumes that you have the right media mix at the right times for the right audience.

[9] *How Share of Voice Wins Market Share*, IPA report, 2009.

CHAPTER THREE

AGENCIES, AND HOW TO GET THE MONKEYS YOU NEED FROM THEM

"You can buy a man's time, you can buy a man's physical presence at a given place, you can even buy a measured number of skilled muscular motions per day or per hour. But you cannot buy enthusiasm, initiative, loyalty; you cannot buy devotion of hearts, minds, and souls, you have to earn all these things."

Clarence Francis, 1888–1985
Former Chairman, General Foods Corporation

THE TALENT PARADIGM

Brands' relationships with their agencies trade on a number of assumptions about how agencies, and the talent within them, work – most of which are incorrect to a greater or lesser degree. These assumptions include the following:

- Brands know the best talent when they experience working with it.
- Brands know their account's importance to an agency.
- Brands understand how profitable agencies are.
- Brands know how much money the agency makes from their account.

Above all, brands believe that they can change the value of their agency's advertising without significantly changing their relationship in terms of process, behaviour and remuneration. Clients who are satisfied with their agencies generally believe that they have the optimal available talent working on their accounts. Therefore, they are receiving optimal value from the agency. Dissatisfied clients usually believe that there are a number of ways their agency could improve, e.g., the agency could reduce turnover of talent on their account, reduce costs and improve their access to better talent. Failing that, clients tend to change agencies altogether.

However, clients get the talent they deserve according to how they pay and how they work with their agencies.

THE MONKEY HOUSE TALENT PARADIGM

Agencies are repositories for talent. They attract talent by a number of means that amount to an agency's employer brand.

An agency's role is to broadly match its talent with the client's needs. In doing so, agencies have to ensure that their matching of talent and clients is appropriate; otherwise their talent is likely to leave and/or the client will fire the agency.

The better the talent, the more influence the talent has over which accounts they will work on. Better clients get better talent, who then deliver greater value; worse clients get worse talent and derive less value from their agencies.

No amount of threatening, table thumping or pitching will get great advertising talent to work on undesirable accounts. Paying over the odds might do it. Instances where this may have happened in the past should be considered false positives or exceptions to the rule, and they are not reliably replicable as strategies to access talent.

Agency talent can be attracted to a particular client in their agency by the relationship that client has with its agency. The kind of talent a client needs varies according to their business problem – some need strategic and creative superstars and others need safe pairs of hands, and every nuance in between.

By designing the way clients work with agencies, by changing the way clients behave with their agencies, and finally by paying agencies appropriately, clients can attract and retain the right kind of agency talent to solve their business problems optimally.

Doing these three things is the best way to ensure the right talent is assigned to – and stays working on – the accounts appropriate to the client's needs.

In the same way that a restaurant has good customers and bad customers, ad agencies have good clients and bad clients. And likewise, restaurant customers who are respectful, spend a lot of money and tip well will have a better experience than those who don't.

In part two we'll explore the landscape of the agency market in some detail. For now, in our analysis of the failings of the current client/agency relationship paradigm, we'll just look at how large creative advertising agencies work, how they all tend to respond to their clients, and what they have in common. In examining how agencies work we'll look at how creative agencies:

- Make money
- Get talent to work for them
- Get their talent to prioritize clients.

… in other words, money, people and clients.

MONEY

It's not a minority opinion among clients that ad agencies make a lot of money, and it is a view that apparently prevails among most of the marketing procurement community. Although there has long been evidence to the contrary, this perception persists, and it is what often informs the procurement teams' buying strategies. It is worth putting these perspectives in some historical context, so let's look back on how creative agencies used to be remunerated. Way back when, the creative agency that developed the selling strategies and the ideas, and the media agency that selected and bought the media, were one and the same.

In their heyday, full-service agencies enjoyed a number of revenue streams, which were both plentiful and profitable. The standard media commission they would receive was 15% of their clients' gross media spend. Put simply, if their client spent £1,000,000 on TV media, the agency would earn £150,000 in fees. Additionally, some clients would also pay their agencies up to 15% of their gross production costs. So, if the client also spent £100,000 on the production of a TV commercial, the agency would calculate their mark-up by multiplying the principal by 17.65%, so the client was charged £117,650 and the agency made £17,650 (i.e., 15% of the gross total). In this scenario, the agency fee was £167,650 for planning the media, buying the media, writing the creative strategy (the brief), writing the creative work (ideas, scripts), pre-production of the commercial, oversight of the production company and project management, and tracking the advertising's effectiveness. When a client made several commercials a year, the agency would also do the brand planning; it would design or participate in brand research projects, and do all the things that we find in a typical service-level agreement for a big advertiser today.

Although, back then, commissions of 15% included media planning and buying services, the commission did not usually allow for the development, duplication and distribution of artwork. This was an additional and monumental task before the age of automated resizing and digital distribution. The computerization of the agencies' studios and the subsequent efficiency this transformation provided took some time to saturate the market, so extensive press campaigns required large amounts of resource and money, which was also profitable to the agency.[10] In fact, many agencies also established separate artwork and production companies that could charge their clients healthy rates for these services, and the more audacious agencies even charged their clients the same pass-through markup of 17.65% on their own subsidiary's services.

These fees only covered the development of the campaigns that would populate the media space their client bought. Although the fees would include peripheral services such as brand strategy, they did not include creative work for other communications channels. So, integrated agencies would charge for the development of direct mail campaigns, in-store materials and so on – on top of their fees and pass-through markups.

International accounts also often required a dedicated international agency team. Their role was to fly from country to country putting out any fires there might be (sometimes starting a few) and generally coordinating an agency's resources regionally or globally. These were sometimes charged in addition to the fees charged on a national level. Sometimes these roles were used to justify the maintenance of commission levels on national levels, so that the global or regional teams could demand levies from the local ones to pay for them centrally.

In addition, agencies also realized that they themselves had quite a lot of buying power over their own supply chain, with the result that many of them negotiated rebates from their bigger suppliers. The media budget was an obvious starting point and an area over which some contention persists today. For example, the combined spend of a number of clients on the printing of out-of-home posters could also produce a healthy rebate to the agency at the end of a year, which was not then necessarily redistributed to their poster-using clients. Likewise, post-production facilities for TV commercial production and other supplier categories provided other lucrative rebate revenue streams. The more entrepreneurial agencies even had interests in the travel agencies that provided their flights on international accounts.

During the 80s and 90s, most large ad agencies also began to uncouple their media planning and buying services to form what became termed 'media independents'. These independents (although often formed from the media departments of one or two agencies owned by one holding company) could pursue greater buying power opportunities from their clients by consolidating their media spend into one agency while often maintaining a roster of creative agencies. The move also cleverly mitigated the financial exposure of account reviews, which more often became limited to creative or media rather than both. However, it meant creative agency profits were reduced, as revenues for media services were diverted.

Time passed and agencies undeniably made some very big money. It became quite conspicuous when in 1987 the Saatchi brothers made a play to buy Midland Bank but failed, where HSBC succeeded five years later.

Enter procurement from stage left. With a gleeful look in their eyes, shotguns in hand and ready to shoot fish in a barrel.

As procurement started to move into marketing and technology, they made some of the high-cost aspects of the production process vastly more competitive; one by one agency revenue streams began to dry up. Procurement started asking their agencies lots of awkward questions and, as the right of audit started to appear in more agency contracts, other opportunities for savings were painfully and sometimes embarrassingly uncovered. As services extra to the core creative product (such as artwork production) were put out to tender through competitive procurement processes, agencies saw their revenues decline further and – depending upon the legitimacy of the streams that had dried up – they also found it difficult to protest or justify an increase elsewhere.

As this flow of money into agencies changed from what was, without doubt, a healthy torrent to something much more modest over the years in the latter end of the 90s and the noughties, agencies began to adapt. Technology assisted in this regard as, for example, the ratio of secretarial support to billable staff changed as computers became less expensive and more and more staff typed contact reports and presentations for themselves. And the introduction of the internet and email into day-to-day office life made account management and planning even more efficient and self-reliant. Also, agency offices became more populated; open-plan spaces became the norm.[11] Some agencies moved out, and others started up out of cities' central business districts, and enjoyed lower rents and business rates, which reduced their overhead. So, although the agencies' revenues were decreasing, agencies became significantly leaner and more efficient in order to make good their losses and to protect their margin for profit as best they could.

Having successfully sustained service levels despite reduced fees, agencies naturally found the continuous provision of such savings unsustainable. They started to operate on significantly narrower margins and some started to lose money. According to reports from Kingston Smith,[12] published in *Campaign* magazine in December 2015, in 2014 agencies had an operating margin performance of 10.7% – the worst in nine years.

So how did agencies allow fee reduction to get this far?

One of the many challenges to the agency business is to escape the perception of their profligate past. As we gradually emerge from a global financial crisis, the problem of this perception is compounded by the fact that agencies will, when forced, agree to silly deals – deals that procurement would believe are actually profitable to agencies, despite their agencies' protests. In fairness to clients, most folk believe that it must be a lie if an agency claims they won't make a profit – why would anybody agree to such a deal? Well, there are a number of reasons, but here are three for now that I think are worth registering:

First, the business-to-business model of an agency is different to that of many of their clients' businesses. Most big creative agencies probably won't have more than approximately 20 big clients, largely because the ones they have insist on being exclusive to the category or categories in which they compete. Therefore, if an agency loses a client, there is a significant contribution to overhead that needs to be replaced. Faced with the option of losing a client over a failed deal, compared to keeping one that makes a contribution to overhead but makes no profit, of course you will keep the unprofitable client. Think of it this way – if your house was on fire and you needed three extinguishers to put it out, you wouldn't turn down two if they were to be made available to you.

Losing a significant piece of business is not only a body-blow to an agency's bottom line, but also to its employer brand reputation and its staff morale. If an agency finds itself in a downward flat spin, then staff and clients both lose confidence in it, and like rats they will jump ship, even if they only think it is sinking. Therefore, if procurement over-play their buying-power hands, agencies will sometimes rather keep an unprofitable client versus taking their chances on replacing them.

Secondly, and perhaps understandably, clients believe there are legitimate savings to be made; as agencies continue to suffer from the hangover of their profligate behaviours of yesteryear, so procurement will ignore agencies' protests. Agencies have got to shoulder some responsibility for their reputations, but now it is little more than a perception, and it's not in their clients' interest to continue punishing them for sins of the past. The days of regular extravagant lunches are over – reserved mostly now for occasionally entertaining clients. Flash company cars at relatively junior levels are long gone. These perceptions are wrong, and procurement needs to take its foot off the negotiation gas – or their agencies' throats, whichever metaphor you prefer.

Lastly, and unfortunately, many agencies aren't terribly good at the negotiation and renegotiation processes, for a number of reasons:

- Few, if any, have the resources to match their clients' procurement teams' time to prepare properly for their negotiations. And, an agency's clients are vastly larger organizations with much greater resources to allocate to such activity.
- Agencies are in the service business. Many find it counter-intuitive to stand their ground with their clients because it might cause conflict – even more so if the agency's business performance is already weak.
- It's very difficult for an agency to tell its client that if they reduce their fees then their service and/or value will suffer. But the procurement fraternity knows this from the supplier preference model, which we'll look at later in this chapter.

The result is a little like over-fishing. Agencies' financial liquidity, profitability and their ability to hire and/or retain talent is like a diminishing stock of fish. Their clients are the fishermen – but they can't see that the stocks are diminishing because whenever they cast their line the hungriest fish eagerly swim towards them. This is why reports like those of Kingston Smith are so important. And there's plenty more being written about the decline in agency financial health – Michael Farmer's *Madison Avenue Manslaughter*[13] is a good read for starters.

Like any other business, advertising agencies need to be profitable to be stable, so they can invest in their growth, the development of their services and even intellectual property in the form of proprietary research, for example. Moreover, profitability is a legitimate business interest. Most of the top agencies are publicly listed companies with shareholders that need to be compensated in the same way their clients' shareholders are. Likewise, independent agencies have founders who deserve a return on their hard work, innovation, investment and risk.

Clients should be content to be with agencies that are successful creatively and successful financially, and clients are collectively responsible for both.

PEOPLE

Raymond Chandler once observed that playing chess was the greatest waste of human intelligence to be found outside an advertising agency. While his cynicism is entertaining, the difference between chess and advertising is that computers are able to play chess, and very well, but if you want ideas, you need people. Chess is certainly a strategic game, though the strategic variables are limited such that they are programmable, but only people can solve strategic and creative advertising problems. There are no machines or computer programs capable of the kind of complexity, intuition and intelligence required. There are myriad variables involved in the process of developing an ad campaign, and they are not things that will ever be mechanized or derived out of formulae. Ad campaigns are about persuasion, and persuasion is an art.

Therefore, to succeed, the advertising business and businesses have to attract and retain the best available talent in order for them to compete effectively with one another.

The kind of people the agency world needs varies enormously from wildly creative rebel artists to extremely efficient, detail-focused, multi-tasking project managers who respond well to pressure, to lateral thinking strategists who can see the world in a different way and find business opportunities in it that others can't. What they have in common is that they are all intelligent, persuasive, creative (in the broadest sense) and usually quite likeable – though there are notable exceptions. There are many other industries and many agencies that would like to attract and hire the best talent, so the individuals determine their own careers. If you're good enough to go to a better account or agency, you go.

The advertising business is an exciting, vibrant, stimulating working environment, but at the same time it's also a bear pit where only the strongest, toughest and ablest can survive. Not everybody who starts in advertising can finish in advertising, and at a certain age or stage – if you're not part of an agency's future – your career can come to an abrupt end. Those who do succeed are usually deserving of their success, though sometimes not, and those who are forced out or down are sometimes undeserving – though usually not. And many just leave to pursue a different career direction. But in any event, talent attraction, development, management and retention are absolutely essential to business success in advertising.

The way talent behaves in agencies is consequently quite organic. Better agencies (making more interesting ideas that create bigger returns – Gorillas and Spider Monkeys) get better clients, attract better talent, and establish an upward spiral of value creation (*figure 7*, below). If an agency's reputation starts to slide, it will struggle to attract the same calibre of talent, and consequently, it won't win or retain the kind of clients that need that talent. For the most part, large creative agencies have a range of talent, from the stars of the future to the departure lounge, and a range of clients, from the flagships to the little-spoken-about nasties that make them just enough money to make it worth keeping them. Big-agency reputations ebb and flow a little over the years, but rarely to any significant degree in the short term – greater volatility is to be found in the smaller agencies and the fast-growing newcomers. So, the calibre of big-agency talent is pretty stable, and within a big agency, the better clients attract the better talent and the worse clients much less so.

So, agencies' reputations and employer brand management have become vital to their sustained success in the long term.

Figure 7

The Virtuous Circle of Value Creation and Talent

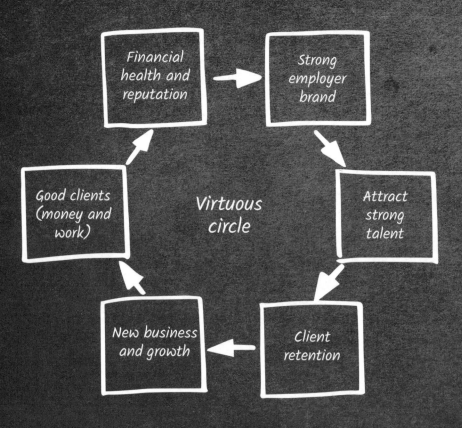

When I was working in ad agencies, I had long believed that agencies' own brands were vital for new business, to attract and reassure clients by the stature and appearance of the agency brand. While they do have a role in that regard, I later came to believe that the other vital roles they play are those of beacons to potential employees and as brands of reassurance and pride to existing employees – they are employer brands. On reflection, the power of the agency employer brands in the 80s was nothing short of phenomenal. Such was the excitement, intrigue and glamour surrounding the advertising business that those wanting to get a foot in the door would gladly work in the post room as a runner – just to be in an agency. Agencies like Collett Dickenson Pearce (CDP) were considered almost magical, and revered industry-wide as the best, as the creators of groundbreaking campaigns for brands such as Heineken, Hamlet Cigars and Harvey's Bristol Cream (and that's just the Hs). These campaigns were spoken about and adored by ordinary folk – and they worked. No wonder people would start in the post room. I had thought these stories of humble beginnings apocryphal until I met one or two who admitted they had started their careers exactly that way.

The power of the agency's employer brand can be used as a short hand for its value. Better employer brands indicate the first qualification in the creation of the virtuous circle. Better people make better ads, get better clients, make better employer brands and so on. Consequently, weaker employer brands should ring alarm bells to anybody searching for a new agency.

"If you think it's expensive to hire a professional to do the job, wait until you hire an amateur."

Red Adair, 1915–2004
American oil well firefighter

So what makes a strong employer brand for an advertising agency in the 21st century? There isn't a clear set of rules. But if I were a client looking for a new agency, some of my criteria would be: overall brand recognition and reputation in the market, CPD[14] status and industry accreditations for staff training, low staff turnover, stability (an absence of account losses), who their other clients are and the calibre of the creative work that they produce for them. Awards are a good measure of both good talent and good clients. On a national level, the likes of the IPA effectiveness awards, reputedly one of the toughest measures of advertising effectiveness, are a very useful indicator; internationally there are the likes of the Cannes Festival awards and also the Gunn Report.[15] Last, but not least, leadership. The ad agency business is one of heroes – some names in the industry inspire awe and admiration and add huge kudos to employer brands. With leadership comes a lot of the good, powerful agency culture, staff motivation, productivity and value. Strong leaders are beacons to talent, creating employer brands people will fight over to work for.

But the world is changing, and the battle for talent has never been tougher than it is now. In recent years, the advertising industry has been battling different competitors in the war for talent with Google, Facebook and the like. In addition to super-famous brand names, they offer city-centre offices with playroom atmospheres, free lunch buffets and free soft drinks all day, staff events and even unlimited holidays in some American companies, so the battle for talent intensifies.

There has been some significant migration at senior levels from the advertising industry to new tech companies, but at graduate employee entry level, the new tech companies' employer brand strength makes many ad agencies look positively conservative – even dull. Improving an agency's employer-brand demands investment but, while margins are being continually squeezed by the very clients that are relying on that talent, agencies are feeling more and more like they're in between a very large rock and a very hard place. These combined pressures are unsustainable without the agency's value suffering significantly.

Additionally, for decades there has been a predominant culture of presenteeism in creative ad agencies. People would brag about the all-nighters they had pulled as badges of honour to prove their commitment and stamina. Plus, long hours and weekend work both clocked up extra hours on the time sheets, some of which might be billable and hence revenue-generating efforts. It had been the case, in an almost perverse manner, that working conventions like 24-hour access to offices and so forth actually contributed to agencies' employer brand status. But more recent management philosophy and competition from the likes of Google and Facebook are making agencies rethink how they can improve their working conditions.

HOW WIEDEN+KENNEDY CHANGED THEIR STAFF CONTRACT TO IMPROVE EMPLOYEE WORK/LIFE BALANCE.

Founded in 1982 by Dan Wieden and David Kennedy, with Nike as its first client, Wieden+Kennedy (W+K) has never suffered any significant reputational damage, because it consistently produces arresting, engaging and sometimes breathtaking creative work. Despite the employer brand strength, in March 2016 W+K London started a trial of new ways of working to improve staff's work-life balance, productivity, satisfaction and retention. The trial consisted of four key guidelines for staff that were developed by the champion of the initiative, Helen Foulder, the Deputy Managing Director, and the HR team. The changes were:

1) Between the hours of 7.00pm and 8.00am an email program called Boomerang will queue outgoing mail. At 8.00am anything that you may have written and sent will then be delivered. So, people who feel more productive or at ease writing their emails late at night can do so, but they will no longer impose on others to receive them when they are written.

2) Days worked on weekends or national holidays will be repaid with days off in lieu. The primary purpose of this is to pay back the time staff may have spent from their allotted days off. A secondary benefit is that staff have to apply for days off in lieu and the process of application acts as an alarm bell, identifying more extreme cases who may be overdoing it or feeling pressured to work harder and longer more regularly.

3) Internal meetings should take place between 10.00am and 4.00pm. This protects staff members who may be commuting for as long as 90 minutes from having to get up in the middle of the night to attend an 8.00am meeting. It also means that daytime working hours are more precious and staff are more reluctant to call meetings to share information that can be managed more efficiently as pre-reads.

4) Early finish on a Friday. As long as your 40 hours for the week have been worked and the clients' needs have been attended to, staff can go home early. (Or to the pub, or the cinema or the seaside or whatever.)[16]

It's unsurprising that Wieden+Kennedy might be a pioneer of such positive interventions. As an agency business model, it is different to many insofar as it is a large but still privately-owned agency, and it makes a promise to all employees that W+K is the agency where they will do the best work of their lives. Such a promise depends upon the creation of a mutually dependent client/talent relationship, where all the clients are there to get the best work possible and all the talent is there to make it. Such a relationship would not be possible without Wieden+Kennedy being highly attractive to both clients and talent alike, and also highly selective from those on both sides. But, as difficult as it sounds, this is what W+K has done. Essentially, according to W+K, all their clients are either 'Develop/Showcase' or 'Core' (see *figure 8,* below).

As can be seen, there is an emerging conflict between creating these new working conditions (flexible hours, remote working, repayment of discretionary effort) and a time-based remuneration model. Agencies that are not manacled to the time sheet can afford to be much more innovative about how they create these attractive working environments. Agency culture plays a huge part in their employer brand status. Although a media agency, not a creative one, the7stars has been noted to be ahead of the cultural curve. Jenny Biggam, a co-founder, was quoted as saying: "My staff can work what hours they like with unlimited holidays."

When I asked Jenny more about their initiative, she replied:

"We treat our people like adults and they respond accordingly. Everybody shares a responsibility for the success of the business and therefore people don't abuse the freedom of unlimited holidays – and if they did, their team would let them know anyway. It means we can dispense with unnecessary, tedious, time-consuming bureaucracy and get on with delivering value for our clients. And it makes the7stars a place where people want to work."

Jenny Biggam
Co-founder, the7stars

The Results Only Work Environment (ROWE) – a human resources strategy pioneered by Jody Thompson and Cali Ressler in their subtly titled book *Why Work Sucks and How to Fix It*[17] – would provide some excellent initiatives for the advertising world but for the fact that the drive in efficiency proposed by their outputs-only model is entirely scuppered by the inputs-only remunerated advertising industry.

CLIENTS

So what does this mean for marketers and procurement? If your brand needs great talent, you'll find it in the agencies with the great employer brands. Unless the client owns all or a share of the agency (the way Innocean is an agency owned outright by Hyundai, or Specsavers has its own in-house agency), then agency management and talent respond to two sets of stimuli from their clients: the financial value and their attractiveness. These two things determine the priority that accounts receive from their agencies. By priority I mean how they decide which talent is allocated to work on which account, but it also indicates how motivated that talent is likely to be, i.e., whether the client receives any discretionary effort from their agency team or its management and so, ultimately, it means the value the agency provides.

Figure 8 shows these two factors as two axes on an agency's client portfolio matrix – what the procurement community calls a 'Supplier Preference Matrix'.

Figure 8

The Supplier Preference Matrix

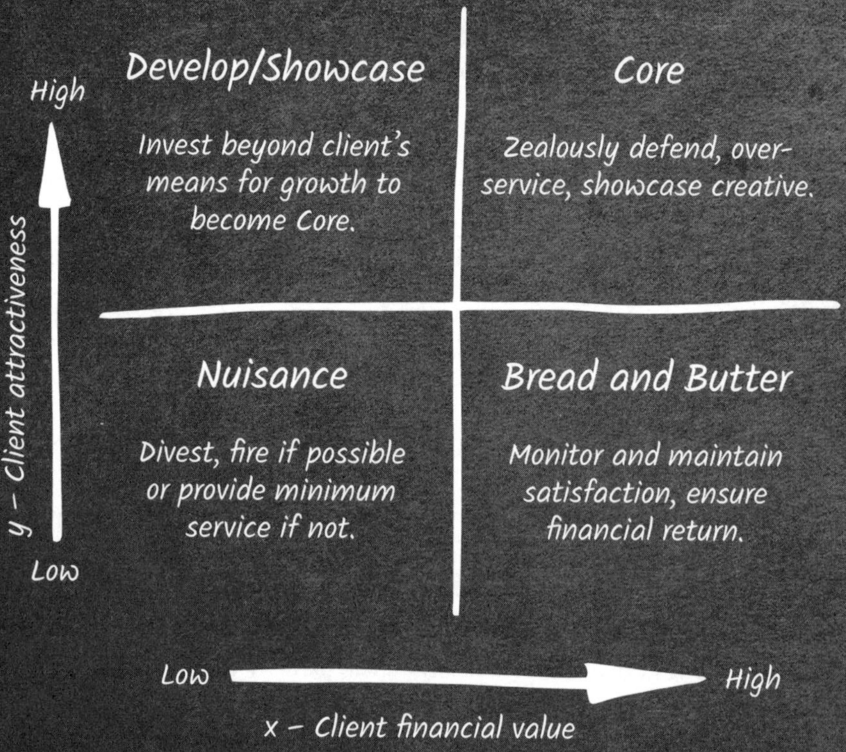

y – Client attractiveness (vertical axis, Low to High)

x – Client financial value (horizontal axis, Low to High)

Develop/Showcase
Invest beyond client's means for growth to become Core.

Core
Zealously defend, over-service, showcase creative.

Nuisance
Divest, fire if possible or provide minimum service if not.

Bread and Butter
Monitor and maintain satisfaction, ensure financial return.

The y-axis represents the attractiveness of the account, which is both relative and subjective. The qualities of an account's attractiveness might include:

- The client's brand reputation
- The client's people (fame, reputation)
- The client's appetite to buy creative work that will enhance the agency reputation
- The opportunity to win industry awards
- The client's processes
- The client's behaviour.

The x-axis represents the relative value of the client business; it can be determined by a number of different measures:

- Overall profitability
- Contribution to agency overhead
- Profit conversion
- Payment terms and cash flow contribution (chapter eight)
- Performance-related bonus (chapter eight).

Most of the factors contributing to the x-axis have been covered above, and some (indicated) will be covered in chapter eight, but it is worth spending a moment on profit conversion. Generally speaking, agencies charge all their clients for a contribution to overhead and profit, as well as the direct costs of staff time spent specifically working on the client's business. But, because the overhead represents fixed costs, when an agency's accounts have already covered the overhead, if the agency wins another piece of business, which it charges at the same overhead rate, there will be a much greater conversion of that revenue to profit. However, before any brands rush to cry foul or use this in their negotiation – there are three important points to consider:

1) For smaller brands, this improves their supplier preference position, but if they negotiate based on their high profit conversion, they may become a Nuisance client.
2) Agencies have to continue to charge on this basis, because if they lose one of their other larger clients the agency will be financially unstable.

3) Perhaps most importantly, agencies rarely recover more than 80% of their time on a client's account, so higher conversion on some is important for the financial wellbeing of all.

The buying strategies that we will look at in chapter five will indicate to a great degree – though not entirely – where a client might sit on the x-axis. Likewise, the Meikle Matrix in chapter four will indicate to a great degree where the client might sit on the y-axis. What's interesting is that the negotiation or renegotiation of contracts with procurement usually moves an account from right to left instead of left to right. As can be seen in *figure 9,* below, this means moving away from the agency's best talent.

The agency's policy for the clients that might sit in these quadrants could be described as follows:

Develop/Showcase

Clients in this quadrant will usually have two qualities that will be attractive to the agency: they will buy reputation-building strategy and/or creative work, and they have the potential to grow and become a 'Core' client (though the potential for growth is not necessary if the contribution to the agency's reputation is great enough). The agency will be able to win creative awards on these clients.

Core

These clients are the flagship accounts of the agency, the ones for which the agency is primarily known as an employer brand and as a prospect to other clients. They will consistently buy creative ideas that build the client's business, but also improve the agency's reputation, providing the agency with case studies in order to persuade new clients to appoint them. Usually, Core accounts have long-standing relationships with their agencies, and the agency will vigorously defend them from poachers. The agency will often overdeliver for these clients with their responsiveness, initiatives and best all-round service. These clients will dominate the agency's awards cabinet.

Bread and Butter

The standard procurement model would describe this quadrant as 'exploitable', but this term isn't appropriate to the agency business model.

Whereas in the standard procurement model these clients would be driven to pay a price premium at the risk of losing them, in the agency world they form the backbone of most agencies. These clients are predictable and buy less exciting strategy and creative work. From time to time there might be an effectiveness story that will win an award, but rarely. However, if they become dissatisfied with the agency, then the agency will usually do their best to retain them. Some clients, though, will behave in such a way that the agency will resign the account or not re-pitch for it because of the damage being done to agency talent and morale.

Nuisance
As rare as these clients are, they do exist. They might be international clients that are vitally important to the agency in another country, such that the agency must service them despite their low revenue and unattractiveness. These clients may also be heritage clients that the agency has grown up around and doesn't have the heart to fire, but in any case, they are usually serviced with minimum effort and little or no interest. If they choose to leave the agency, they will go without a fight.

So when matching talent to task, it stands to reason that an agency would allocate its very best talent to the Core accounts, but it is not quite that straightforward. Agencies will also make sure that their very largest clients have well-qualified or even overqualified staff assigned to them because the consequence of such clients' loss to the agency would be too great. In particular, if an agency has one client that is not very attractive but represents a disproportionately high share of the agency's revenue, then the agency will usually throw money at great talent to keep them happy. Similarly, although a Develop/Showcase client will not usually have the money to attract talent, if they represent an opportunity for the agency to win industry awards, they will surely be assigned the talent that can realize that potential.

So, the hotspots in the Supplier Preference Matrix, the accounts that the agencies' best talent is attracted to and that the best talent will be allocated to, and where the agency people will be most motivated, looks like this:

Figure 9

Supplier Preference
with Talent Hot Spots

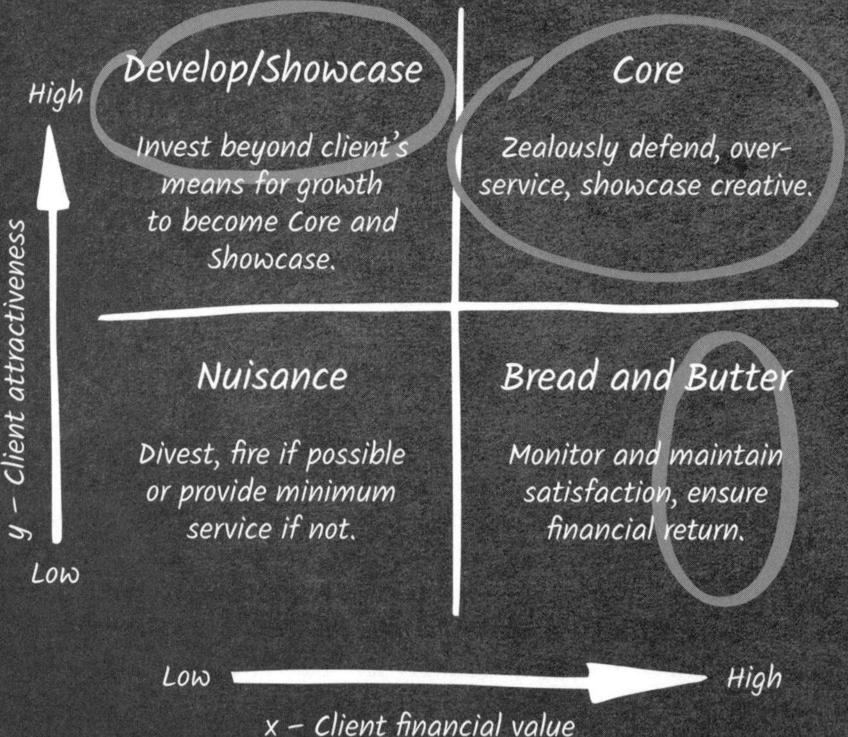

	Develop/Showcase	**Core**
High	Invest beyond client's means for growth to become Core and Showcase.	Zealously defend, over-service, showcase creative.
	Nuisance	**Bread and Butter**
Low	Divest, fire if possible or provide minimum service if not.	Monitor and maintain satisfaction, ensure financial return.

y – Client attractiveness

Low ———————————→ High

x – Client financial value

What is important to understand about this model is the number of clients that might occupy each quadrant. For example, the big creative agencies are likely to have two or three in Develop/Showcase, two or three in Core, one or two Nuisances and the rest in Bread and Butter.

The challenge for marketers and procurement is to select an agency with the right level of talent and then employ the right processes and behaviours to motivate that talent to provide the value the advertiser needs. The clients' greatest barrier to being able to do this effectively is low self-awareness of their position in their agency's portfolio and what determines this position. Three major factors compound this barrier of low self-awareness:

1) No client likes to think that they are less important than another one. Although a client may know that their agency doesn't win awards on their account, they are likely to believe that they are an important enough brand and nice enough people and represent great enough revenue to be considered a Core client of the agency.

2) This factor, which fuels the first, can be answered with a straightforward question: When have you ever heard of an agency tell one of its clients that it is NOT one of their most important accounts?

3) Clients that have not experienced the best advertising talent available don't know what it is like to have access to it. These clients believe they are Core clients because they simply don't know any better.

Interestingly, this is one of the reasons that procurement, in many instances, has a greater advantage in agency selection than marketing. Marketers often fall foul of their own egos and lack the objectivity to know what their agency's supplier preference would be. Procurement strategies are better equipped to determine that difference if executed correctly.

THE MONKEY HOUSE AND AGENCY TALENT

By now, the more attentive readers might have noticed that the different levels of attractiveness of accounts and the varying value of accounts might also correlate to the differing nurturing needs in The Monkey House (see *figure 10*, below).

Figure 10

Supplier Preference and The Monkey House

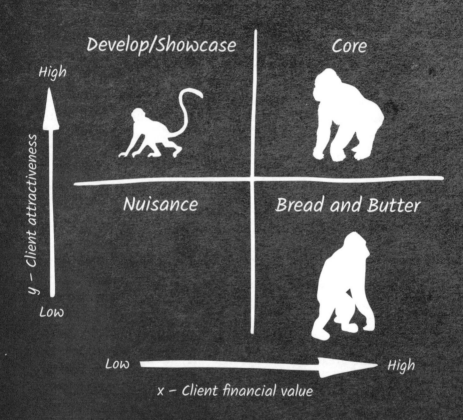

While *figure 10* holds true of agency talent in general, it is worth noting that there are differences between client-facing and value-creating roles and how they behave towards different accounts within an agency. Account management and planning are usually more visible to clients than creative folk. If a client is happy with the people visible to them, then these people become more valuable to the agency because the provision of suitable talent on the business isn't a problem that needs to be solved. Those less visible to a client are more manoeuvrable – as long as moving them is not inconsistent with their calibre in the agency pool.

Account management and planning also usually stay on an account longer than creative people. Although some larger accounts like to have greater longevity with creative directors, and specialist categories such as fashion or cosmetics often demand it, for the most part creatives are assigned to a brief according to the brief's need, its opportunity and their availability, whereas the continuity of account management and planning and their handling of multiple briefs is their fundamental remit.

The key point for advertisers here is that there is nothing they can do in the long term to improve their agency talent unless they change their relationships. To underline this point, here's an exercise in empathy to see how two different key roles might think about which accounts they want to work on.

Creative:

- Will working on this brief improve my showreel and my long-term employability if I want to move agencies?
- Have the people before me been able to get good creative work out of this client?
- Are the people in account management and planning able to sell good work to this client and keep it sold?
- Is the brief any good? Can I write good work to it?
- Is this account important to the agency?
- Will it build my internal reputation?
- Does the client use research sensibly or will it ruin my ideas?
- Does the client have a good process?
- Could I win awards?

Account management:

- Will this account improve my CV and my long-term employability?
- Is this account important to the agency?
- Will I get decent creative teams working on it?
- Will it build my internal reputation?
- Will I get good work out of the agency?
- Will I do so without killing myself trying?
- Does the client know what they're doing?
- Does the client behave well to the agency and the agency's people?

They will both also ask if it will be fun.

The client that manages to answer yes to all of these questions most likely doesn't exist, but those who provide more yeses than noes will get better talent.

A common tactic for brand teams and procurement is to try to stipulate certain agency people in their agency contracts. But if the client is deemed a Core account, the specification of agency staff is an unnecessary measure and one that may simply limit the client's access to the agency's other, and sometimes better, people. For Bread and Butter clients, the agency will not agree to assign their best people to such an account for two good reasons:

1) If they did, those people will not be happy and are likely to leave the agency.
2) It would be insane to assign your best people to anything other than your best clients. Why on earth would you unless your client was Tony Soprano?

So when clients succeed at including the names of individuals in the contract, it's because they won't be securing anybody the agency wouldn't have assigned by choice anyway.

Also, unlike account management and planning, copywriters and art directors in creative departments can manage which accounts they work on differently, depending on their relationship with their executive creative director. Some will be able to negotiate directly which briefs they will work on, some are assigned by their experience versus the complexity of the brief, some because they've worked on that account before and know the brand, or they have important experience in the category, such as automotive or financial services. More often than not, creative teams will either give you work that they are prepared to make or they won't give you any work at all. One of the most difficult things to do is to get a creative team to make an ad that they think is awful. And this is a keen observation about creative people in any profession: you cannot force them to have a great idea, and – even if they have one – you cannot force them to let you have that idea, because you can never prove that they had an idea that they didn't show you. Hence, brands that want great ideas have to encourage and motivate their agencies and the agencies' people to give them their best. This point is most critical for Gorilla and Spider Monkey brands, but applies also to Orangutan brands that can benefit from working to a tighter brief and process.

The unshakeable truth here is that it is an unsustainable strategy for clients to force agency people to work for them unless it is already in those people's interest to do so – in which case the force is unnecessary anyway and could even be harmful to the relationship. Circumstances where agency personnel might accede to such force could include a financial downturn, for example. If the advertising industry starts to shed staff during a recession, everybody – talent included – plays it safe, so the interests of the client and talent are aligned, it's just that the talent's interest has changed from creativity to financial security.

In conclusion, clients' ways of working, their behaviour to their agencies and their financial value to their agencies determine the calibre of talent that works on their business – and this correlates directly to the different kinds of advertising they need from The Monkey House. Therefore, clients get the work that they deserve from their agencies, and there's nothing they can do to change this unless they are prepared to change the procedural, behavioural and financial aspects of their relationships. Brands *can* get the advertising monkeys that they require by designing the relationships they need in accordance with the business problem they want to solve.

Clients' relationships determine agency talent, motivation and therefore value.

SUMMARY

- The agencies of yesteryear made oodles of cash from lots of different revenue streams, but those days are now gone.
- The introduction of procurement into the client/agency mix has cut agency revenue streams and volumes, as have greater transparency and improved technology, enabling competitive threats to some agency services like third party production.
- The nature of the agency business, and its reliance on each client to contribute to their overhead, combined with relatively low profitability, forces agencies to do silly deals when their clients negotiate heavy-handedly.
- Agencies are entirely reliant on their talent to deliver client value. As profits are squeezed and the competition for talent increases from new tech companies, there is a real and present danger that agency value will diminish with its calibre of talent.
- It's hard for marketers to know their agency's priorities because they will almost always be told that they are a Core client.
- Talent is allocated to accounts according to the account's value and its attractiveness to the agency. Management won't allocate great people to bad accounts, nor would bad accounts be able to get the good out of great people if they did.
- Great ideas can't be forced from anybody, ever; they have to be nurtured and encouraged.
- So, clients get the talent they deserve and hence the work they deserve, and there's nothing they can do about it unless they change their processes, behaviours and remuneration.

[10] As an aside, it is perhaps worth noting that the complexity of a large account before the computerization of production often created a killer application for the agency. The explosion of information technology and its impact on production made the movement of a complex account from one agency to another much easier, less expensive and much lower risk.

[11] Though in my view, not without a significant indirect cost in productivity. Open-plan spaces are not conducive to concentrated thought and are, I believe, a false economy for many agency roles, not least strategy and creative roles.

[12] A London accountancy firm specializing in marketing services.

[13] LID Publishing, London.

[14] Continuous professional development as opposed to Collett Dickenson Pearce (CDP) – advertising hot-shop of the 60s, 70s and 80s.

[15] https://www.gunnreport.com

[16] Restricting working hours creates an interesting conflict of interest in agencies that mostly charge their staff out by the hour. How does the agency make more money while ensuring they're a strong employer brand and their people are most effective? Many agencies rely on the extra hours of billable but unpaid overtime – another reason to move away from a remuneration platform unfit for most purposes.

[17] Penguin Publishing Group, 2010

CHAPTER FOUR

BUILDING THE RIGHT RELATIONSHIP FOR YOUR MONKEY

"Where there is great power there is great responsibility,
where there is less power there is less responsibility, and where
there is no power there can, I think, be no responsibility."

Winston Churchill, 1874–1965
British statesman and former Prime Minister of the United Kingdom

THE CONTROL PARADIGM

Marketers are being held increasingly accountable to their boards for the return on their marketing investment.

In turn, this accountability is being passed on to their media and creative agencies, often being asked to prove advertising effectiveness in various ways prior to investment.

However, marketers are also increasing their control over their creative agencies in a number of ways: strategy, creative routes, qualitative and quantitative research key performance indicators (KPIs), time available and the client's stakeholder management.

Therefore, agencies are increasingly responsible for advertising effectiveness, but with decreasing control over their work.

Accountability or responsibility without appropriate control is a recipe for stress and, as such, marketers' prevalent practice is having a detrimental impact on their agencies' talent and their agencies' overall performance, diminishing their value.

THE MONKEY HOUSE CONTROL PARADIGM

Marketing and their agencies design their processes, action standards, etc., according to the kind of advertising they need for their business problem: Spider Monkey, Gorilla or Orangutan.

Because high control can stifle originality, control is calibrated according to the role of creativity – the kind of advertising monkey the client requires.

Likewise, agencies' accountability to their clients varies or changes according to the client's business problem and their relative importance to the agency.

Once designed, client/agency relationships are actively managed in a process of continuous improvement to ensure ongoing, optimal performance.

One of the reasons I enjoyed my time running Ogilvy Russia so much was because of the working relationship that the owner and I established when we met the evening before my first day in the office. I had said something like:

"Over the coming months I'll check in with you on major decisions, of course, to make sure you know what I'm doing and that you're comfortable with my choices."

Leonid Shutov was the owner of what was then called Propaganda Ogilvy, an affiliate of the Ogilvy network, that he wanted to sell to Ogilvy and WPP outright.

"No," he replied. "Oh God," I thought to myself, "I've got myself a Russian control freak."

"No," Leonid continued, "I want you to take full control starting tomorrow. Make decisions as you have to. I'll be around if you need me, but it's your business to run from now on."

There was a lot to do with the company, but I was given clear objectives and free rein to achieve them. I began by recruiting a management team, departmentalizing the process of advertising development more clearly and allocating goals, responsibility and authority to the management. And I applied the same principles of responsibility and control to my management team. By way of example, the agency was once invited to pitch for a high-profile advertising and customer-loyalty programme called Malina.[19] The Russian advertising market was showing growth of about 20% a year, and the agency was growing its revenue by 100% annually from my first year, every year, so resources were stretched. The ad agency was beyond full capacity, as was the activation department, so I approached the head of my direct marketing group, Brian Lee, and offered him the pitch. Brian replied along the lines of:

"You have to be kidding," with a voice of worried disbelief. "We can barely manage as we are. We have IBM briefs coming in, Pfizer … Lenovo have just given us two new projects – I hate to say no but we just can't do it."

So I asked Brian if he would hit his revenue targets for the year.

"Yes," he said without flinching, "and then some!"
I said:
"Fine, I'll tell Malina we can't take part."

I didn't want to take control from him by demanding he dilute his stretched resources further for the chance of winning another piece of busness that our forecasts didn't need – and if I did I would have to take responsibility for all the consequences. Brian did what he said he would do and delivered the revenue, and then some.

Examining responsibility and control in my client relationships began to show a pattern – that there is a diminishing return on an agency's value if a client applies too much control to what the agency does and how it does it. I have expressed this principle like so (see *figure 11*):

Figure 11

The Diminishing Return of High Control

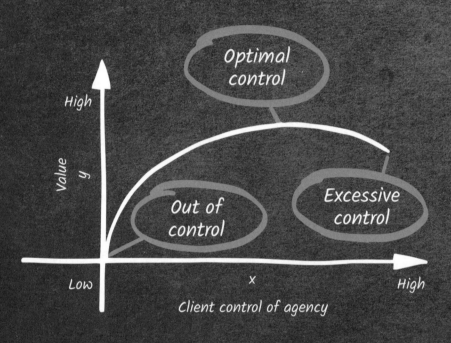

The y-axis represents the value the agency can deliver for its client in the form of effective communications and overall service. The x-axis represents the degree to which client processes and behaviours control the agency.

What's interesting is that when one party deliberately reduces the amount of control it has over another, it does not necessarily result in chaos; indeed when done intelligently it has the opposite effect.

By way of illustration, when I researched the idea further I came across the story of Hans Monderman, a Dutch road traffic engineer, perhaps not the most likely role to inform the marketing world but, nonetheless, bear with me …

Monderman was responsible for a road safety concept called Shared Space. With an understandably cautious beginning, the idea was to reduce traffic controls in the interests of improving driver and pedestrian safety. You may need to read that last sentence again – I did. Drachten, a town in Holland, was a pioneer of the concept.

Drachten has a population of approximately 50,000 people and had a total of 15 sets of traffic lights. On average, the town suffered from one road accident fatality every three years, but after removing 12 of the 15 sets of lights, at the time of reporting there had been no road deaths for seven years. According to Monderman, there had been a few small collisions, but they were almost encouraged, insofar as minor accidents in which nobody is hurt are far preferable to large ones that result in injury or even death.

As counterintuitive as the initiative may seem at first, when you consider the position of a driver approaching a junction with no traffic lights, they will slow down, take responsibility for themselves and their vehicle, and be cautious about the behaviour of others. Instead of devolving responsibility for road safety to the traffic lights, drivers assumed the responsibility themselves. Monderman said:

"Essentially, what it means is a transfer of power and responsibility from the state to the individual and the community."

The initiative was so successful, it was developed further as a concept that was then implemented in many countries such as Australia,

New Zealand, Sweden, Switzerland and Germany. As Monderman himself stated, succinctly:

"When you treat people like idiots, they'll behave like idiots."

The important thing to understand here is what the consequences are of sustained exposure to conditions where somebody has responsibility without control. In trying and failing to take control – which is very stressful – the only way to alleviate the consequent stress is either to change your situation, i.e., quit and leave, or to stop caring, i.e., relinquish responsibility – quit and stay.

Returning to the world of advertising, I considered the question: how does a client typically control an agency? There are a number of ways in which they do this and it's not an exhaustive list:

- Controlling the roles and responsibilities of the agencies within the client's roster
- Creative controls and brand controls: the imposition of creative mandatory inclusions, such as demonstration sequences or brand registration, pack shots and range pack shots – logo size
- Brand guidelines and their inflexible application
- The use of action standards in qualitative or quantitative research
- Dictatorial behaviour
- Poor stakeholder management of others in the client organization
- Providing insufficient time
- Insufficient investment in agency resources.

So, I developed a model I call the Meikle Matrix (*figure 12*).

The Meikle Matrix sets varying levels of responsibility against varying levels of control. It proposes that there are four different agency behavioural responses to the high and low combinations of the two axes. Each of these responses has a different and predictable kind of outcome in the form of the value the agency provides to the client.

Figure 12

The Meikle Matrix

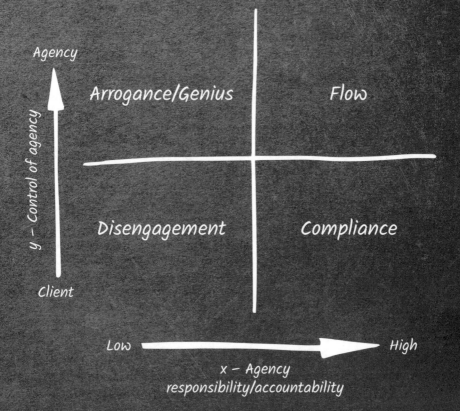

The y-axis represents the degree to which client processes and behaviours control the agency; the optimal level of agency control is achieved at the top. The x-axis represents the degree to which the agency is accountable to the client according to a number of subjective measures; it may be that the account is large or important or just too big to lose, or that the agency has been warned the account may be moved to another agency – or any number of different pressures.

We'll first take a look at how agencies will respond, i.e., what would be their likely attitude to these four different circumstances. Then we'll look at the outputs.

Top Left
Response: Arrogance/Genius
High agency control, low agency responsibility. The client listens attentively to the strategic and creative recommendations the agency makes, and collaboratively engages with the process of campaign development. This is an opportunity for the agency to do what it does best. Under these circumstances, the agency is usually motivated to do its best work. A good agency will assume responsibility for the outcome of the work and do its very best for the client – the outcome of which is 'Genius'. The cynical agency might satisfy its own creative agenda first, or pander to internal egos, and the result will be 'Arrogance'. Arrogance does not necessarily mean that the result will be ineffective, just that the client will only have the choice to take it or leave it.

Top Right
Response: Flow
Optimal agency control, high agency responsibility. The agency is both highly motivated by the relationship (the way the client and agency work and behave together) and also by the client's value to the agency – the ongoing success of its campaigns and the retention of a happy client. The agency is accountable for performance in any or all of the ways described earlier. In this scenario, the agency team often feels like they are in what Mihaly Csikszentmihalyi (pronounced 'CHICK-sent-me-high-ee' if you were wondering) describes as 'Flow'. In a challenging environment, they are working to the peak of their collective ability.

Bottom Right

Response: Compliance

Low agency control, high agency responsibility. In this corner, the agency is held responsible for its performance, but the client exerts excessive control over the agency. Although the agency team will almost always start by doing what they think is right, either they will be too afraid to fight hard for their beliefs or their client will simply mandate that the agency does their bidding. The client's importance means the agency will ultimately capitulate and comply with the client's demands. There are, however, business circumstances where it is appropriate to be in this quadrant, which we will investigate later in this chapter.

Bottom Left

Response: Disengagement

Low agency control, low agency responsibility. In this quadrant, the agency has little or no responsibility for this client or indeed any real commitment to their satisfaction. In many agencies, this is the kind of client that is likely to be fired. In other scenarios, it might be a local branch of an international client trying to throw its weight around. The agency's response is disengagement. If the client is unimportant and tries to tell the agency what to do, the client will likely be ignored.

It stands to reason that these different responses will generate different kinds of output from agencies with different kinds of value for clients. This is indicated below (*figure 13*).

Figure 13

The Meikle Matrix and Outputs

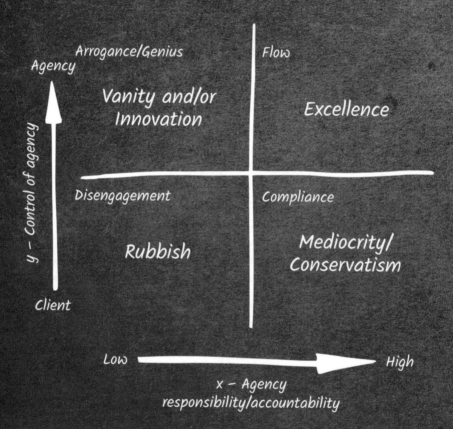

Top Left

Response: Arrogance/Genius

Output: Vanity/Innovation

The agency will create either a vanity project or breakthrough innovation. A vanity project will have a singular purpose of improving agency and/or staff reputation (usually creative) with self-serving work that will please awards judges. It may well work, but less attention or thought will be given to whether it will work or not, because the agency is not accountable for the client's satisfaction. If they don't like it, the client can either decide to START liking the work or go elsewhere. Think of pro bono clients or small clients going to big agencies, wide-eyed and hopeful.

The agency that chooses to be responsible will endeavour to make breakthrough strategy and creative work, and develop innovative, highly effective work for the client. Think of savvy, start-up brands showing signs of strong long-term growth into which an agency would be wise to invest its discretionary effort.

Top Right

Response: Flow

Output: Excellence

Most clients that are investing in active, competitive markets should be in this box. Here a client applies the optimal amount of control to the agency, and their investment is most likely to return 'Excellence' or, in other words, the highest-growth definition of agency value. This is not to say that such clients are undemanding or a soft touch. Clients here can be very demanding, but they understand the strategic need for bravery, innovation and creativity, and they have the capacity to buy breakthrough work. Sports brands, alcohol brands and automotive brands, among others, are routinely found here, not least because their categories demand great advertising. In the UK, brands that are renowned for getting the very best from their agencies in this way include John Lewis, comparethemarket.com, Cadbury, the BBC and, in more recent years, Direct Line Insurance. Global brands include Nike and VW.

Bottom Right

Response: Compliance

Output: Mediocrity/Conservatism

Agencies usually resist high control, at least initially in their relationship.

But if the agency feels like it's fighting a losing battle, talent will exhibit what psychologists call learned hopelessness. Once its people give up hope they comply, and the work will only be as good as the client can make it, because the agency will lose the will to fight for something better.

However, when there is a need for strategically conservative work, agencies mostly understand the specific role of the advertising and resist less from the outset. Instead, the challenge to which they might rise could be one where they must satisfy the specificity of the brief precisely and for good reason; i.e., to make the advertising as good as it can be within the strategic constraints.

Bottom Left
Response: Disengagement
Output: Rubbish
If the agency responds to the client brief at all, it will be with their worst and least-motivated staff. Compared to any other sector, the output would be considered rubbish. Clients with needs such as this would be better off going to an alternative service, such as an independent production facility or even a high-street print shop.

SO, WHAT IS CONTROL?

There are two key areas that contribute to a client's control – the processes a client applies and their behaviour towards their agency. Most aspects of control fall within these two categories, but there's one other thing that I will deal with first, and that is the client's share of agency revenue.

If a client represents such a large proportion of their agency's revenue that it would have a deeply painful or even catastrophic impact if that revenue were to be withdrawn, with the best will in the world the client may unwittingly have more control over the agency than is good for either of them. An agency's dependence on a client can deter its talent, even the best talent, from telling the client what they really think. Larger, established agencies will know better, and will try to ensure that no client has too high a share of their revenue. However, younger agencies can quickly find themselves depending on one or two large pieces of business. And for all parties' sakes, this either needs to be avoided or managed carefully so that the agency doesn't slip into the 'Compliance' quadrant out of fear of upsetting a client upon which their business depends. But back to the main two areas that determine control …

CONTROL FROM PROCESSES

Most big advertisers have 'their own way' when it comes to developing marketing communications. But the needs of different campaigns are so variable, and clients' ability to adhere to their own processes so volatile, and the nature of these processes is so demanding – in particular their often-prescriptive nature – that they end up being counterproductive to achieving the clients' objectives.

Some rare clients deliberately reject or change their own processes from time to time when the nature of the campaign idea and the motivation of the team and the agency demand it. But these processes aren't changed as a matter of course to achieve these different objectives. And that's the point. Rigid processes are made up of prescriptive steps – from how to write a brief to how to evaluate creative work. Their structures are such that they are applicable to the most common kinds of advertising creativity – which logically means that they are unfit for anything extraordinary. Any client with 'their own way' is unlikely capable of producing a Gorilla or a Spider Monkey because of the nature of their process, let alone because such processes may have deterred the talent that could deliver that kind of advertising in the first place.

CONTROL THROUGH BEHAVIOUR

Client behaviour describes the manner with which they deal with their agencies and how they apply their working processes. Some clients are collaborative, some issue instructions, some are friendly, some are stern and demanding. Managing agencies effectively requires the same emotional intelligence and management experience as managing people within your own company. And here is where many can go wrong, even when they think they're doing it right.

For some reason, we're not reticent to sing praises publicly, and we're happy to openly recognize the efforts of individuals and teams – as long as they are our own company's people. But as soon as it's an individual or team in another company, we can't do it. Likewise, with our own people, most are reluctant to raise their voices, use threatening language, or speak in an instructional manner – but when a distance is perceived between a client and agencies, these behaviours become more commonplace. But these behaviours, even down to the habitual use of the words 'thank you', can make an enormous difference.

A good friend and occasional colleague of mine, Paul Burns, told me the following story, which he sometimes uses in his training courses.

There was an advertising agency whose client was a famous national newspaper. The advertising for a national newspaper is always demanding. The nature of the newspaper business dictates a very fast turnaround of work.

The agency got into a regular weekly routine of getting briefed on a Monday morning to write a TV commercial about what would be in the following week's paper. The TV script was written and approved on a Tuesday, pre-production was done on a Wednesday, and it was shot on a Thursday. On Friday, the agency would spend all day in Soho – editing, putting the voiceover on and finishing the commercial, ready for presentation to the editor of the paper. The editor would be driven to the editing suite at about 5.00pm. The creative team, the agency producer, the film director, the account handler and the film editor would all be squashed into the editing suite, nervous, tired and praying that the editor of the newspaper would approve the commercial. If he didn't like it, it meant a late night fixing it, because come what may, something had to get done and on the air.

This particular newspaper editor was brilliant at being an editor, but he was also very dour, a taskmaster. Rarely, if ever, did he say 'thank you' and he ruled by fear. When he arrived in the editing suite, the whole team was always on edge. He'd say 'good afternoon' and ask to see the commercial. They would play it to him, all holding their breath. He gave nothing away and would ask to see it again, then a third time. He'd always watch it in silence and always with no facial expression at all. He'd then turn to the team and say, "Could you make the logo bigger and make it stand out more, maybe make it rotate a few times?"

The agency team would then all dive in at once with why this was a bad idea. It would take too much time. It would cost more money. It would make the brand look cheap and it would be distracting. The newspaper editor would reply, "Just do it, send me a copy later and play it out."

J.F.D.I.

The agency eventually did what he wanted and then they would drown their sorrows in the pub afterwards, feeling more than a bit deflated. Time passed, and the editor eventually moved on and became editor of another title, so a new editor arrived, and so he and the agency got into the same routine.

However, there was a huge difference. The new editor was fun.

He was also appreciative, and he valued everyone's contribution. All of his team and the whole of the agency team loved working with him.

He would also arrive at the editing suite at about 5.00pm on a Friday, just like the previous editor. The whole team would be on edge, just as before. He'd then say, "I can't wait to see the commercial, I've been really excited about this one all week … BUT before I look at it, I've got to tell you all this great joke I heard at lunchtime."

He'd tell them all the joke (and it was always a great joke), they would all laugh, then he'd ask to see the commercial.

They would play the ad for him. He gave nothing away and would ask to see it again and then a third time. He'd always watch it in silence and always with no facial expression. He'd then turn to the team and say, "That's fantastic, I can't believe you've all done such a great job in such a short amount of time. It's brilliant and I'm thrilled. One small thing though, it might be a crazy idea, but would it be possible to make the logo bigger and make it stand out more, maybe make it spin around a few times. What do you think?"

The whole team had no issue with this minor request, they fixed it in five minutes and then they all went to the pub – with the newspaper editor. A great end to a great week. Both editors got what they wanted, but the second one got it with a grateful, enthusiastic and motivated agency team. If you create the right atmosphere and you have mutual respect, then difficult conversations become much easier. However, if something had gone wrong and the first editor had to rely on his agency to get him out of a hole (as can often be the case in the newspaper business), how enthusiastically would they have done it, and how well? But if the second editor had needed the agency's help, they would have been climbing over each other to provide it.

And it cost the second editor nothing.

Before we continue to explore the rights and wrongs of occupying each quarter of the Meikle Matrix, we will first get rid of the bottom left quadrant – Disengagement – as these circumstances are rare and do not really warrant our time. Next, we'll look at some of the other insights the matrix can apply by considering responsibility and control's impact on agency talent, agency efficiency, clients' risk and return on investment.

Figure 14

The Meikle Matrix and Talent

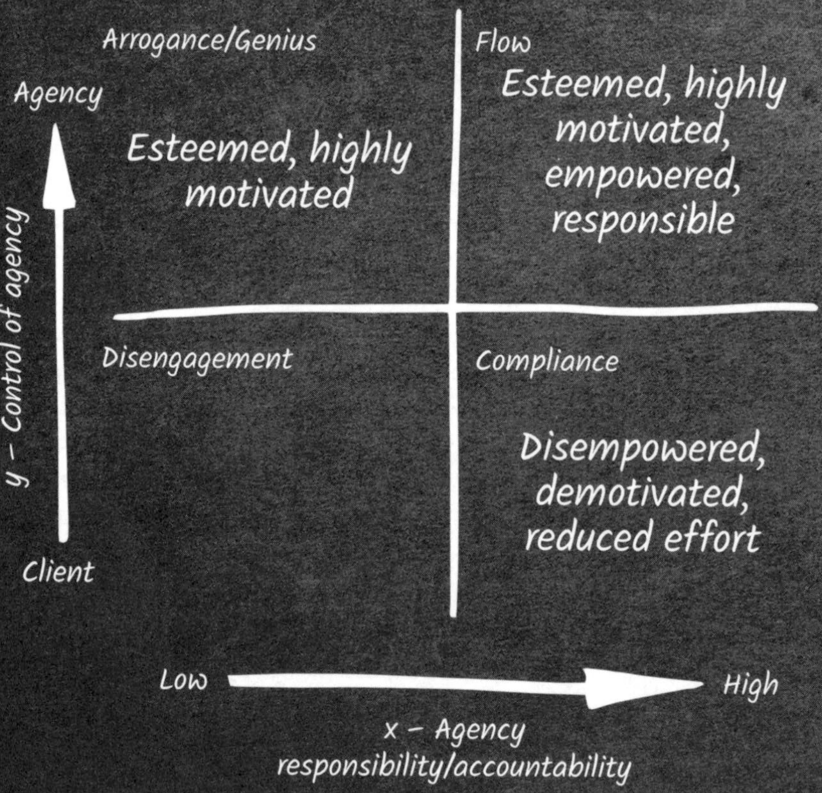

Arrogance/Genius

Agency

Flow

Esteemed, highly motivated

Esteemed, highly motivated, empowered, responsible

y – Control of agency

Disengagement

Compliance

Disempowered, demotivated, reduced effort

Client

Low   →   High

x – Agency
responsibility/accountability

TALENT

Different client processes and behaviours affect agency talent in different ways. Let's look at what happens in the three boxes of the Meikle Matrix.

Top Left – Arrogance/Genius

Consistent with the variability of outputs, talent can respond variably to high control and low responsibility. As Arrogance/Genius suggests, the behaviours are either vain or conscientious. Importantly, though, clients operating in this quadrant can attract the highest level of agency talent. Only those who are able to transform clients' briefs into showcase work and/or transform the clients' business into larger and more profitable accounts will be allocated to these clients. People who work on these kinds of accounts feel esteemed by their peers and are largely pretty motivated.

Top Right – Flow

Agency people working in this quadrant are almost invariably the best of the best the agency can offer. From management's perspective, why would you allocate anything less than the best to clients who use an optimal level of control, and who need and routinely buy flagship creative work? From the individual's point of view, why stay in an agency that doesn't reward its best talent with their best clients? People working in the Flow quadrant feel esteemed by their peers, responsible for the agency's success and are highly motivated.

Bottom Right - Compliance

This last group's talent is split between those that produce 'Conservatism' outputs, i.e., for those clients who have a strategic need to be in this quadrant, and talent whose output is 'Mediocrity' because they should not be in this quadrant, but are under too much control from their client.

Conservatism

Agency staff will be sufficiently satisfied with their lot. They will tend to be perhaps a little less ambitious or will have tempered their ambition with the knowledge of their own limitations. Their working life will be less stressful than the 'Mediocrity' group below because they will know exactly what is expected of them and they will routinely deliver against it.

Mediocrity

Prior to the condition of learned hopelessness, people working in this quadrant experience vast amounts of stress. Accounts here should be producing great work (the client's need is for a Gorilla), but the processes and behaviours make their outputs mediocre. Staff members feel responsible to make it better and continue to fight losing battles until they recognize its futility. At this point, the more talented will lobby internally to work on a better account and, if unsuccessful, are likely to move to another agency. The less talented will emotionally quit but stay on the account with vastly compromised performance.

Vitally, agency people working in the top two quadrants are not only highly motivated, but they routinely demonstrate discretionary effort, i.e., they go beyond their personal scope, and such is their enthusiasm for the brand, the business and the agency that they do more than is asked of them. Those in the Compliance quadrant producing conservative work have little need for discretionary effort: they do what's required and then they go home. They are relatively satisfied with their lot; the agency is relatively happy and the client is relatively happy. But, if talented people are assigned to a client in the Compliance quadrant, they will start with great enthusiasm and show discretionary effort and then, gradually, as the hope of producing great work fades, they will begin to reduce discretionary effort. And if they stay there long enough, they will withdraw it completely.

There are circumstances when both the client and the agency find themselves in the Compliance quadrant. Both marketing and the agency believe in the need for breakthrough work, but marketing is constrained by senior management's conservatism. When one of the most famous UK campaigns of the 21st century was first presented to Cadbury's senior management, the marketing director was told it would never see the light of day.

Such was this ad's fame that the story of the Cadbury gorilla commercial was reported by Jo Caird in *The Guardian* on 7 January 2016 – long after the campaign had finished.

CASE STUDY: DRUM BREAKS AND AD BREAKS. HOW CADBURY GOT ITS MOJO BACK WITH THE HELP OF A GORILLA.

Cadbury is one of the best-loved brands in Britain and Cadbury's Dairy Milk is an iconic chocolate brand, so in 2006 when more than a million chocolate bars were recalled amid a salmonella scare, many couldn't believe it. A leaky pipe in Cadbury's plant in Herefordshire was traced as the source of contamination and on Monday 16 July 2006 the BBC[20] reported that more than 40 people had fallen ill as a result.

How does a brand recover from such reputational damage?

The following year, the brief issued to Cadbury's creative advertising agency, Fallon, was: "Give people the feeling they have when eating our chocolate."[21]... to remind them of the benefits of Cadbury's dairy milk. Some might have thought the brief was a brave move after the events of the previous year, but that bravery was to pale into insignificance compared to the advertising that followed.

As can often be the case when solving problems or developing ideas, Juan Cabral, the director at Fallon who wrote the Cadbury's gorilla ad, wasn't working on the brief at the time when the idea came to him. Originally, he spoke with colleagues about making the idea of a gorilla playing a drum kit into a short film, but soon after conceiving the idea, Cadbury approached Fallon in London and asked for their help. Shortly after that, Fallon pitched the gorilla idea to Cadbury.

Phil Rumbol was Cadbury's director of marketing at the time. Rumbol was quoted in *The Guardian*[22] as saying that he and his team had had an instinctive and immediate reaction to the ad when it was first proposed to them, a sentiment that was not later echoed by Rumbol's superiors.

The client and agency team wanted to launch the ad in a 90-second format during the finale of *Big Brother*. Cadbury's senior management could not believe that the plan was to run an ad three times longer than the normal (and most cost efficient) 30-second format. Furthermore, there was no chocolate in it. None of the usual taste cues of pouring chocolate in swirls of deliciousness; instead there was just a gorilla, a drum kit and Phil Collins. To add insult to advertising convention's injury, there wasn't even a clear message, just an end line of "A glass and a half full of joy."

What is now commonly referred to as the "aggregation of marginal gains" (thanks to the success of Dave Brailsford, the Performance Director for Team Sky, Great Britain's professional cycling team) is a principle that works in the mind of every great art director. They have an obsession for detail, knowing that even the slightest compromise on quality or style can facture the story they're telling or distract the viewer, so Cabral frantically searched for a gorilla that would do justice to his idea. He rejected Computer-Generated Imagery and finally settled for a costume from a film studio in Hollywood that they augmented with a gold tooth.

The ad was completed, edited and presented far faster than it was approved, but after four months of relentless persistence, Rumbol finally got the green light to run the ad.

And the hard work paid off. In the first half of 2007, value sales of Cadbury's Dairy Milk had fallen 4% year-on-year. In the month Gorilla broke, value sales increased by 5.9%.[23]

In my view, this is as near a perfect example as there ever could be of how to get the best from an agency. The client issued the brief, bought the work, relinquished control to the agency for their areas of expertise in production and allowed them to scour the earth for a gorilla outfit that they liked, even down to the gold tooth (even drummer gorillas have an image to maintain, you know). When Rumbol championed the work, he didn't fix it, change it, add the bits that would make it more like work they had run before; he championed the work as it was, and finally got it on the air.

"The Gorilla did three things for us: Put a smile on our consumers' faces; Put a buzz in our organization and made us feel proud of being part of it again; Made us go back to the iconic advertising we were once famous for."

MD Trevor Bond at the Cadbury UK
Senior Managers' Conference, February 2008[24]

The level of commitment and the level of discretionary effort, attention to detail and bloody-minded determination of everybody involved were phenomenal.

Why is this important? Discretionary effort – i.e., trying harder than you have been asked to try, innovating, thinking beyond your initial brief – is where much of an agency's greatest value can be found. It may be additional opportunities to implement a campaign idea through another channel, it might be a creative idea that has sat in a drawer until the right client brief came along, it may be thinking about client problems in the shower, any number of things.

As I noted in the introduction, throughout the rest of 2007, 2008 and into 2009 the new business pitch briefs were saying 'we want a gorilla'. The problem is that it takes a certain type of marketing director, employing a certain set of behaviours with appropriate responsibility and control, to get a gorilla. On countless occasions this ad could have died – indeed it could have been shot in the paddock after its first presentation. It's the partnership and implicit mutual trust between a client and an agency that can make this kind of transformative work. Gorillas come from high agency responsibility and optimal agency control.

EFFICIENCY

Before we examine the impact of responsibility and control on the efficiency of an account, it is worth considering efficiency in the agency environment. There are some aspects of the role of a marketing services agency in which efficiency would be a clear benefit, but much of what they do would be harmed or hampered by efforts to be efficient. The administration of the account: communication, organization, meetings, finance, provision of materials and so on are all better managed efficiently rather than inefficiently. On the other hand, the development of strategy, the process of developing creative ideas, the business of exploring different propositions, and considering how to execute an idea require agencies to prospect different territories with some speculation in order to find what they think will best deliver against a brief. Some of the explored territories won't yield any value and are therefore wasteful, but the inefficiency of the exploration is usually a necessary part of the creative process.

It is also worth noting that different client categories can have different demands on efficiency. Product categories that need always-on advertising – such as retail and insurance – cannot afford the inefficiency of time speculated on, because the timing of their campaigns is business critical. But in such instances the agency might assign more people rather than demand a longer lead time.

This means we need to be wary of a relentless pursuit of efficiency across all things. There is a danger that a finely-tuned, highly efficient process is incapable of the flexibility required to accommodate the unpredictable. Efficiency is brittle.

Figure 15

Meikle Matrix and Efficiency

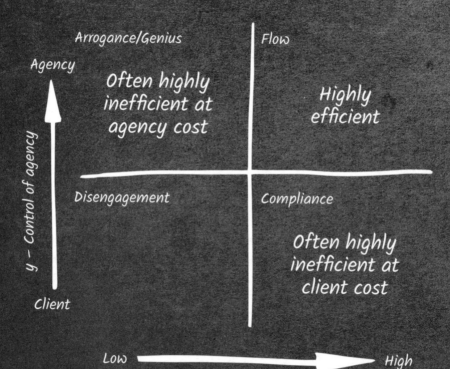

Arrogance/Genius

Flow

Agency

Often highly inefficient at agency cost

Highly efficient

y – Control of agency

Disengagement

Compliance

Often highly inefficient at client cost

Client

Low ⟶ High

x – Agency responsibility/accountability

Accounts in the top left quadrant are often inefficient at the expense of the agency. The client cannot afford the resources needed and the agency chooses to invest for the potential of the creative work, the growth of their client or hopefully both.

Accounts in the Compliance quadrant that shouldn't be there are often highly inefficient (and one way or the other this is at the client's cost, as can be seen below).

Brands whose portfolio strategy or business or market conditions demand a conservative strategy and creative work (for example, a client with multiple brands in the same category – such as Procter & Gamble has in fabric softeners) would not want advertising on one brand to be limitlessly effective at the expense of the market share of its own other brands. Instead, such a client will use more prescriptive processes and rigid selection criteria for strategies and creative ideas to ensure one brand doesn't cannibalize another – i.e., high control.

In my experience, almost all clients brief their agencies by asking for 'breakthrough creative work' – many despite their rigorous processes and conservative needs – in the belief that this will rouse and motivate the people on their account. Others will often say that the agency can stray from the established campaign idea as long as they do so in addition to the briefed route. Clients do this thinking that it will make their account more attractive, but in both instances an expensive process of attrition wears down the agency's best efforts into something much more mediocre and safe while simultaneously demotivating its people.

This process of attrition costs clients more in multiple ways. Large clients usually operate on a retainer, the rates of which are determined by hours expended, so at the end of a year the stacks of unsold work will contribute to evidence to maintain or increase a fee. The higher relative turnover of agency staff means clients' products, brands and business have to be relearned by the staff who replace those departing. And there is the cost of client and agency time in repeated engagements, meetings, re-briefs and rounds and rounds of research.

The most efficient, or perhaps I should say optimally efficient, accounts are in the Flow quadrant. The agency has the incentive, the talent and the client relationship best suited to satisfy the client's needs. This is not necessarily to say that this efficiency is inexpensive, merely that it is more efficient than the practices of over-speculation by the agency in the Genius/Arrogance quadrant (compared to the revenue afforded by the client) or the processes of attrition in the Compliance quadrant.

GLOBALIZATION AND CONTROL

Over the last few decades, more and more global organizations have developed advertising designed to work in multiple countries. The likes of Unilever, SC Johnson, Procter & Gamble and Mars have found different ways of making their need to advertise in multiple countries more economical. Countries where such global advertisers' brands are present are grouped by any number of factors – size, importance, growth opportunity, brand name on the product, cultural commonality, etc., such that one country's agency or an appointed regional 'hub' agency can create campaigns to be used in multiple markets.

Global research organizations such as Millward Brown and Ipsos Mori have further facilitated the growth in globalization by checking the suitability of an ad in a number of markets prior to its production. Different advertisers apply the same principles in different ways. One may create an ad campaign centrally, swapping in different language pack-shots and changing the voiceover and titles only. Another may take an idea or an execution from one country and reapply it to another by having the whole ad recast, reshot and totally remade but using the same original idea. And, as ever, different brands and different product categories have different levels of multinational relevance – fine fragrances may travel more easily than mayonnaise.

If we think of the highest level of multinational application, the level of control exerted over the creative process grows very high indeed. The central client, the research they use and usually a local stakeholder all have to check that the ad will be relevant and sufficiently engaging through strategy, creative idea, casting, wardrobe, location, set design and use of music. This makes the advertising process become a research and consensus process rather than a creative one, the best possible result of which is a steady, safe Orangutan, which is fine if that suits a brand's need, but dangerous if the competition deploys Gorillas or Spider Monkeys.

RISK AND ROI

Having explored the impact of responsibility and control over the agency, we can now look at how the Meikle Matrix can be applied to different advertising monkeys. In *figure 16,* below, The Monkey House has been overlaid on the Meikle Matrix and it becomes clear – assuming clients are in the right quadrant – that the most likely outputs from the agency in any quadrant are consistent with the needs of the client.

The challenge for brands with demanding processes or conservative cultures is that if they need a Gorilla or a Spider Monkey, they will need to loosen the reins over their agencies to a degree of likely discomfort.

But my overriding observation here, the greatest cause for concern and also the greatest opportunity, is that very many clients brief for Gorillas but run relationships for Orangutans. This is actually worse than briefing for an Orangutan in the first place, because it results in inefficiency: higher agency staff turnover, higher costs and a mediocre output.

Figure 16

The Meikle Matrix and The Monkey House

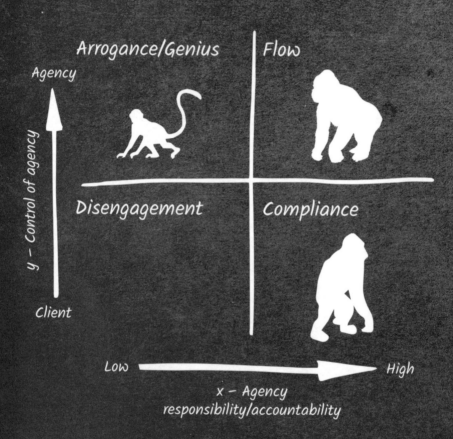

Levels of responsibility and control have to be designed according to the advertising monkey brands' need.

SUMMARY

- Clients whose processes and behaviours control their agencies too much diminish their agencies' value.
- Agencies' talent and agencies' efficiency are influenced by these client processes and behaviours.
- By designing processes and ways of working with agencies, clients can better determine the kind of monkey and the value they can derive from the agency.
- In many instances, reducing control over the agency has significantly improved the advertising's return on investment and, in turn, overall ROI (see case studies in chapter six).
- Lower control over an agency, but with high accountability to the client for advertising performance, will attract and motivate the agency's best talent and produce more effective Gorillas for growth brands.
- Brands with risk-averse strategies, either Orangutans or brands within a portfolio that includes competitive products, may need higher controls to avoid risk or cannibalization of sister products.
- Inappropriately high controls for a Gorilla will elicit a worse result than briefing for an Orangutan.

---

[19] Russian for 'raspberry', if you were wondering. Customers would collect loyalty points much like picking raspberries.

[20] http://news.bbc.co.uk/1/hi/england/6900467.stm

[21] IPA Cadbury – "How a drumming gorilla beat a path back to profitable growth: a real-time effectiveness case study", Magali Barreyat-Baron and Rachel Barrie.

[22] Jo Caird, *Guardian Media*, 7 January 2016.

[23] IPA Cadbury – "How a drumming gorilla beat a path back to profitable growth: a real-time effectiveness case study", Magali Barreyat-Baron and Rachel Barrie.

[24] As above.

CHAPTER FIVE

MARKETING PROCUREMENT AND FEEDING YOUR MONKEY

"There is hardly anything in the world that some man cannot make a little worse and sell a little cheaper, and the people who consider price only are this man's lawful prey."

John Ruskin, 1819–1900
Victorian art critic and social thinker

THE MARKETING PROCUREMENT PARADIGM

More often than not, brand owners' procurement departments do not apply appropriate buying strategies to the procurement of marketing services in creative agencies.

Fees paid to agencies in the provision of such marketing services represent investments for their clients, from which clients expect to receive a return greater than the principal.

However, the process of procurement sees hard-nosed negotiation over these *investments* in the same way as a company might manage *costs*.

Marketing procurement people are also usually incentivized by 'cost savings', regardless of whether the 'cost' is expected to deliver a return and should therefore be managed as an investment.

While some of the work creative agencies undertake for clients does not contribute directly to the client's return on investment, ultimately they contribute to the effectiveness of the client's advertising investment overall. This means they should be procured according to a strategic buying strategy that allows the agency to benefit from the relationship.

Reduced investments in agencies, like any other investments, either increase the risk of not generating returns or simply provide lower returns.

THE MONKEY HOUSE PROCUREMENT PARADIGM

In the same way that client processes and behaviours influence agency talent (which is ultimately responsible for client value), so too will the way the agency is selected, remunerated and financially incentivized.

Procurement's buying strategy for marketing services will be consistent with the nature of the client's business problem or marketing objective. Spider Monkey problems will use a 'Critical' buying strategy; Gorilla brands a 'Strategic' buying strategy; and Orangutan brands an appropriate 'Leverage' buying strategy.

Marketing procurement will be incentivized on savings only against hard costs, which do not have a variable return on investment.

Marketing procurement will share performance measures with marketers for all marketing activity in which it is involved.

In October 2011, I delivered what turned out to be – through no fault of their own – my last training course for marketing procurement professionals. I had been running a number of open courses through an industry association for a couple of years to provide marketing procurement with some insight into how to manage agencies more effectively. My intention had been to develop a network of marketing procurement professionals who would go on to buy my consultancy services, but the leads I had been making had not been converting into business. I realized that this could have been because they didn't like or trust me but, increasingly, I felt that there was something else I was missing ...

With this in mind, I began what would be my last training course with two questions for my attendees. There were about ten delegates in the room, representing marketing procurement for categories such as automotive, telephony, cereal manufacture and financial services. My first question was this:

"Can you please raise your hand if you are personally incentivized to save money from your expenditure on marketing services?"

Pretty much immediately ten hands went up around the room. My second question was this:

"Could you please leave your hand up if your bonus is in any way contingent on the value of the marketing services you procure?"

The second question took longer to answer than the first and needed to be repeated a couple of times. Slowly, but surely, every hand that had been raised by an incentive was lowered by a lack of accountability. I had found my problem. My presentations and my arguments had been clear – that marketing is an investment from which its investors expect a return greater than the principal – but my delegates didn't want to bite the hand that fed them. To change the status quo would be to choose to be more accountable and to purposefully make their lives more difficult. In short …

"It is difficult to get a man to understand something, when his salary depends on his not understanding it."

Upton Sinclair, 1878–1968
American author

However, the time I spent with marketing procurement people was not fruitless. During the process of delivering a number of these courses, I started to learn a few things about procurement. One of the first things I learned was a directional policy matrix for buying invented by Peter Kraljic – the Kraljic Matrix (*figure 17*).

Figure 17

The Kraljic Matrix

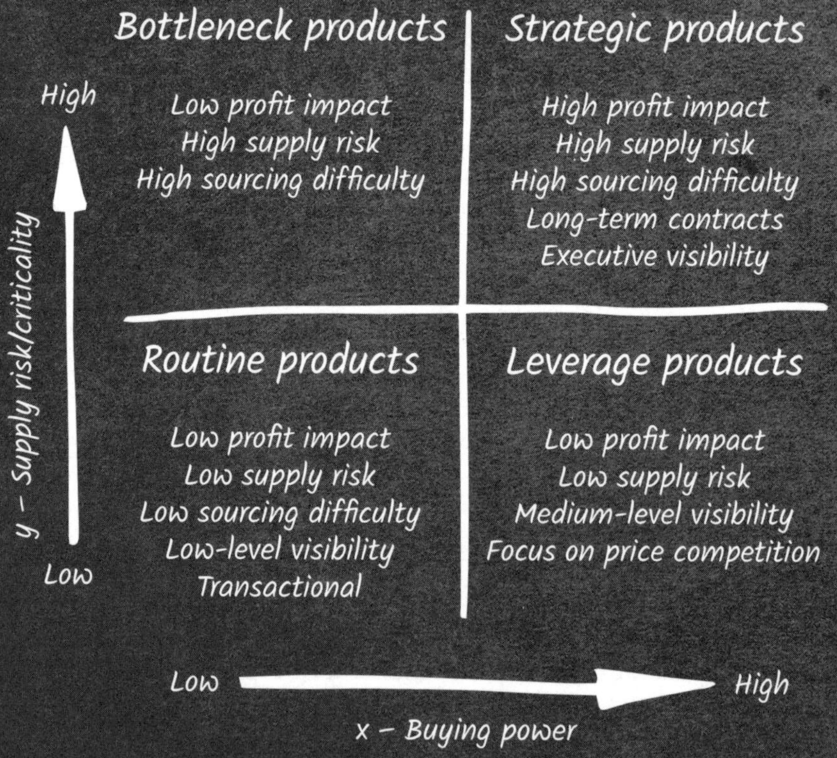

Bottleneck products

Low profit impact
High supply risk
High sourcing difficulty

Strategic products

High profit impact
High supply risk
High sourcing difficulty
Long-term contracts
Executive visibility

Routine products

Low profit impact
Low supply risk
Low sourcing difficulty
Low-level visibility
Transactional

Leverage products

Low profit impact
Low supply risk
Medium-level visibility
Focus on price competition

High

Low

y – Supply risk/criticality

Low ⟶ High

x – Buying power

The y-axis represents the importance of the goods or services being procured to the company procuring them, and the risk of these goods not fulfilling their purpose or delivering the value for which they are intended.

The x-axis represents the impact these purchases will have on the buying company's profitability. It can be seen in terms of the magnitude of the outlay for them but, equally, as its relative importance to the vendor – in other words, the purchaser's buying power.

In the version above, the model describes the features or nature of the products or services being procured. In *figure 18*, below, developed with my colleague Phil Massey, each box instead contains the strategies for purchasing against each quadrant. For the purposes of the buying strategies in terms of marketing services, I have also made the following changes: The y-axis is the variability of return on investment for the purchase or the relative importance of the purchase – its criticality. The top left quadrant is now simply called 'Critical'.

Figure 18

The Buying Matrix
for Marketing Services

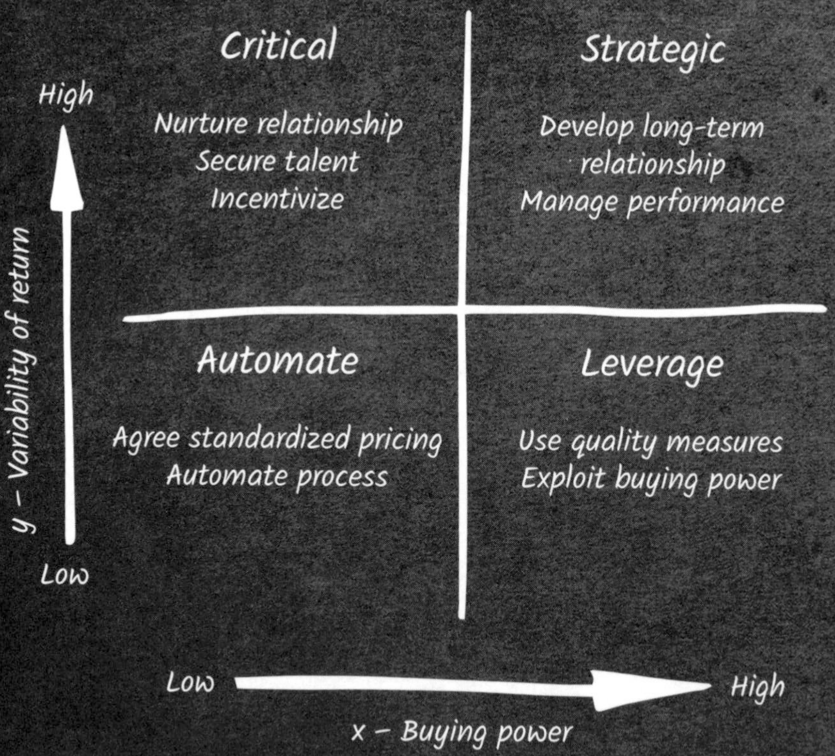

Critical

Nurture relationship
Secure talent
Incentivize

Strategic

Develop long-term
relationship
Manage performance

Automate

Agree standardized pricing
Automate process

Leverage

Use quality measures
Exploit buying power

y – Variability of return (High / Low)

x – Buying power (Low / High)

The original Kraljic Matrix was first published in the *Harvard Business Review* in 1983. The language of the matrix and our knowledge of the advertising industry at the time indicate quite clearly that this was not a model designed for developing directional policy for investments. At that time, procurement departments had their own mandates and had not really ventured into the world of marketing – in fact, as Gerry Preece and Russel Wohlwerth noted in *Buying Less for Less*, procurement in the 80s was just beginning to enjoy some business limelight when they came to the rescue of the automotive business in the US. But there was tangibility about the products they bought, which could be anything from agricultural commodities to manufacture their consumer goods, or steel to make cars. But, this tangibility is something the procurement industry would not find when procuring many services for marketing. It's worth getting familiar with this matrix as a variation of it comprises a key part of The Monkey House.

Another way of looking at it is that the Critical quadrant represents a seller's market, the Leverage quadrant represents a buyer's market and the Strategic quadrant is where both parties are invested in their mutual success. So, with this purchase model in mind, let's return to marketing procurement.

As the procurement discipline grew in size and reputation and migrated toward the realm of marketing, procurers could see quite quickly that marketing expenditure made up a significant part of many big advertisers' profit and loss accounts. If marketing expenditure could be reduced, it would have a significant and positive impact on their business's profitability.

As with most approaches to new categories in procurement, they looked at the greatest expenditures first: media, then production – simpler and tangible – then agency fees. The problem is that the buying strategies they employed were almost universally Leverage, i.e., they were focused on price reduction because it was what they knew and it was how they were incentivized.

Buying media services provides a useful illustration as to the difference between costs and investments. To apply a buying strategy for media properly, we will first need to differentiate between the fees paid to the agency and the capital spent on media space/time with media owners. Mainstream media channels have vast amounts of data (audience demographics, opportunity to see, frequency of exposure), which are quality standards that justify their price. Likewise, you can see for yourself whether your ad actually got the early right-hand page you paid for by buying the newspaper. So, this is a natural Leverage buy.

But that's why brands have media agencies in the first place. Although they began as sales agents for the media owners, for a long time already media-buying agencies have been outsourced procurement specialists who have consolidated the buying power of their clients so that they can negotiate better deals with the media owners.[25]

Media planning is a different story. This involves the solution of problems with unlimited possible solutions. On even the most basic level, media planning requires the development of an optimal media plan against a given budget and set of objectives. It involves using consumer insight (of products, behaviours and consumption of media), media selection and mix (TV, radio, press, out-of-home, online), format (size, shape, duration, position), development of a channel plan identifying the roles of the media, and timing.

There can be no effective quality measures for media planning given this number of variables. An experienced marketer will have a point of view. They will be inspired by a media strategy to a greater or lesser degree. They will know their consumers and have judgment about the media planner's insights. But they will not have the insights, strategies and plans that were never presented because they didn't invest sufficient funds in the planning service. It might be a financial saving to reduce media planning fees, but it could represent a significant economic loss of ROI. Media planning is therefore a Strategic buy.

A financial saving that creates an economic loss is not a saving, it's a loss.

"I can put down on a page a picture of a man crying,
and it's just a picture of a man crying. Or I can put him down
in such a way as to make you want to cry. The difference is artistry
– the intangible thing that business distrusts."

Bill Bernbach, 1911–1982
Founder, Doyle Dane Bernbach

Similarly, production cannot be taken in one bundle, it must be split between what we can call 'upstream' and 'downstream' production; let's briefly define these terms.

Upstream production is the start of the production process; it is the realization of creative ideas by creative specialists such as photographers, illustrators and film directors. Upstream production involves the unlimited variability of artistry, and therefore represents an investment – it can be invested in either heavily or lightly depending upon the need and the available budget. Downstream production is the duplication, simple adaptation and distribution of production materials to the media in which they will run/appear. Downstream production has very clear quality standards.

To illustrate the difference, consider a campaign of newspaper ads. The upstream production, including photography, typography and design, will determine the visual appeal of the ad and its ability to grab and hold the attention of the reader. Do it badly and the return on media investment is diminished because the ad will be overlooked; do it well and more readers will be engaged and then persuaded (see *figure 6*, chapter two). The downstream production has limited value – the requirement is to get the right ad at the right size with the right colours to the right technical specification delivered to the right medium at the right time. Not only is this the minimum requirement of the production company, but also it is difficult to add any greater value than competent completion of the requirement. The bigger the number of ads to be duplicated and distributed, the greater the advertiser's buying power. Downstream production therefore demands a Leverage buying strategy and upstream production requires either a Critical or Strategic buying strategy.

BUYING CREATIVE AGENCY SERVICES

Creative agencies solve problems with unlimited possible solutions – as such, the returns on investment are highly variable. Although they provide myriad services to their clients, whether they are developing brand strategies, advertising ideas, campaign management, creative development of ideas in upstream production or the integration of communication ideas across a media mix, all of these services have open-ended solutions. Campaigns in any medium that are counting on originality and persuasive creativity need to be bought Strategically; they cannot have effective quality measures applied before their effectiveness is proven when a campaign goes live.

However, procurement departments of marketing services almost always employ Leverage buying practices, because that's what they've always done – and they're incentivized by the savings.

But this is all rather abstract. What is the actual difference between a Strategic and a Leverage buying strategy?

There are a number of tools and tactics brands use with their agencies that can collectively, or sometimes individually, determine the overall buying strategy. Many people in marketing procurement believe that they are buying strategically, but their practices would indicate they are not. Agencies' financial and contractual terms include a number of transactional variables that affect the agency's ability to make money (which they should be able to do in a strategic purchase).

TIME-BASED REMUNERATION

Since the early 90s, creative agencies began transitioning from commission-based fees, based on the media spend of a client, to hourly-based fees. To calculate the fee for most big agency contracts, the agency determines which of their people need to spend what proportion of their time on a client's business, then they calculate the total staff cost per person, multiply that by their time allocated, factor in the contribution to overhead (usually about 100%) and add a margin for profit (usually agreed with the client at somewhere between 15 and 20%) (see *figure 19*). 'Cost plus' is the term applied to this fee model.

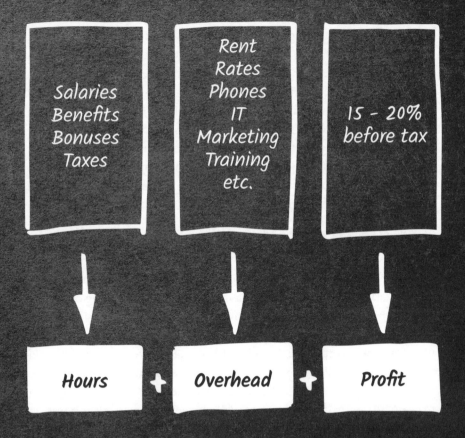

Figure 19

Cost Plus Equation for Agency Fees

Salaries
Benefits
Bonuses
Taxes

Rent
Rates
Phones
IT
Marketing
Training
etc.

15 – 20%
before tax

Hours + **Overhead** + **Profit**

By 2000, the majority of advertisers paid their creative agencies by the hour, and now almost every sizeable agency is paid by the hour. However, there are a number of issues attached to the use of hourly rates – a theme I will return to in chapter eight:

- Hourly rates are two steps removed from the value clients seek to procure. Hourly rates assume that in a given hour somebody is both trying hard *and* knows what they are doing. There's no value to be had from busy fools.
- The agency's ability to make a profit is limited by their chargeable assets, and it is finite in the form of the maximum hours their chargeable staff represents. There is no benefit to the agency to do good work faster; on the contrary, agencies are arguably incentivized to spend the maximum available time on any given brief.
- Ironically, however, agencies mostly fail to recover the hours they expend on their clients in billing, usually only charging for about 80% of hours and some I've come across recover as little as 55%.
- Many clients reconcile agency hours such that if the agency goes over time it's at their own cost, but unexpended hours are to be reconciled and either refunded or not charged. The worst of both worlds for the agency.

RECONCILIATION OF HOURS

Some clients are better than others at paying for hours they may be responsible for wasting, and some agencies are better at negotiating these reconciliations. The point is that clients are increasingly taking control of their agency resources, but not taking the responsibility consistent with that control. To elaborate: as much as the commission system at 15% of media was overpriced, agencies at least had both responsibility and control for their clients and were accountable to them insofar as then, as now, the agency could be fired. Equally, when clients made lump sum investments in the form of commission, if agencies over-burnt hours on some briefs and under-burnt on others, it was the agency's responsibility to make them balance out.

In summary, when agencies are paid by the fairly reconciled hour, they will take the time allowed to do their best possible work and hope to recover the hours they expend and turn a profit. If agencies are paid a lump investment against a scope of work regardless of how long it takes or not, they are incentivized to deliver their best work in the most efficient manner and potentially make more profit from it. If the agency fails to convince the client to buy their recommendation, however, they may have to go again at their own expense. The first is more consistent with a Leverage buying strategy and the second with a Strategic one.

REVERSE AUCTIONS

When it comes to new business, many in procurement have been re-applying tools they have used in other categories. By way of example, we have seen a rise in the use of reverse online auctions as a means to establish an agency's fees or hourly rates, particularly as part of a pitch.

For those who are perhaps unfamiliar with the tool, a reverse online auction is a competitive pricing tool that takes the form of an anonymous auction. Competitive suppliers bid and compete with one another for contracts within a limited period of time. They are notified of their bidding position versus their competitors – and given the opportunity to revise their rates down in order to win the contract. When they submit a revised bid, they can see if their position has changed. The auction continues until competitors can cut their own throats no further and a winner is declared.

Reverse online auctions represent Leverage buying at its most brutal and are very effective at lowering costs. E-auctions, as they are also known, are simply a race to the bottom, but they are also wrong on many other levels. Even though some of the more sophisticated procurers of marketing have, they believe, applied the tool strategically, they are still exposing their companies to significant risk of diminished value. Here's why:

- Cynical agencies can bid low and simply deliver low. They can allocate weaker, cheaper talent that is just sufficient to retain the client but not enough to satisfy their needs.
- Equally, agencies can deliver unsatisfactory services according to what the client pays and then renegotiate a proper deal when the client complains.
- Desperate agencies can bid whatever it takes to win as long as the client's revenue will make a contribution to their overhead. Desperate agencies are less stable and don't represent appropriate assurance of supply to the client (see *figure 14*, chapter seven).

Procurement people are awarded bonuses on cost savings, making e-auctions a savagely effective tool. However, their incentives have no good relation to the value of the services being procured. And consider the danger of their application – the result of a reverse online auction diminishes the agency's value – but the value at question is not just the agency's fee. If the agency consequently produced less effective advertising, the value consequence is the brand's return on investment, which is greater than the agency fee, the production, the media spend and other campaign investments combined. The lost value is the market share that was instead won by a competitor. Once again, a financial saving creates a greater economic loss.

PAYMENT TERMS

In June 2015 *Campaign* magazine published an article about Heinz with the headline: "IPA slams Heinz pitch process". The article revealed that Heinz was running a competitive pitch for its advertising account and that one of the conditions of the pitch was that the winning agency would agree to payment terms of 97 days. Quite understandably, the incumbent agency AMV/ BBDO declined to re-pitch.

> *"They are risking not getting the best agencies in town to compete, to save a small amount of money in an area that could be potentially transformative for their business. It's so short-sighted. The long hand of procurement is driving this."*

> Paul Bainsfair
> Director General, IPA

Payment terms have been creeping up across many clients and can significantly harm agencies' cash flow. Agencies that do accede to these kinds of demands for whatever reason ultimately have to pass on the cash flow problem to their suppliers, the smaller organizations often suffering more than their agency clients.

Sadly, we've known for a long time that buying on price alone isn't wise – we just have a knowing-doing gap because procurement incentives are almost universally inappropriate. John Ruskin got it right as early as the 19th century when he observed:

> *"It's unwise to pay too much ... but it's worse to pay too little. When you pay too much, you lose a little money – that is all. When you pay too little, you sometimes lose everything, because the thing you bought is incapable of doing the thing it was bought to do. The common law of business balance prohibits paying a little and getting a lot – it can't be done. If you deal with the lowest bidder it is well to add something for the risk you run. And if you do that, you will have enough to pay for something better."*

John Ruskin, 1819–1900
Victorian art critic and social thinker

What's more, there has never been much that could stop agencies pitching in poetry and delivering in prose, which is why brands will usually get less for less, as Gerry Preece observed.[26] And in a market as competitive as creative ad agencies, there's also nothing to stop agencies low-balling their offers to win the business only to 'discover' six months into their four-year contract that unless they're paid significantly more they will be unable to deliver the kind of quality the client needs, despite having made the promise that they would. Interestingly, the subsequent increases in fees do not trigger claw-backs from the savings bonuses paid to procurement.[27]

All of this is not to say that there are never brands or business problems for which Leverage buying strategies are appropriate. However, it would be fair to say that most brands are currently employing a Leverage buying strategy for their marketing services and that many might improve the value delivered by their agencies if they bought strategically.

PROCUREMENT AND SHAREHOLDER VALUE

A common argument from the procurement community in defence of their Leverage buying practice is that they do it because the savings maximize shareholder value. That is to say, that by reducing agency fees, the money saved can be either be added straight to their bottom line, spent on media[28] for greater exposure of their ads and consequent return on investment, or spent on anything else they wanted. There are a number of arguments to challenge this assertion. First is that transferring marketing investment in the brand to the bottom line is not a sustainable means of creating or maximizing shareholder value. What will you do the following year, or the year after that? Brands work best over time. Short-term divestment from brands creates long-term problems, as salience weakens and increases risk from competitors. As John Kay argues very convincingly in his excellent book of 2010, *Obliquity*, the most profitable companies are not the most aggressive in chasing profits, much like the happiest people do not pursue happiness:

> *"No one will be buried with the epitaph: 'He maximised shareholder value' ... The epitaph of men such as Henry Ford, Bill Allen, Walt Disney or Steve Jobs reads instead: 'He built a great business which made money for shareholders, gave rewarding employment, and stimulated the development of suppliers and distributors by meeting customers' needs, which they had not known they had before these men developed products to satisfy them'."[29]*

Likewise, regardless of how it may or may not influence your procurement of marketing services, before adopting any strategy in the interests of maximizing shareholder value, it would be worth reading *Shareholder Value Myth: How Putting Shareholders First Harms Investors, Corporations, and the Public* (2012), by Lynn Stout.[30]

As Steve Jobs noted, when he returned to Apple in 1997, *"The cure for Apple is not cost-cutting. The cure for Apple is to innovate its way out of its current predicament."*[31] Within eight to ten weeks of Jobs' return to Apple, they launched the 'Think Different' campaign and shocked the world – in a good way – with this breakthrough work for the IT category.

There may be some circumstances when the client's cash would indeed be better spent on market expansion, for example, or competitor acquisition. When this is the case, then this is the business problem that should be shared with the agency, marketing and procurement: "How can we best improve our cash position in the short term without compromising our brand and market share?"

However, most of the time it is in an effort simply to improve the bottom line. If it were the case that reducing agency fees did not diminish their value, then this would stand to reason. But the problem with buying ideas is that the client can never tell whether they would have had a better, more effective idea if they had paid their agency more. They don't have that alternative history to 'prove' their lower negotiated rate was without a consequence to quality.

> *In advertising, you never get to see the work you didn't pay the agency enough to create.*

What is a certainty is that if the better agency talent is given the opportunity to work on an account that is sufficiently resourced by reasonable fees – so that the process is enjoyable – the talent will seize that opportunity over an account that squeezed agency resources. It means that fee reductions are not made without consequences to talent, and talent equals value. Therefore, the interests of the shareholder may not be better served by the short-termism of adding to the bottom line, but rather in the longer-term provision of more effective marketing and its impact on the bottom line.

Plus, agencies have much greater experience in knowing what resources they need to get that great idea. Deriving a return on an investment to achieve a specific goal is a question of balancing whether your investment has achieved the critical mass it needs or has gone beyond that to a diminishing return.

For example, if you are prospecting for oil and only invest in a little territory in which to search, the chances of you striking it rich are smaller, i.e., you are unlikely to have reached the critical mass needed to provide your target return. In contrast, if you are investing to prospect all available territory and even territories beyond where geologists think oil is likely to be present, you may achieve your target but much of your investment will have seen a diminished return. It's the same in marketing services.

An example of a Strategic buying strategy, though more by default than by design, would be my experience of working on the account for Allied Dunbar Financial Services. It was about 1998 or 1999 and I was a Board Account Director working at Grey Advertising. I had been steadily rising up the ranks of the agency towards the more attractive accounts and was finally asked to work on Allied Dunbar, which at the time was the flagship account for the agency.

Allied Dunbar had been producing award-winning campaigns with Grey for about five years and the campaign idea was a Gorilla that had transformed the fortunes of their business. When Allied Dunbar came to Grey, they were among the least-trusted financial services companies in the country, known for hard-nosed sales tactics and nicknamed 'Allied Crowbar' due to the persistence and aggressive sales tactics of their door-to-door salesmen.

Grey developed a campaign idea based on the unpredictability of life events. In a 60-second TV commercial we would see our hero encounter a life crisis and instead of panicking, our Allied Dunbar customer would start dancing to Nat King Cole's "Let's Face the Music and Dance" because Allied Dunbar's financial plans adapt "for the life you don't yet know". On the top floor of the agency was the suite of meeting rooms where the awards cabinet lived. At least three quarters of the agency's awards were won on the Allied Dunbar account. The client's ability to buy great advertising was one part of their success, but what many people didn't know was that the client paid the agency 17.5% of their media investment as a commission and 15% of their gross production investment. Consequently, when a new brief for a TV campaign came into the agency, I was told that every team in the creative department could work on the brief. Between 30 and 40 people in the creative department submitted scripts for the brief.

I've used an extreme case here to make a point. Arguably and logically there is a point of diminishing return on the investment a client can make in their agency's services and Allied Dunbar had far surpassed that point. Nonetheless, the result was a long-standing campaign that saw Allied Dunbar's fortunes blossom and their trust rating exceed that of NatWest Bank, which at that time had the highest trust rating for financial services in the UK.

BUYING STRATEGIES AND THE MONKEY HOUSE

In a similar fashion to how we overlaid The Monkey House onto the Meikle Matrix and the Supplier Preference Matrix, we can overlay it onto the Buying Matrix (*figure 20*).

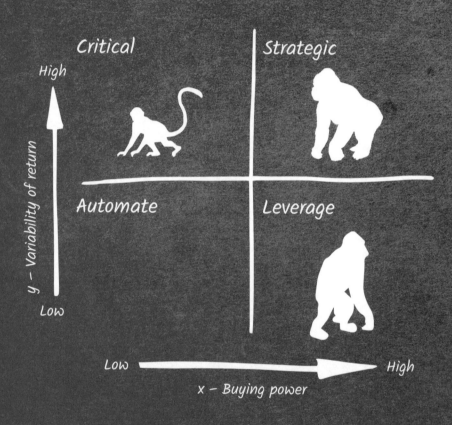

Figure 20

The Buying Matrix
and The Monkey House

Critical

Unless the owner of the brand, which needs a Spider Monkey, has huge funding that they are prepared to gamble on a large marketing investment, they will likely have limited buying power. They could be with a smaller agency, but that will simply improve their buying power without changing their need for a Spider Monkey. A brand that needs a Spider Monkey needs truly transformative advertising, something that punches above its weight. Therefore, the money alone is unlikely to be enough to motivate the agency, so the relationship needs to be nurtured to ensure that the best talent available will be enthused and motivated by the brief and the client's potential to buy a Spider Monkey.

Strategic

Already a big spender, here the brand needs to resist the temptation to exploit its buying power, instead behaving consistently with a strategy for a two-sum game. By ensuring that the agency is a financially-motivated business partner, in whose success the brand makes a clear and strategic investment, the agency is most likely to deliver the kind of work that the brand needs over the long term. Again, the degree to which the agency is a strategic partner is relative. If pressed to define categorically a Strategic buying strategy, I would say it must allow or even encourage the agency to profit financially from the account as well as by reputation.

Leverage

Brands that need Orangutans believe there is limited scope for growth, therefore the variability of return is narrowed. The brand has achieved critical mass of market share, so it should be otherwise stable. As the brand that is steadily delivering a predictable amount of profit, it is the brand owner's strategic decision to play it safe with the advertising. The agency's ideas and ads can be quality tested for their adequacy against the task, with the use of qualitative and quantitative tests. However, the prescriptive nature of the research's application may demotivate the agency from providing their most original thinking – but this doesn't matter. In this quadrant, it is entirely consistent with the Orangutan brand's portfolio strategy to pay the minimum necessary to maintain their brand's performance, as any overpayment would simply diminish the purpose of the brand – which is to provide a healthy bottom line.

Automate

This quadrant is a moot category in the realm of agency services that provide strategic or creative services.

In conclusion, as the behavioural economist Dan Ariely noted, by rewarding effort we are more likely to tip a locksmith who does a bad job than a good one. When a locksmith tries harder, takes longer to open your door and, consequently, costs you more, you are more likely to tip him or her than one who easily picks your lock in two minutes and charges you the minimum call-out fee. Despite the inconvenience of the former, we resent the efficiency of the latter.

The reason for this is that we instinctively reward effort over utility. Perhaps it is because there is an irrepressible child in us who thinks, 'it's not fair' if somebody gets paid a significant amount of money for seemingly little effort, regardless of its value to us.

My belief is that the greatest part of the challenge here is down to the human condition. There isn't a default of cooperation between different teams, let alone different companies. So the idea of doing a deal with a supplier that might allow that supplier to make a significant amount of profit, in this instance an ad agency, is counterintuitive to most, but that is the nature of managing investments rather than costs. Likewise, until we change the way most people in marketing procurement are incentivized, we will continue to see investment levels reduce without a compensatory strategy by which the return on that investment might be increased with a different approach to risk.

> *Investments cannot be managed the same way as costs; they're value judgments determined by the business need.*

SUMMARY

- The predominant practice in marketing procurement does not sufficiently differentiate between costs and investments, where costs are purchases of goods or services with finite value and investments have a variable return.
- Appropriate buying strategies are seldom employed, because they are inconsistent with cost-saving and cost-avoidance objectives against which marketing procurement personnel are incentivized.
- The billing of agency time as a means of remuneration forces agencies into a time-commodity business rather than a value-creation business.
- Agencies are vulnerable to large clients making significant contribution to their overhead and often accept negotiated deals they should reject.
- Effortlessly talented individuals are more valuable than effortful less-gifted ones. Agency fee platforms need to accommodate this insight.

[25] It would be remiss of me not to note here that there are some different models for media agencies, but the consolidation of multiple clients' buying power, either bought collectively or individually by the agency, provides all media buyers with the greater leverage they need to drive better prices with media owners.

[26] See *Buying Less for Less*.

[27] Interestingly, for marketers perhaps, when agencies have successfully low-balled to win business and fees have later been 'adjusted' upwards, procurement savings records and bonuses are rarely also adjusted retrospectively.

[28] See *Working vs nonworking marketing investment*, chapter two.

[29] *Obliquity*, Chapter 8 *Pluralism*, (Kay, London 2010).

[30] Distinguished Professor of Corporate and Business Law at Cornell Law School.

[31] *Apple Confidential: The Real Story of Apple Computer, Inc.*

CHAPTER SIX

THE MONKEY HOUSE PARADIGM

"You never change things by fighting the existing reality; to change something, build a new model that makes the existing model obsolete."

Buckminster Fuller, 1895–1983
American architect, systems theorist and inventor

In this chapter, we'll put together what we've covered in the preceding chapters and look at how the logic of The Monkey House has worked for campaigns that have produced what we could describe as Gorillas, Spider Monkeys and Orangutans.[32]

All of the matrices we have looked at share some generic qualities to their axes. The horizontal axis 'x' is the simplest. In each matrix it is indicative of scale:

- Supplier Preference (*figure 8*, chapter three) – scale of financial value of the client to the agency.
- Meikle Matrix (*figure 12*, chapter four) – scale of responsibility or accountability of the agency to the client.
- Buying Matrix (*figure 18*, chapter five) – scale of the client to the agency in terms of buying power.

The qualities of the y-axis are a little subtler, but revolve around risk or control one way or another:

- Supplier Preference – the variability of client attractiveness and its implications for talent and therefore value.
- Meikle Matrix – the uncertainty of relinquishing control to the agency.
- Buying Matrix – the uncertainty of the value of return.

The relationships between risk (originality) and scale of investment (money) and return (value) are the points at which the conflicting agendas of marketing, procurement and agencies inevitably collide. The fundamental principles of economics prohibit big wins from low stakes without high risk. Likewise, in a low-risk environment, high investments will only deliver proportionately low yet more predictable returns, but nonetheless usually greater than the principal. These principles are visible in the stock markets of the world, the returns we're expected to gain on our pension funds, the roulette wheel and odds on the races. Despite this, the increasingly prescriptive ways of working and the diminishing fees that clients are prepared to pay their agencies are trying to both lower the stakes and reduce the risk without harming the return – but of course it has harmed the return, it must have – but neither I nor the brands have an alternative history we can use to prove it. Although brands don't have alternative histories, when we look at these outlier case studies below – i.e., the high performers in their categories – and we interrogate how they came to be, how clients pay,[33] and how they manage risk, it becomes clearer to see that risk and its return are the central issues. Those who are achieving extraordinary returns create the circumstances suitable for Spider Monkeys and Gorillas, whereas the returns of the others are more predictable as the nurture they provide is suited to Orangutans.

But by no means do I suggest that brands everywhere need to be more risk-savvy. My argument is that their risk strategy needs to be consistent with the needs of their business problems – i.e., right for their monkey. Orangutans are most consistent with a risk-averse approach. But risk aversion for a Spider Monkey defeats its very purpose – i.e., to over-commit, embrace risk and hope for a disproportionately higher return. Likewise, Orangutan processes that seek to limit risk when a brand needs a Gorilla ironically create greater risk for the brand. They can leave it more susceptible to innovative, more interesting and more attractive Spider Monkey and Gorilla brands. By managing our relationships according to the business problems we need to solve, and the necessary role of risk, the result will be appropriate – the brand will attract the right agency talent to best meet the brand's business objectives with the right kind of advertising monkey.

Now that we have looked at the financial and procedural aspects of nurture individually, and in some depth, we can put them together with the brand need and see how they coordinate and align.

We'll look at each brand need as characterized by The Monkey House in turn. A diagram at the beginning of each section plots how that brand's need then corresponds to each of the other quadrants and illustrates the way that this alignment has worked in a case study.

Figure 21

The Monkey House for Spider Monkeys

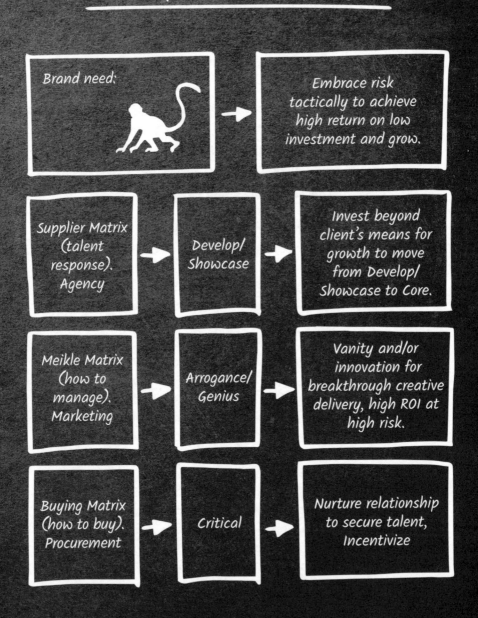

| Brand need: | → | Embrace risk tactically to achieve high return on low investment and grow. |

| Supplier Matrix (talent response). Agency | → | Develop/Showcase | → | Invest beyond client's means for growth to move from Develop/Showcase to Core. |

| Meikle Matrix (how to manage). Marketing | → | Arrogance/Genius | → | Vanity and/or innovation for breakthrough creative delivery, high ROI at high risk. |

| Buying Matrix (how to buy). Procurement | → | Critical | → | Nurture relationship to secure talent, Incentivize |

1) SPIDER MONKEYS

As we overlay the corresponding quadrants of each of the matrices, we begin to see that the interests of each of the parties, and their actions or strategies for their roles, are aligned (*figure 21*).

A brand that needs a Spider Monkey requires breakthrough strategy and advertising. A Spider Monkey brand often doesn't have the buying power to pay for the best people from its agency. But, because the agency's reputation will benefit from developing breakthrough work, the agency will provide discretionary effort to exploit the opportunity to make award-winning and distinctive advertising.

CASE STUDY: BEN SHERMAN – HOW A 60s ICONIC BRAND WAS RELAUNCHED WITH THE HELP OF BRITPOP AND AN AD AGENCY THAT WAS MORE USED TO PROMOTING PILLS AND POWDERS.

In the late 90s, the musical and cultural phenomenon of Brit Pop was capturing the hearts, minds and pockets of the British nation. From its roots, early in that decade, the bands that epitomized the movement, such as Blur, Oasis, Pulp and Supergrass, were expanding their followings. In 1993 in Northern Ireland, what had become a little-known brand, Ben Sherman shirts, was in receivership – and with the backing of a private equity firm went through a management buyout. The brand's heritage was incredibly potent. Founded in 1963 and opening its first store in Brighton in 1967, Ben Sherman was to become an iconic brand of the late 60s and 70s – synonymous with the Mod subculture as much as parka coats and scooters. As the subcultures evolved, Ben Sherman became a part of the skinhead uniform in the 70s and as the subculture waned, so did their popularity.

Back to the 90s, and the newly backed Ben Sherman management knew they had something of great value in the Ben Sherman brand, but they were not experienced marketers. By chance they approached a subsidiary division of Grey Advertising to help them develop their brand strategy. Subsequently, they were then referred to Grey Advertising to relaunch their brand with a limited advertising spend.

Brand Need – Spider Monkey
Low market-share in UK men's shirts sales with less than £1million in revenue. Low brand salience and diminished awareness.

Buying Matrix – Critical
The brand had little money and no buying power in the big agency market. Smaller agencies could have been too hit-and-miss for talent, so better to nurture the relationship with the big agency and access the talent there. Equally, Grey Advertising had few or no clients in the Develop/Showcase quadrant at the time.

Meikle Matrix – Genius/Arrogance
With limited marketing experience, Ben Sherman loosened the reins and was led almost entirely by the agency on the brand strategy, the advertising strategy and the creative work.

Supplier Preference – Develop/Showcase
Grey Advertising vastly overinvested in Ben Sherman both by design and by default. There was little concern among the management that the brand made no money for the agency or that the account would even lose money. Creative teams were regularly pitching speculative work to the account team.

The Result
Ben Sherman was relaunched with a poster campaign developed by Grey. The idea played directly to the skinhead heritage, but with a humorous or attitudinal twist to disempower the once thuggish, aggressive and even racist reputation of the skinhead subculture and breathe new life into the brand in a relevant and challenging way.

The photography was done as a favour to the agency's executive creative director for little more than the price of the film and the processing. The models for the shoot were mostly Grey staff or friends of friends and so they charged little or nothing.

Within 18 months of the campaign breaking and with the improved distribution the investment helped to leverage, Ben Sherman increased their sales from £1m per annum to £14m (mostly limited by the speed with which they could increase their manufacturing base).

2] GORILLAS

For a brand that needs a Gorilla, the client uses a two-sum buying strategy and applies optimal control over the agency to form a genuine and equitable partnership (*figure 22*). Breakthrough work serves the client's need to defend its base, stave off newcomers and also enhances the agency's brand and employer-brand, contributing to the virtuous circle (see *figure 7*, chapter three).

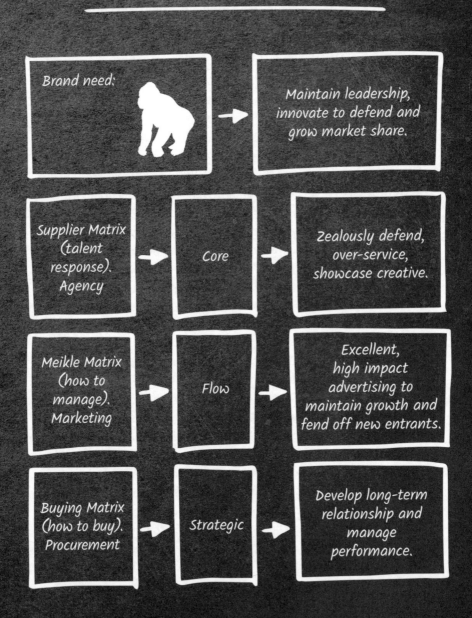

Figure 22

The Monkey House for Gorillas

Brand need:	→	Maintain leadership, innovate to defend and grow market share.
Supplier Matrix (talent response). Agency	Core →	Zealously defend, over-service, showcase creative.
Meikle Matrix (how to manage). Marketing	Flow →	Excellent, high impact advertising to maintain growth and fend off new entrants.
Buying Matrix (how to buy). Procurement	Strategic →	Develop long-term relationship and manage performance.

CASE STUDY: HOW WINSTON WOLF LAUNCHED THE THIRD REVOLUTION IN CAR INSURANCE.

"Insurance is a weird business – for a number of reasons, not least because we don't know what the cost of an insurance policy will be when we sell it, ranging anywhere from our admin costs through to many millions of pounds."

So explained Mark Evans, Marketing Director for Direct Line Group.

"Understandably, this inherent unpredictability creates a corporate environment of risk aversion; we want to be as certain as we can of everything."

Direct Line Insurance was launched in 1985; it was the UK's first telephone-only insurer, i.e., there were no expensive brokers in between the customer and the insurer. Within just nine years, it had become the UK's biggest insurer of private vehicles. Its brand mnemonic of a red telephone on wheels became instantly recognizable, with or without its equally memorable car-horn-like beeped jingle. With the advent of e-commerce, the red telephone was joined by a little red computer mouse, and with these strong iconic brand devices, an almost constant TV advertising presence and a competitive product portfolio, Direct Line became the market leader in both domestic motor and home insurance.

Products came and went and Direct Line largely maintained its competitive edge – even with the introduction of price comparison websites (PCWs) – such was the strength of Direct Line's products, its brand and a healthy degree of critical mass. Fast-forward nearly 30 years and Direct Line was still the UK's biggest insurer, but with a proliferation of other direct sales propositions and more significantly, the growth of PCWs, the insurance market was becoming commoditized. Whenever somebody bought a new car, the first thing they would do would be to use a PCW to find the cheapest insurance from familiar brands – or even ones they were not familiar with. Consumers had become conditioned to buy on price.

Direct Line was clear that it would have to do something to avoid being sucked into a price-war business, so they decided to shake things up. As the leader in a market that is responsive to advertising – indeed dependent upon constant advertising – Direct Line had to do something significant to maintain and grow their leadership position.

The insurance market had already seen two revolutions: the first, initiated by Direct Line themselves, was to cut out the middleman. The second addressed complexity with the birth, and subsequent rise to dominance, of the PCW. Direct Line was ready to lead the third – to get rid of the unnecessary worry and hassle associated with insurance. It was to be the next insurance revolution and its job was to lead consumers back to a value-based proposition – insurance isn't just about price: it's about getting stuff sorted out.

Brand Need: Gorilla

In January 2014, Direct Line invited a number of agencies to pitch for their brand relaunch. The brief to agencies was inspiring, clear, focused, and it invited agencies to challenge the brand's pitch team with breakthrough, transformative ideas. It made clear the size and scale of the business and was open and honest about the challenges that faced the insurance business, including the financial authority's regulations.

Meikle Matrix: Flow

The scale of the account indicated the agency's accountability and the brief relinquished greater control over previously stringent brand rules and guidelines. Plus, of course, when an agency is working on a pitch it has both the control over its resources and high accountability because it wants to win the business.

Evans was sticking his neck out with this brand strategy and knew he had to get the very best agency support. In one preliminary meeting with Saatchi & Saatchi, Evans recalled what he believes was a pivotal moment:

"I said to the agency team something like, 'I think you're being safe and telling us what you think we want to hear. Sometimes a creative brief talks about needing a revolution, but the client doesn't really mean it. We absolutely mean it, so tell us what you really think.' At this point the dynamic changed and the remainder of the meeting went a long way towards defining the eventual outcome of the pitch." Evans had given them the strongest indication possible that they would have an optimal amount of control over the process. Magnus Djaba, Global President of Saatchi & Saatchi, was leading their efforts as CEO of Saatchi & Saatchi, London at the time: "I remember that moment in the chemistry meeting vividly; it was pivotal. Richard [Huntington – then the chief strategy officer, now chairman] suddenly became very animated. He said, 'Often we get a brief for a comms problem, often we get a brief for a brand problem, but you've got a comms problem, a brand problem and a category problem.' There's nothing more motivating than a big hairy challenge to get your teeth into when a client genuinely wants a game-changing idea. We get loads of approaches to pitch every year and we have to choose carefully which ones we want to go for. With Direct Line, we knew they wanted the very best we had to offer and we knew it would be a big prize."

Supplier Preference: Core

The prospect of a high-value client and the appeal of the creative opportunity attracted and motivated the best talent Saatchi & Saatchi had to offer.

Saatchi & Saatchi won the account by using the Harvey Keitel character from *Pulp Fiction*, Winston Wolfe, as the new face of the Direct Line brand.

Buying Matrix: Strategic

The financial aspect of the pitch was not unimportant to the Direct Line pitch team, but the primary goal was to find a winning agency that could challenge them as like-minded partners in creating a revolution. If Direct Line was to succeed in such a significant brand repositioning, it would need to buy agency services in a fair, motivating way, whichever agency won. Direct Line was ready to invest significantly in the winning agency's services if they found the value that they sought.

The advertising was an instant success.

Mark Evans: "It is without doubt the most transformative advertising campaign that I have been involved in so far in my career. It has played a key role in helping to turn around the fortunes of our flagship brand, moving from a significant and systemic declining trend into strong growth and market share gain. On a like-for-like basis, the creative is 53% more effective at driving quotes for motor insurance than prior to the relaunch. It has also been tremendously galvanizing internally as a symbol that our ambition to revolutionize insurance again is in our grasp if we are prepared to be brave."

Figure 23

The Monkey House
for Orangutans

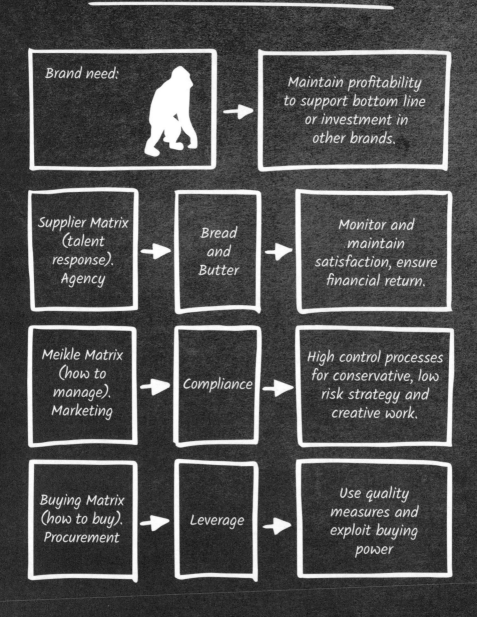

Brand need:	→	Maintain profitability to support bottom line or investment in other brands.
Supplier Matrix (talent response). Agency	Bread and Butter	Monitor and maintain satisfaction, ensure financial return.
Meikle Matrix (how to manage). Marketing	Compliance	High control processes for conservative, low risk strategy and creative work.
Buying Matrix (how to buy). Procurement	Leverage	Use quality measures and exploit buying power

3] ORANGUTANS

Most brands that need an Orangutan should adopt risk-averse strategies (*figure 23*). Flat or declining markets don't attract newcomers so readily as growth markets, so the roles for innovation and risk are reduced. The need for advertising per se is regrettable, because the role of a brand in these circumstances is usually to deliver profit; therefore what has to be invested must be done efficiently – including agency fees, production and media spend. High control of the agency will produce conservative work consistent with the low-risk need, and will neither attract nor require the agency's greatest talent.

The creative engagement of Orangutans covers a broad spectrum. It can be highly engaging creative work (see the Snickers' case study, below) or an information-based, highly rational, proposition-led infomercial at the other end of the scale. The important insight about Orangutans is that they only perform badly when they should be Gorillas – and when the agency is trying to produce a Gorilla, despite a high-control client.

CASE STUDY: PAY DAY LOANS COMPANY.
HOW A SEEMINGLY CYNICAL DEAL FOR AGENCIES CAN BE AS LEGITIMATE AS ANY OTHER IF IT IS CONSISTENT WITH THE BUSINESS PROBLEM.

This case study is based on an anecdote, but it is nonetheless very useful as an extreme example to make a point. In most instances, Orangutans are creative and engaging, but this example illustrates the alignment of objectives very well.

I once heard another advertising consultant complain about the behaviour of a client; more specifically, he was critical of the way this client was handling its advertising resources. The client was something like a short-term loans company, direct response advertiser. At the time I heard the story, we were still deep in the global financial crisis and there was a proliferation of this kind of advertiser. The recession would have a limited life span, so the business had to exploit their opportunity quickly and economically.

As I recall, the complaint was that the client pitched their business every nine months or so and that they insisted on a 40%

discount from the winning agency's fee proposal. This was deemed outrageous by the consultant. So, in reply, I offered an alternative way of looking at what the agency world would generally see as horrendously bad client practice.

The Brand Need – Orangutan:
The brand is in a distress-purchase category; customers are buying according to their need and not because they have developed an affinity with the brand or like an advertising idea. The category and the business don't require great creative work from their agency. In fact, if anything, cheaper-looking advertising would appear more authentic and suggest that the brand was austere and operated on low margins so it could offer the best rates for its customers.

The Buying Matrix – Leverage:
Agencies were not forced to pitch, and if they won they weren't forced to make the 40% discount. Agencies would only do so because a small account will have offered them high profit conversion and still have made a contribution to their fixed and variable costs.

The Meikle Matrix – Compliance:
Highly prescriptive work with little or no interest in building anything other than brand awareness and direct responses. On the scale of agency creativity, this would have been rock bottom – it didn't need to be anything more than that. Money spent on the ad was money not spent reaching their audience through greater media investment. Ironically, this is one instance where reducing non-working marketing capital was an appropriate strategy.

The Supplier Preference Matrix – Bread and Butter/Nuisance:
Depending on the size and nature of the particular agency, the client would have been assigned the agency's least talented staff. For the agency, this account would have made their least talented people productive; for the client, they didn't need the strategic and creative geniuses, they needed 'doers' who would listen and obey.

The point of this example is to illustrate that if the agency perceives its role exclusively to be the producer of great advertising ideas, regardless of the client's business problem, it isn't hard to see there will be a clash with certain kinds of briefs if that isn't the requirement. Imagine a continuum with transformative creative ideas at one end and quick, cheap ads at the other. The Monkey House and its models are designed to navigate from the business problem to the right agency talent, through processes of payment and ways of working to hit the right point on that continuum.

If we consider all the variables that determine the outcome on this continuum, what is critical to understand is the consequence of getting some or many of them wrong. One of the reasons this is overlooked is that there are some brands that can get away with extremely mean Leverage buying and a very demanding, high-control process, who still get the best talent. The world's super-brands vary in this regard. Some are extremely adept at forging productive, high-value, lasting, loyal relationships with their agencies, and others forge love-hate relationships with their agencies, whereby the agency's reputation is so enhanced by this client that all else is forgiven.

You would also be forgiven for thinking that the rules of economics about risk and return that I mentioned earlier don't always apply. But if a global super-brand abuses its agency, it has simply moved the risk from one place to another – because the agency gets a say as to whether or not they want to continue the relationship.

For example, in July 2010 Levi's discovered where they had moved their risk. Their relationship with Bartle Bogle Hegarty (BBH) had apparently been deteriorating when the agency suddenly announced they were parting company with their client after 28 years. It was news that shocked the industry – Levi's was one of BBH's founding clients – and rumours quickly circulated that the agency had fired their client over creative differences, although Nigel Bogle commented in a joint statement:

"The Levi's brand has been an enormously important part of the BBH story since BBH London won the business as a founding client in 1982. We feel it is best that we part company, which we do on good terms. We wish Levi Strauss & Co. all the very best for the future. It has been a privilege to work on this iconic brand."

In the short term, it might be possible for some iconic brands to get away with poor relationships or Leverage remuneration and still derive value from their agencies. However, they will always be taking the chance that at some point the pay will be too little or the relationship so intolerable that their agency will no longer stand for it. Poor client relationships can demoralize entire agencies and, as such, agencies are aware that they sometimes need to lose a hand to save an arm. And if advertising is critical to the client's business success, this can be a risk with catastrophic consequences if it goes wrong and the client discovers they've pushed their agency too far.

For mid-range big advertisers whose brands are not yet iconic, the agency's tolerance level of poor or difficult relationships decreases, landing a client that needs a Gorilla in the agency's Bread and Butter zone of supplier preference, potentially even edging towards Nuisance. For brands that routinely need Orangutans, there's nothing wrong with being in the Bread and Butter zone, because that's where they're meant to be.

The brand's need is what defines the shared interest between marketing, procurement and agencies. The need determines the monkey and thereby the talent, the relationship and the remuneration.

OTHER CASE STUDIES:

CASE STUDY: HOW SAINSBURY'S AND AMV/BBDO BUCKED THE TREND OF CHRISTMAS ADVERTISING WITH A CAT CALLED MOG.

In recent years, Christmas in the UK has become the advertising battleground that the Super Bowl has long been in the US. It wasn't always the case, but when Adam&Eve won the John Lewis account in 2009, the advertising that followed seemed to raise the game, in particular across the retail sector. It was to be the start of a beautiful relationship between the two companies that was sustained through the acquisition of Adam&Eve by DDB to form their currently double-barrelled agency.

Many other advertisers responded by also trying to raise their game – not just out of a sense of pride in their advertising, but because the growth that Adam&Eve managed to achieve in a time of global financial crisis was unheard of. Other retail brands did their level best to compete for the goose bumps and tears of the British public throughout the Christmases that followed, but John Lewis's status of most-loved advertising brand at Christmas seemed unassailable, and the advertising they produced continued to be cherished and shared. The arrival of the next John Lewis Christmas ad became another cultural event in the run-up to the big day itself.

However, in 2013 the gloves came off when another leading UK retailer, Sainsbury's, peeled away from the retail pack by doing things differently. Despite an overall deflation in shop prices, Sainsbury's and AMV/BBDO stuck to their strategy and achieved outstanding results in some of the worst possible conditions. As a leading mid-market supermarket brand, Sainsbury's was being squeezed by both the upmarket and discounter supermarket retailers and had a declining share of voice. Conscious of that challenge, Sainsbury's and AMV/BBDO elected to change the battleground by making fame their objective and abandoned traditional strategies that relied heavily on big media budgets.

Their successful strategy began in 2013 when AMV/BBDO produced Sainsbury's *Christmas in a Day*, inspired by the critically acclaimed *Life in a Day*, a crowd-sourced drama/documentary. Using the same award-winning director, Kevin MacDonald, *Christmas in a Day* was a moving documentary using more than 400 hours of crowd-sourced footage. Despite consecutive months of shop price deflation, despite being outspent by Tesco, Asda and Morrisons, and despite being squeezed in between the discounters (Aldi, Lidl) and the upmarket retailers (Waitrose, M&S), Sainsbury's delivered their best ever Christmas results in 2013 and learned the value of shifting the game from share of voice to fame.

Christmas 2014 was the centenary of the First World War and Sainsbury's next Christmas campaign was developed in cooperation with the Royal British Legion, with whom Sainsbury's has had a partnership since 1994. Christmas 2014 was the 100th anniversary of the Christmas truce, the moment when German and British soldiers stopped fighting, shared Christmas gifts and treats and played a game of football with one another between the trenches. An integrated and phased campaign using paid and earned media also included fund-raising activity, social media and even sending beautifully packaged WW1 chocolate bars to media influencers. The TV ad clocked more than one million views on YouTube in little over 24 hours and Sainsbury's raised £2 million more than the previous year for the Royal British Legion. Sainsbury's outperformed all their brand tracking measures since their tracking began: recognition, likeability, involvement, standout, relevance. But overall, the campaign delivered a return on investment of £24.34 for every pound spent.

The Christmas 2015 campaign focused on the importance of storytelling at Christmas time and featured the tale of Mog the cat. *Mog's Christmas Calamity* featured one of the nation's best-loved children's book characters, Judith Kerr's Mog. The new advert was a charming saga of a sequence of highly improbable and entertaining events that befall the iconic and calamity-prone Mog in the early hours of Christmas morning, before the family are awake.

Such was the popularity of *Mog's Christmas Calamity* that it became the most viewed Christmas ad on YouTube ever – outperforming in popularity every John Lewis ad, including their

2015 campaign. The Mog plush toy stocked by Sainsbury's to support the campaign sold out in a week, and a few days after launch, *Mog's Christmas Calamity* became the bestselling book in the UK and stayed there for four weeks, selling more than 450,000 copies. Once again, Sainsbury's defied market expectations and was the only one of the 'big four' UK supermarket chains to increase its market share over the Christmas period.

Interestingly, by the conventional application of a working versus nonworking investment strategy, *Christmas in a Day*, *Christmas Truce* and *Mog's Christmas Calamity* would all have never seen the light of day. It was strategically necessary to invest differently, and although the lower investment in conventional media felt risky on one hand, Sainsbury's ability to attract the highest calibre agency talent, and AMV/BBDO's ability to provide that talent, mitigated the risk to the highest degree possible. And the business results make a compelling case that these risk-savvy strategic decisions were very well taken.

Brand Need: Gorilla

Sainsbury's needed breakthrough, transformative and powerful work, not only to compete with the fame of the increasingly popular Christmas advertising, but to fight off challengers to market share from retailers above, below and beside.

Meikle Matrix: Flow

Sainsbury's highly collaborative approach involves a combination of rigorous business and consumer research and a broad-reaching strategic approach to business problem solving. This encourages the agency to think unconventionally and much more creatively in the broadest sense of the word.

Buying Matrix: Strategic

Sainsbury's is an always-on advertiser and was one of AMV/BBDO's largest accounts, representing a comparatively significant proportion of the agency's revenue and billing.

Supplier Preference: Core
As one of the agency's largest accounts and with their appetite to consistently demand and buy Gorillas, Sainsbury's attracts and motivates the agency's very best talent. (The brief for the Christmas 2015 campaign was taken by Adrian Rossi and Alex Grieve, AMV/BBDO's executive creative directors.)

CASE STUDY: THROWING CAUTION (AND 250,000 RUBBER BALLS) TO THE WIND. HOW SONY ELECTRONICS BOUGHT INTO CREATIVITY AND SOLD OUT OF BRAVIA TELEVISIONS.

When the Sony account planner at the advertising agency Fallon in London first saw the script, it was the shortest he had ever seen in his career. It read:

"We go to San Francisco and let a million brightly coloured balls loose down the steep hills of the city."

Title: 'Colour Like No Other'

Fallon won the Sony account in 2002. Sony had sought to differentiate themselves and their products through their "… like no other" end line. Its intention was to convey Sony's confidence in their product superiority and it was doing the trick. The construct was focused on the product benefit, rather than the features of the product, i.e., the technical specifications, where the rest of the market's propositions were focused. It allowed Sony to significantly differentiate its brand in an increasingly price-sensitive and competitive market. The final proposition for the ad was:

"Sony Bravia Brings Incredible Colour into Your Life."

However, the simplicity of the advertising idea didn't sit comfortably with all the Sony stakeholders. Questions were asked about how the product would feature in this commercial.

David Patton, now Global President of Young & Rubicam, was at the time the European Senior Vice President for Sony Electronics. Patton had recently moved over from PlayStation and was committed to the idea and knew that its creative integrity was key to its success. There was significant internal pressure from product teams to highlight technical improvements and show off the product, but Patton knew that if the sight of these bouncing balls cascading down the streets of San Francisco was interrupted by the usual product demo and voiceover, the whole impact would be ruined.

An entire block of the city was cordoned off for the shoot. Dumper trucks holding 35,000 balls 50 feet above the ground and 12 specially-made canons, which fired 5,000 balls into the air each, ensured the balls achieved the height they needed so they would bounce and not just roll down the steep hills. The production company believes it bought every available bouncy ball in the whole of the US. The 23-man camera crew needed body armour and crash helmets to protect themselves from the rubber balls, which were breaking car windows as they bounced down the San Francisco hills at about 60 miles per hour.

But such was the spectacle of the multi-coloured bouncing balls being fired out of canons down the streets of San Francisco that images and video started to go viral on the internet before the ad was finished.

The commercial was first aired across an entire ad break on Sky Sports One, just before a soccer match between Chelsea and Manchester United. The ad lasted the duration of the song, two and a half minutes.

Within hours it had become a YouTube sensation. Within seven weeks of the campaign breaking, Sony had sold out of Bravia TVs in the UK.

Brand Need: Gorilla
Sony was a market leader and televisions were its greatest source of revenue. Newcomers in television manufacture are rare but, nonetheless, the market is constantly growing and new technologies, innovations and advertising affect shifts in market share between the leaders.

Meikle Matrix: Flow
Patton's commitment to the agency, their collaboration over the communications strategy, the single-mindedness of their idea and the simplicity of the final execution kept the agency highly motivated and engaged throughout the process.

Buying Matrix: Strategic
Details of the nature of the numeration are unavailable, but Sony was one of Fallon's largest accounts.

Supplier Preference: Core
High revenue and high attractiveness of the brand and its appetite for genuinely breakthrough creative work made Sony a Core client of Fallon's.

CASE STUDY: SNICKERS – HOW THE WORLD'S BIGGEST CHOCOLATE BAR BRAND BOOSTED ITS SALES BY EMPLOYING A HOLLYWOOD BLOCKBUSTER APPROACH TO TALENT.

Snickers is one of the biggest and best-loved global chocolate brands. Launched in 1930, it now enjoys annual revenues of almost $2 billion (USD). AMV/BBDO has managed the Snickers brand since 1995.

In 2009, Snickers' global value market share dropped dramatically – competitors were encroaching on Snickers' position as the world's most popular chocolate bar. In response to this threat to one of Mars' greatest revenue streams, AMV/BBDO developed the current Snickers advertising campaign idea: "You're not you when you're hungry" (YNYWYH).

Between 2009 and 2011, the YNYWYH campaign helped Snickers regain a global market share of $376.3 million (USD). Category pressures in 2014, such as high-profile concerns about sugar intake, saw Snickers' volume market share drop 1.59%, about 60 million Snickers' bars, so the YNYWYH needed a rethink.

The core creative idea was built on a simple but powerful insight: being hungry can compromise your ability to behave like one of the male pack, it makes you irritable, weak, off your game. Snickers can sort out hunger and restore your place in the pack. In the commercials, we saw everyday situations where celebrities such as Joan Collins, Betty White and Aretha Franklin replaced one of the lads who was hungry, turning him into a diva. One of his mates tells him to eat a Snickers and he returns to his normal self. The ads were effective, but wouldn't work across all markets. There was caution and some hesitation about moving from a locally-generated idea to a global brief – an IPSOS ASI study indicated that advertising copy informed by local insight tended to struggle outside their originating markets.

Then AMV/BBDO proposed an idea with Mr Bean. As a globally-recognized character played by actor Rowan Atkinson, the development of the idea was a departure from real-life celebrities to a well-known character. In addition, instead of the scenario being a real-life situation such as a football changing room, or a road trip, the idea used a Kung Fu genre movie where one of the Kung Fu expert protagonists was transformed into a bumbling Mr Bean by his hunger. These two departures from the original construct represented some risk, so there was understandable hesitation; consequently, the idea was researched repeatedly until it finally launched in October 2014.

By summer 2015 it was running in 49 markets worldwide in which *Bean Kung Fu* helped Snickers to grow value sales by almost 9.91 %, way ahead of the category. But in addition to its effectiveness, because the solution was global, *Bean Kung Fu* also saved $14.1 million (USD) in production costs in addition to providing incremental sales of more than $70 million (USD).

Brand Need: Orangutan

As Mars' and the worlds' best-selling chocolate bar, Snickers is a brand that is handled with care. The market is somewhat responsive to consumer trends, but is relatively stable. However, as a highly valuable market on a global scale, even small percentage shifts in market size or market share can have a significant impact on business revenue. The chocolate bar category demands high-quality, engaging creative work with good production values, taste cues and brand appeal – a loveable and engaging Orangutan.

Meikle Matrix: Compliance

There is a strategic need for Mars to have a higher-control relationship between the brand and the agency, given the size of the brand's business and the potential consequence of failure on revenue. However, the processes and protocols for the development of creative ideas are clear, so the resultant work is conservative (i.e., not high risk), but not mediocre.

Buying Matrix: Leverage

Mars' confectionery business is both consolidated within the Omnicom Group and, in turn, Snickers is consolidated within AMV/BBDO with other Mars brands: M&Ms, Maltesers, Mars, Pedigree,

Whiskas, Uncle Bens and Wrigley. This consolidation drives efficiency and hence brand profitability. The group of Mars' accounts represents significant revenue to the agency, which is now the largest billing agency in UK history.

Supplier Preference: Core
In addition to high revenue status within supplier preference, Mars also has the attractiveness of some of the world's best-known and best-loved brands. Despite the high demands of pre-test KPIs, Mars therefore still manages to attract the finest industry talent to work on brands like Snickers.

These case studies, and there are many more of them, illustrate that if your business need is for a Gorilla, you have to create an environment – the 'nurture' – conducive to a Gorilla.

You may want a world-class Orangutan that performs like the Snickers one, but to achieve this you still have to attract the right talent and manage it well. Much like the case with Mars, the bigger the Orangutan, the better the talent it can attract. Problems for brands arise when their need is for innovative, breakthrough work and the relationship, process and remuneration aren't right for a Gorilla. The resultant mediocrity is far worse than a well and efficiently developed Orangutan. The Monkey House is designed to provide three key benefits:

1) Identify the kind of monkey your brand needs.
2) Align the interests of marketing, procurement and agencies behind that need so you secure the talent that can deliver it.
3) Provide a chain of logical reasoning from your brand's market circumstances and its competition, to your brand ambition, your communications strategy, creative idea and its ultimate execution that even the most stubborn senior stakeholders will understand.

For Gorillas and Spider Monkeys, this means you can explain the business need for stakeholders to live with their discomfort and for them to trust both marketing and the agency.

SUMMARY

- So far, each model has involved the relationship between scale and some form of risk.
- Risk manifests itself in different ways: the competitive threat in a growth market, the relinquishment of control to the agency, the variability of the marketing return on investment, the client's reliance on their attractiveness as an account compared to other agency clients, or a poorer standard of advertising.
- It is impossible to break the rules of economics to secure a high return from a low stake without increasing risk one way or another. If it appears that this has been achieved, then it is more likely the risk has been moved to a different aspect of the relationship or the return has been diminished.
- Similarly, high investment at low risk will only deliver a relatively low but more predictable return.
- The Monkey House is the appropriate application of risk in each part of the agency relationship according to the needs of the brand's business problem.
- All aspects of agency engagement – remuneration, client behaviours and ways of working – need to be aligned to the business problem.
- Outliers – brands that achieve a higher than normal return on marketing investment – invariably manage their agencies and the aspects of risk in their relationship in ways consistent with the return they achieved.

[32] I should be clear at this point that though the case studies I have included illustrate the principle of The Monkey House, they were not developed using this framework.

[33] Understandably, most of the detail of agency fees has been withheld by the brands due to confidentiality policies, but I have indicated their buying strategies as well as I can.

PART

TWO

CHAPTER SEVEN

SOURCING AND PITCHING

"Whatever course you decide upon, there is always someone to tell you that you are wrong. There are always difficulties arising which tempt you to believe that your critics are right. To map out a course of action and follow it to an end requires courage."

Ralph Waldo Emerson, 1803–1882
American essayist, lecturer and poet

THE SOURCING AND PITCHING PARADIGM

The agency market is seemingly oversupplied and complex, making it difficult to differentiate between agencies and assess their suitability to solve client problems. Brand owners and intermediaries largely use the same pitch processes and procedures, regardless of the business problem, both with and without the aid of procurement.

Useful procurement tools and methods are often overlooked or wrongly applied by marketing, procurement and intermediaries – such as those that can help identify risk. Ironically, inappropriate procurement tools such as e-auctions are becoming more commonplace.

Leverage buying strategies are employed almost exclusively in agency appointments, again regardless of the business problem the appointed agency is being asked to solve (the kind of monkey the brand needs).

Pitch gimmicks, such as 'speed-dating' and expensive, over-elaborate responses to Requests for Information (RFIs), offer little other than entertainment to help what is a vastly complex and important decision-making process.

Hunger and passion are frequently cited by clients and their intermediaries as means to differentiate agencies, but passion is any agency's stock-in-trade and hunger is potentially a counter-indication of an agency's success, not a measure of it.

Agency fame and history are used as a proxy for the calibre of their talent, though within most agencies the standard of talent is quite variable.

175

THE MONKEY HOUSE PARADIGM FOR AGENCY SOURCING

The process of agency selection starts with the characterization of the business problem the client needs the agency to solve: a Gorilla, a Spider Monkey or an Orangutan.

The characterization of the business problem identifies the kind of agency talent needed to best solve it (see the Supplier Preference Matrix – chapter three).

Use the brand's approximate annual budget for agency fees to determine the appropriate size of agency for it:

- A smaller share of the agency's revenue will require high 'attractiveness' levels for brands needing a Spider Monkey. Smaller, highly creative 'boutique' agencies might be an alternative.
- A higher share of agency's revenue is necessary for a brand needing an Orangutan to avoid becoming a Nuisance account in supplier preference and deprioritized within the agency. The largest Orangutans can enjoy the same calibre of talent as Gorillas.
- A higher share of agency revenue is also necessary to access Gorilla-quality talent in the agency.

Assess the brand's processes and ways of working for their suitability to access the agency talent needed – and change these processes and KPIs if necessary (see the Meikle Matrix, chapter four). Consider the attractiveness of the account and the level of control the brand exerts over its agency.

Determine the brand's appropriate procurement buying strategy for agency services according to The Monkey House characterization of the need and accessibility to the talent required (see the Buying Matrix, chapter five).

Make a first assessment of the available agency market. Establish a long list of no more than ten agencies, eliminating agencies servicing clients that would be in irreconcilable conflict.

Use prescriptively simple RFI forms to access any agency data that is not otherwise readily available. Eliminate outliers to achieve a top five.

Select from a number of tools and processes to design a pitch process with the right procedures to appeal to and motivate the agency talent you need. Share the process with the agencies using appropriate detail, commit to the process and stick to it, never bending or breaking your own rules.

Apply a qualitative assessment of talent and agency suitability (leadership, culture, knowledge, team), eliminating the bottom two scoring agencies. Do not include wild cards, only qualifying agencies by your own criteria.

Include the top three scoring agencies in a full pitch.

In every instance and at every opportunity, be a brand that the talent you need will want to work on – and continue operating based on this principle once the account has been awarded. Focus relentlessly on the agency you most need, not necessarily the agency that most wants you. Applied properly using The Monkey House, they'll be one and the same.

THE CREATIVE ADVERTISING AGENCY MARKET

Before setting out how to find an agency and how we might design a sourcing and pitching process that would satisfy your Monkey House needs, it's first necessary to understand a few things about the advertising agency market per se.

In the UK, as in many other countries around the world, the market for creative and integrated advertising services is vastly complex. To start with, it seems very overcrowded – hence, it is extremely competitive – and its landscape changes almost week-by-week with new agencies launching, acquisitions, account moves and talent appointments. However, I do not subscribe to the belief that the market is oversupplied; some sections of it are, but others are not – once again it depends on a brand's need.

The market is much more dynamic now than it used to be. Once upon a time it was a much bigger and more difficult endeavour to start a new agency. Technological developments over the last two decades have enabled the quicker and more efficient movement of talent, clients' accounts and their creative assets from one agency to another. Consequently, agencies are far more elastic in their headcount now than they have ever been.

The job of the agency is to stand out from this messy crowd. There are ways in which agencies actively approach differentiation and there are ways where it can be useful to clients to differentiate agencies themselves (which agencies might like a little less) and it is worth spending some time examining these different ways. All agencies will almost always profess to be able to satisfy your Monkey House needs, whichever advertising monkey or monkeys you want, but some will be better than others. Similarly, if you have additional specific needs, you might differentiate one agency that can develop a Gorilla for you from another based on their aptitude for providing other services or satisfy other needs. Size, geographical reach, specialist units, different operating models, leadership, industry recognition and culture, to name a few, are perhaps worth examining more closely here.

SIZE

An agency's size, usually estimated by their headcount and billings[34] or revenue, is an important factor in agency selection. Some accounts are simply so large that only agencies of a certain scale would possibly be able to manage them – so their ability to manage other similarly bulky accounts can quickly cut through the complexity of the market. Other clients, that own multiple brands, will operate a roster of agencies. This will ensure that they can benefit from their agencies competitively vying for position and can more efficiently manage pitch processes from a pre-selected shortlist. They will also hopefully ensure they never have too great a share of one agency's revenue.

Revenue-share[35] is a criterion some agencies dislike, but it is a useful measure to indicate how the agency is likely to respond to a client with their supplier preference (see chapter three). If a client's revenue is too large, then there can be a danger of the agency becoming reluctant to challenge the client's thinking or judgment, scared of losing them by speaking truth to power. If a client's revenue is too small, then the best talent can overlook an account. Most agencies will protest that neither is the case, but as I have already argued in chapter three, to some extent it has to be.

There are also multiple super-groups of operating and holding companies like WPP, Omnicom, Interpublic, Publicis and Havas, to name a few. The way these different behemoths operate, the kinds of agencies they own and the cultures they encourage can be quite different from each other. The level of control they exert over one agency in their group compared to another can change depending on the agency's performance. This can impact their employer brand, their clients – or not – it all depends. For large multi-national accounts, it can be useful and portfolio clients might like to do a deal at a group level.

Size and breadth of an agency's client base also provide reassurance that an agency is stable, that it's likely to be around for a long time. There is similar reassurance from the likes of WPP, Omnicom and Interpublic. These groups would be reluctant to allow a failing agency in their group to go under if it hit upon hard times, just in case clients might lose faith in the group's other agencies. Hence, there's a higher degree of safety in larger agencies and those owned by holding companies.

GEOGRAPHICAL REACH

Geographical reach also differentiates agencies (global, regional and national) for brands with needs across multiple regions or countries. Network reach varies from half a dozen key markets around the world to offices in more than 150 countries, depending on which agency you go to. Affiliations and associations exist in more remote markets, so the presence of their own office doesn't necessarily represent a go/no-go criterion in a pitch. Likewise, brands that are increasing their globally aligned presence commonly look for hub-and-spoke models whereby, depending on the need for strategic and creative involvement on a local level, a regional hub agency will develop campaigns that are then implemented by their network of offices or production facilities. Agencies use their networks, their ownership and their facilities to differentiate from one another. The calibre of talent, leadership, agency capability and services within the same agency network can vary significantly from one country to another. Global brands that require in-country strategy and creative work need to consider the highest common standards across a network, not just the head office or regional hubs.

SPECIALIST UNITS

Specialized services – from behavioural economics units, econometrics, in-house post-production and content production facilities to brand activation divisions – can be used to entice clients and also to broaden agencies' remits and revenue streams. Some fully integrated agencies have all of these in one single resource; larger agency groups offer access to other more traditional offerings such as interactive[36] direct marketing, PR and so forth through sister companies. But how these agencies and offerings work together is important. The consolidation of multiple channels can, of course, be used to improve your supplier preference.

OPERATING MODELS

Creative agency operating models can vary, from the individual agency, to how a group of agencies of different communications disciplines can work together in a single country, to how different agencies work together in a global network. The models for integration produced by collaboration between agencies can vary enormously, too. In turn, this can affect their ability to integrate effectively. This can be influenced by their ownership, their leadership, their incentives, the client's process, the client's behaviour and many, many more factors. If you are pitching an integrated piece of business, i.e., one that would draw on the resources of multiple agencies, it is vital to understand how these companies work together, how they are incentivized and what to do if something goes wrong so that client fees aren't eaten up by needless inefficiency and in-fighting.

Additionally, there is the question of the agency model – so when looking for a new agency you would have to know what kind of agency you need. This particular subject has had its waters further muddied by endless industry chatter around the question of whether or not the agency model is broken. Of course, the agency model is not broken, because there isn't one right agency model – it's difficult enough to even cluster agencies on some of the criteria they use to differentiate themselves. Some agencies have differentiated themselves by their model, and sometimes the points of difference can be so significant that pitch processes and procedures might need to be modified to accommodate them. For example, the agency Anomaly, founded in 2004, has been cited on a number of occasions as one that won't be remunerated on the basis of hours expended.

AGENCY LEADERSHIP

The world of creative agencies is still, to some extent, one where some people enjoy something similar to rock-star status, though perhaps a little less now than it used to be. There are a few leaders of high intelligence, wisdom, gravitas and raw strategic and/or creative ability who can transform an agency's power to hire and retain talent and solve client business problems. Often those of rock-star status will have established themselves off the back of multiple Gorillas. Most clients cannot access these people directly and, if they do, they probably get to see them only a couple of times a year. So it would be best to register what they do for the employer-brand reputation of the agency more than anything. It is only the most extraordinary of accounts that will have the rock-star agency folk working on them regularly.

Another important aspect of leadership is ownership, which can have a significant effect on the agency's culture. The priorities of privately-owned agencies that are establishing themselves, versus those that are readying themselves to be sold, versus those in the process of an earn-out, versus those owned outright by a holding company, can all be significantly different from one another – and not always in the ways you might think, but in ways that will impact how they work with their clients.

> *Agency ownership can have a significant impact on agency culture.*

For example, an earn-out is the period after the acquisition of an agency by another company during which the previous owners stay on. During this period, the company's performance determines the final sale price of the agency. At the end of an earn-out, net profits have a multiple applied to them (usually around eight) to determine the final sale price. So, if net profit were £1 million, then the sale price would be £8 million. Therefore, during the earn-out period the agency might be run quite differently to how it might be run normally. If a pencil normally costs one pound, essentially it becomes an £8 pencil during an earn-out because it is a cost that would otherwise be profit – i.e., a pound of profit would have been £8 in earn-out. But what if the training budget was £35,000? Suddenly that represents a quarter of a million-pound loss from the sale price – so the conditions of an earn-out (and evidence that the business isn't being fleeced for profit at the expense of its staff and facilities) can be very important.

AWARDS

There is a vast range of industry awards, from the general to the specific, from international festivals to local awards run by trade magazines. Creative awards such as Cannes Lions, Clios, D&AD Pencils and the like, plus effectiveness awards like the IPA's Effectiveness Awards, Effies and so on – all contribute significantly to an agency's industry reputation among clients and their employer brand reputation for existing and potential staff. The number of awards also contributes to their overall value as a business. The City uses the Gunn Report – an annual record of all agencies and the awards they have won – as a factor in the calculation of their share valuation. As mentioned earlier, the conclusions of the thorough IPA research paper by Les Binet and Peter Field suggest that agencies with the most awards have produced the most successful, long-term brand campaigns for their clients. Most awards for creativity will be awarded to Gorillas and Spider Monkeys, so awards indicate an agency's track record in The Monkey House, too.

CULTURE

Agencies can differ significantly in the principles by which they operate – their culture. First, there are those that will stand by their principles – and as Bill Bernbach once said, "A principle isn't a principle until it costs you something." These agencies might resign a client for bad behaviour or creative disagreements. Then there are others that will suck it up and bite their lips to keep a client – even though it might be demoralizing to a toxic degree for the agency. Some agencies have a brave culture that encourages their people to challenge clients, while others are more compliant. It isn't difficult to see how differences in agency culture can be aligned or in conflict with their provision of different advertising monkeys. Highly creative, daring cultures are much more consistent with Gorillas and Spider Monkeys. However, although more compliant agencies are likely to have more Orangutans on their reel, it doesn't necessarily mean that they can't deliver other advertising monkeys, just that they don't do so often.

Many agencies will also claim to have unique approaches to solving their clients' business problems consistent with cultural differentiation. Agencies may have strategic planning tools or campaign development methodologies from brand thumbprints, brand footprints and brand pyramids, to processes for developing integrated ideas. These approaches can be anything from painfully similar to radically different and need some investigation as part of the pitch process. Agencies often use these at the start of the differentiation process, when in fact the more basic, factual criteria are the most useful to marketing and, even more so, to marketing procurement.

HUNGER/PASSION

> # Why isn't hunger considered a counter-indication of an agency's success?

Agencies will routinely declare their passion and commitment to a prospective client's brand and affirm that they have an insatiable hunger, not just to win their business, but also to make the brand phenomenally successful. It is a rarity to find an agency that isn't falling over itself to declare its passion, regardless of how mundane the product or category in which the brand competes might be. Marketers routinely look for this kind of commitment and hunger, but sometimes we might be looking at hunger the wrong way around. Brands that need the best of agency talent may sometimes need to seek out the agencies that are successful enough not to be desperate for a client's business. They are likely to have a far higher calibre of talent than one that behaves like a scavenger. If an advertiser needs a Spider Monkey, it's important to remember who needs whom most, and to see through superficial declarations of hunger and passion.

There are other means of differentiation that can be useful to marketers or their procurement colleagues. Although these may already seem plenty, such is the complexity of the market and the differing needs of brands that it is a great advantage to be able to choose from a wide selection of criteria with which to narrow the market.

START-UPS

It is a feature of the creative agency world that there is a perpetual life cycle. Start-up agencies are launched, and they build into sufficient mass and reputation that they become attractive acquisitions. They are often then bought – usually by large agency groups – and merged into larger agencies, only to find that some of their best or up-and-coming leadership break off and start up again. Technological advances have enabled this feature of the agency market to accelerate in more recent years, and it can be a benefit to both the founders of the start-ups and the big agency owners who usually end up buying them, because they can revitalize an ebbing agency reputation and boost their portfolio of clients. DDB's acquisition of Adam&Eve and FCB's acquisition of Inferno have both transformed these networks' London offices and seen them grow far faster than they had been growing without these new leases of life.

Before their acquisition, start-ups can make for attractive agency propositions to brands. They often will appear wackier, with quirky offices, different ways of working and can often compete on price much harder than their longer-established and larger competitors. Procurement is wise to refer to a hierarchy of needs (see *figure 24*) when considering a start-up that hasn't been established for long.

Figure 24

Procurement
Hierarchy of Needs

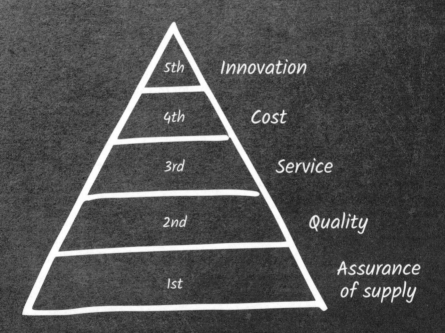

5th — Innovation

4th — Cost

3rd — Service

2nd — Quality

1st — Assurance of supply

1st – Assurance of supply

How stable is this supplier? Will they be able to supply me with the goods and services that I need? Is there any threat to their ability to supply? Is there likely to be any tangible threat in the foreseeable future?

2nd – Quality

Is the quality of the goods/services we require from this supplier good enough to meet our needs? What indications are there upon which we can rely? Are there measures for quality we can use?

3rd – Service

How will this supplier service our account? Will service levels be adequate? What commitments can be made to assure service levels?

4th – Cost

How much will hierarchies 1 to 3 cost according to the scope of our needs? What will be our buying strategy for this supplier?

5th – Innovation

Are there any additional services, opportunities or areas of added value that differentiate this supplier to make it more attractive and beneficial to us versus their competition?

In short, if a supplier has assurance of supply, it means that it can do what it needs to do, reliably and over time. For creative advertising agencies, this means that it has the capabilities to produce the work that its clients need and the stability to be there when the clients need it. Agencies that might balance on a financial knife edge if they lost a big account can't provide the same assurance of supply as one where the largest account represents less than 10% of that agency's revenue. The big brand agencies with holding companies above them, integrated resources around them and geographical reach provide lots of assurance of supply.

Some brands might be lured away from the longer-established agency names to the often-cheaper fees of start-ups, but it can be at the expense of assurance of supply. The reduced fees don't represent a saving without consequence – overall risk has increased because of the nature of the agency and its relative instability. Ben Mark Orlando is a case in point.

In January 2004 it was reported in *Campaign* magazine that a new agency was being launched called Ben Mark Orlando. The partners were Ben Langdon (former UK Group Chairman for McCann Erickson), Mark Wnek (former Chairman of Euro RSCG) and Orlando Hooper-Greenhill (a planning partner from TBWA London). Langdon was quoted on 28 January 2004 in *Campaign* as follows:

> *"The use of our Christian names is a symbol of our personal commitment to our clients and, believe it or not, the relaxed and fun culture we're determined to create in our agency."*

He continued: "We've had a great time working for some brilliant large agencies, but we set up this agency precisely because we share a belief that clients get better advertising if they get direct access to the right people."

So, all well and good one might think – and I certainly can't argue with the premise that direct access to the best talent would provide greater agency value. But fast forward little more than eight weeks to 12 March 2004, and Francesca Newland wrote the following for *Campaign*:

> *"Mark Wnek has hit out following revelations that Ben Langdon is ditching the agency he founded only ten weeks ago to take Wnek's previous job at Euro RSCG London."*

Their company was subsequently dissolved.

As entertaining as this fiasco was for the local advertising industry, who are never averse to a little *schadenfreude* (*Campaign* had also written that, "Both Wnek and Langdon are famed for their fierce working practices."), BMO had won the Bacardi account in February 2004 and until Wnek announced to them that Langdon had quit, it was down to the final two for the Ocado account to be awarded that March.

So, the number-one requirement in procurement's hierarchy of needs: assurance of supply, was left unmet.

(Langdon lasted 18 months in Wnek's old job.)

BMO is not an isolated case. Although it lasted significantly longer than BMO, Johnny Fearless closed its doors just four years after it opened them, reportedly leaving Davidoff, some Diageo brands, Survivors UK and the Imperial War Museum to find new agencies to fulfil some or all of their scopes of work.[37]

CLIENT CONFLICT

Like it or not, creative agencies are also differentiated by their incumbent clients. If an agency has a direct competitor for an account that's looking for a home, in most instances this is enough to exclude them from a shortlisting process. Assuming, of course, that the incumbent competing client is set to stay. In January 2015 it was announced that Tesco had moved its £110m billing account to BBH without a pitch. However, BBH was the agency for Waitrose, which it consequently resigned in order to harbour Tesco at more than four times Waitrose's billing.

In most instances, client conflict is a greater concern for clients than it is for their agencies. Most agencies would be happy to resolve such conflicts in a number of different ways, but more often than not, they struggle to get buy-in from their clients. What constitutes conflict can be determined with consideration of a number of different factors, such as the categories of business in which the clients operate, their categories' target audience, their respective market shares, and whether a conflict category is of sufficient 'critical mass' to constitute a conflict that needs to be resolved. But, in most instances, it is simply a question of a comparable and competitive offering.

Agencies employ a number of means to overcome client conflict. In any event, these different means need to be by the consent of all three parties involved to be successful, i.e., the agency, the incumbent client and the new client. They include:

- Chinese walls: exclusive agency personnel allocation across departments; information barrier.
- Brick walls: separate office locations of the agencies' teams.
- Firewalls: separate servers and/or restricted access to shared servers.
- Separate P&L's: housing the conflict client in the agency's sister company.

Any or all of these can be employed, but consideration should be given to the role of the agency's leadership, too. If the agency leadership is expected to be involved in and contribute to the new client's business, it will be necessary to agree at what level within the agency the splits of resources are effective (CEO, MD, Group Account Director, Planning Director, etc.) and how senior management would manage handling conflicting clients.

The increasing breadth of product offerings made by some brands compounds the issue of conflict for agencies. Many big supermarkets now offer telephony products, car insurance, home insurance, pet insurance, banking, savings, mortgages, etc., with the result that traditional banks often now conflict with supermarkets. Further challenges emerge when integrated agencies are contracted to provide one communications discipline to a client that then precludes them from offering other services to competing clients. For example, an integrated agency might win the account to provide social media services for a bank, but could then be precluded from providing advertising services to a supermarket that offers banking products.

So, an agency's existing clients can help cut through the cluttered market, thanks to advertisers' noncompete clauses, and can make a useful starting point for limiting agencies that could qualify in a pitch process. The result means that when accounts that agencies are allowed to pitch for come up, the competition is usually nothing short of vicious.

Importantly, if you've identified an agency, which in every other way is suitable to your Monkey House needs, it might be a greater risk to exclude them from a process because of your stringent conflict policies than to include them and secure their value.

A process of selection may be better than one of deselection if you know what you want.

The outcome from all of this complexity is that pitch processes can frequently be inappropriate, unfair and opaque, resulting in ill-informed and poorly-judged appointments and deals. Consequently, the kind of talent being allocated to accounts, and therefore the calibre of advertising monkey they produce, is what clients' brands deserve – not necessarily what they want. The clients' returns on investment are thus compromised, accounts are subsequently moved again, marketing directors change jobs and the merry-go-round continues. This may seem like a very jaundiced or prejudiced perspective, but a vast number of advertising accounts will be somewhere on this unfit-for-purpose merry-go-round continuum.

These complex conditions have been a real boost to the intermediary market. The market-leading intermediaries have a disproportionate influence over the agencies – which is even making some marketers nervous about their level of influence.

INTERMEDIARIES

It is also worth pointing out that most intermediaries often demand subscriptions or membership fees from their agencies. They mostly make no secret of this, but I have met many marketers who were surprised to learn about it. I'm sure that 9 times out of 10 it makes little or no difference, as most sizeable agencies are 'members' to most big intermediaries. But, despite offering what I would deem appropriate assurance of supply, quality, service and cost, many small and specialist agency leaders have felt overlooked when a brand is looking for a smaller agency to whom they would be a Core client or if they require a specialism. Advertisers should beware of intermediaries who profess to 'save' their clients money, too. Any fool can reduce investments, and anybody who says that they can do so without either increasing risk or compromising the return carries a heavy burden of proof.

Also, be aware of intermediaries who offer their services for 'free' to the brand, allowing onto any shortlist only agencies that will pay the intermediary a commission of their first year's fee from that brand. This is probably the least questionable of these practices, but it does limit the field to those agencies prepared to play that game, and usually applies to smaller contracts, where the brand cannot get an agreement internally to pay for an intermediary.

Worse still, there are intermediaries who will favour one agency over another if that agency buys training services or suchlike from the intermediary. Intermediaries should be obliged to inform their client of any conflicting interests, pecuniary or otherwise. Brands should demand complete transparency from their intermediary if they are to entrust them with such a role.

NAVIGATING THROUGH THE FOG

Having spelled out most aspects of the nightmarish complexity that surrounds this industry, the question is: how on earth does an advertiser find the right agency for them? It's essential to have a plan, a process by which you'll find an agency to fulfil your need. And once into a pitch process, it is essential to stick to the process you or your intermediary have designed, and for two very good reasons:

1) According to IPA research,[38] in 2009 the average agency investment in one integrated pitch, including staff hours and third party costs, was £209,000. Such investments are not made lightly by agencies. If your company develops a reputation for bending or breaking pitch processes or rules, your brand may not be one in which the agency you need is ready to invest such a stake.

2) Agencies will persuade, cajole and beg to be added to a brand's longlist or shortlist – even to the final three in a pitch – changing other agencies' odds from one in three to one in four on a £209,000 bet – because everyone else does it. However, as soon as an agency, which legitimately made the shortlist, hears about these irregularities, it cries foul. Strict adherence to your own process prevents the pitch from becoming a bear pit.

These underline the need for objectivity, integrity and congruity between word and deed – qualities often missing from pitch processes. And prospective clients have to be the disciplinarians: you can't ask a hungry pack of dogs to form a queue without some serious discipline to make them behave that way.

It would be impossible to write one model approach to pitching because of the variability in the needs of the different brands. However, we can start by at least differentiating our approaches by using the first step of characterizing the brand's need according to The Monkey House. As I have discussed earlier, most big advertisers would benefit from Gorillas – they have a high market share in a growing market or a high market share in a market that may not be in growth but which is responsive to brand/product innovation and/or its related advertising.

There is a chain of logic here that can help us navigate to the kind of agency and the kind of talent a brand might need:

- Gorilla-brands need to innovate, they need creativity …
- Therefore, they need great agency people who are motivated and loyal to their agency …
- Therefore, agencies with strong employer brands are more likely to harbour and retain this kind of talent.

I believe employer brands are the key to agency differentiation.

So rather than allowing agencies to differentiate themselves by the criterion that suits them best, we can use our own employer brand strength measures.

> *Better employer brands attract better talent and better talent produces greater value.*

In an RFI, there are a number of questions a prospective client might ask that would help assess an agency's employer brand status. These include:

- What is their IPA training accreditation status?
- What is their L&D investment and strategy?
- What are their staff turnover levels compared to the market norm?
- What is their maternity/paternity leave policy?
- What evidence can they show of diversity in both staff and management?
- What are the staff working conditions?
- Do they feature in the *Sunday Times'* best companies to work for ranking?
- What are the staff canteen and facilities like?
- Where is the office located?[39]
- What are their flagship accounts and how long have they held them?
- Where do they rank in the Gunn Report?
- What is the industry profile and reputation of the leadership?

Often our reaction to the answers of these questions can be back to front. Instead of being concerned that an agency's new offices must have cost a fortune, clients should be reassured that the agency has created a space where people really want to work or even just hang out. When Ogilvy moved to Canary Wharf in London's Docklands area, it was recognized by general consent that it was one of the worst office choices in advertising history. The new Ogilvy offices on London's Southbank are simply stunning – and these things matter enormously.

So, to differentiate a crowded field, we could consider the advertising market on two more simple criteria: first, agencies' size (and therefore implicitly their appropriateness to handle large or small accounts), their stability and their likely longevity. And second, agencies' employer brand strength – their ability to attract/retain and develop staff. I drew the following in a negotiation training session with one of my agency clients recently (see *figure 25*).

Figure 25

Agency Differentiation

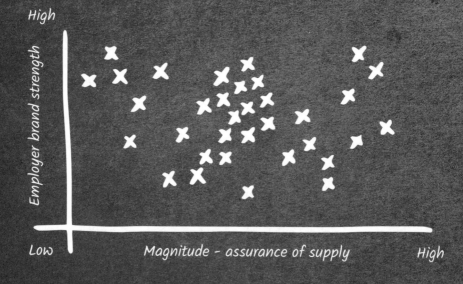

I've taken a guess at what the distribution of the top 30 or so London agencies might look like. Although in this illustration we don't have start and end points on either scale, it would not be difficult to devise a points system for employer brand strength and agency magnitude. Interestingly, it illustrates that if your business requirement is for a very large agency that has the best available talent, there are maybe only two or three comparable agencies to choose from. If one or two of them already harbour a client that would present a conflict of interest, then the market for agencies is a lot narrower than it might first appear. Of course, brands have the option of approaching their competitor's agency at any time, but such a betrayal by an agency is not a decision that would ever be taken lightly.

Depending on the brand's need, and of course the availability of the top three agencies, this mapping shows which agencies might be the next best. The further you go away from the top of the employer brand strength scale, the better you have to be as a client to attract the best talent from within the agency. This is because agency talent is likely to be more variable in their value, so it's likely you'll have to pay for the privilege. And quite right, too: if you want to mitigate the risk of poor talent it costs money, just as with any other investment.

However, if you need to source from mid-range agencies, following the principles of The Monkey House, as an advertiser you are more likely to get the kind of talent you need from within the agency.

CASE STUDY: THE POST OFFICE – HOW A FRESH APPROACH TO RUNNING A CREATIVE PITCH BETTER MOTIVATED COMPETING AGENCIES AND SECURED THE BEST AVAILABLE TALENT.

In 2012, the Post Office split from the Royal Mail and remained a publicly run organization.

Although the Post Office has commercial goals and interests, it is obliged under public procurement rules to review its suppliers and run tenders for its suppliers on a regular basis. In 2014, the Post Office needed to begin the process of sourcing, pitching and appointing a new creative advertising agency because the contract with their incumbent agency was coming to an end.

I was engaged as a consultant to the Post Office to work with their marketing and procurement departments to organize and run the sourcing and pitch processes.

The business problem

The Post Office operates in a number of product categories, some of which it dominates (such as mail and foreign currency exchange), and others in which it has a very small share relative to market leaders (such as telephony and mortgages). At the time of the agency tender, the Post Office was also in the throes of relaunching its brand. The portfolio of products mostly needed Gorillas and Spider Monkeys; therefore, it was essential to run a pitch that would access the greatest available agency talent. The British government had already established a roster of agencies that government departments and organizations could draw from for pitching their accounts. The challenge was not only to identify an agency of the appropriate size and calibre, but also – within that agency – to access and motivate their best talent.

The strategy

In order to access the best available agency talent, the pitch process would have to first identify that talent, and second, motivate it both to win the business and to service the account going forward. Both of these objectives would best be met by making the Post Office an attractive account to work on financially and in relationship terms. To achieve this required an enlightened, sympathetic and intrinsically human approach to both the sourcing process and the management of the pitch itself. There were a number of ways in which the Post Office's pitch approached these objectives differently to what might be considered a more conventional process:

1) Before the shortlisting process began, a member of staff from Post Office procurement and a member of staff from marketing and I went to visit each agency together. Our plan was to describe to each agency the business challenges the Post Office

was facing, describe the pitch process we wanted them to embark upon, gauge their initial interest and identify any areas of potentially irreconcilable client conflict. In doing so, the Post Office demonstrated integrity, congruity and empathy in the pitch process by:

- Stating what the process would be, when it would be, and being completely transparent about how agencies would be assessed and selected
- Sticking to the process initially described
- Communicating openly, clearly and fairly with all agencies and resisting any entrepreneurial work-arounds[40]
- Accommodating the needs of the agency people where the process ran over summer and half-term holidays.[41]

2) Given the number of product categories the Post Office competed in, we developed and agreed on a Post Office client conflict policy for the competing agencies. This document indicated clearly – and in advance of the process – which categories would represent irreconcilable conflict. Of around 20 different promoted products for the Post Office, there were only three categories that were identified as conflicts. Most importantly, the policy stated that the Post Office would be happy to actually assist the agencies in their negotiations with incumbent clients in the other 17 or so categories if they already had clients in them.

3) After making an initial shortlist, based on the size of the agencies and their RFI case study submissions, the second round of the process sought to identify talent more directly through a series of interview-based meetings with the five remaining competitors. Instead of a more common 'chemistry' session in which each agency (and indeed the client) often show their best selves, the interview panel tested the mettle of key team leaders who would work on the Post Office account. The highest scoring three agencies would go through to the final round of presentations against a live creative brief.

4) The pitch document supplied to the final three agencies was thorough and included specifics of the Post Office's expectations for ways of working. It included specifics of the scope of work, but also the number of routes expected and the rounds and nature of changes that would be required within the agreed fee.

5) The agencies were briefed together. Agency attendees' numbers were limited to three per agency and all Post Office marketing and procurement stakeholders were present.

6) All agencies were offered tissue meetings, where they could openly discuss strategy and/or creative work in progress with the client. It was made clear when the tissue meetings could be held that they were not obligatory, and – perhaps most importantly – that they would not be assessed or scored as part of the selection process.

7) The financial aspect of the pitch was handled differently to anything the three final agencies had experienced before. It was designed to influence each agency's supplier preference, should it be successful (see chapter three). Instead of asking the agencies to compete on their fees, we asked them to compete on talent. The Post Office decided on a fee that we believed was an appropriate investment, consistent with the scope of work and experience, and that was not inconsistent with available benchmarking information.[42] The agencies were told the total fee amount, given the performance-based bonus pool, and were asked to submit:

- A weighting for the bonus across various criteria
- An overhead contribution within the fee as a percentage
- A resource plan, using a structured template we provided, such that talent could be compared on a like-for-like basis rather than using the nebulous nature of agency roles and titles. Plans needed to include the leadership that had succeeded in the panel interview round from account management and planning departments. Resource plans had to allow for 15-20% profit for the agency to prevent low-balling.

8) The use of a live brief also made a difference in agency motivation. The knowledge that the work developed to win the business would actually be used meant there was an additional satisfying result that would not require the 'real' work to begin in earnest right after the pitch was won.[43]

The outcome

The result of the process achieved an incredibly high standard of pitch presentations from three agencies. The final award of the account came down to less than a 5% margin between the top two agencies across the combined assessment criteria. The process effectively minimized the risk of a business-critical decision. As it transpired, the winning agency nearly had to withdraw due to unforeseen circumstances, so the risk that had been mitigated was real. Had the final part of the process been a one-horse race, the consequences could have been significant.

From the client's perspective, Pete Markey, former Chief Marketing Officer for the Post Office, who sponsored the pitch, was very satisfied with the outcome:

"The pitch process and overall approach were exactly what we needed to secure the right result. The challenges were measured and appropriate and helped us as a business mould our thinking and select the right agency with which to move forwards. I am delighted with the work from Mullen Lowe. The first campaign alone delivered an ROI of £2.90 for every £1.00 spent. We also saw a step-change improvement in brand metrics. I am delighted with the result."

From the perspective of the agency, the pitch strategy achieved exactly the priority it was designed to achieve. Jamie Eliot, former Chief Executive at DLKWLowe (now Mullen Lowe), the winning agency, said:

> *"We get about 50 new business approaches a year and know that a full pitch process will cost us well over £100,000 in people and hard costs. So, we have to be selective and alert to approaches from time-wasters. But, from the first meeting we knew that the Post Office was a pitch we were going to do everything to win. The way that the process was set up was empathetic to our world and designed to get the best from us; consequently, we were able to manage our resources and make this the pitch the agency got behind in its entirety. Granted, parts of the process were daunting and new, like the interview stage, but this was overall a fair test of our mettle and was managed in a way that set the relationship for success from the off. These things are always a rollercoaster ride but done like this, we'd be in the queue for another go in a heartbeat."*

A NOTE ABOUT THE RFI

RFIs began life as a fact-finding tool used by procurement professionals to collect, collate and assess comparable business information about competitors in a given market from which they would like to find a supplier. RFIs are typically used to determine:

- What products or services the potential suppliers offer
- How big their companies are
- Perhaps how many branches they have and in which locations
- What their turnovers are
- How many people they have working for them
- How long they have been in existence
- Who the companies' biggest clients are.

More sophisticated versions may also request details of things such as business continuity planning or quality management systems. When RFIs stick to well-constructed, well-chosen, specific questions that are appropriate to the category from which the procurement team is sourcing, they help buyers narrow their market of possible vendors intelligently and effectively.

The cost of completing an RFI – which some procurement departments issue without a specific tender in mind, just to assess a given market at a given time – is logically meant to be relatively low. It should require some comparably senior administrative time and that's all. But RFI submissions in the advertising market have somehow morphed from questionnaire responses into creative showcases, requiring significant investments of time and money from agencies completing them. In a normal working relationship, agencies insist on presenting their strategic and creative recommendations, but for some reason they are happy to invest huge amounts in creative showcases that are then sent on to a client, often via an intermediary, to have their suitability as a potential supplier assessed.

There are a number of reasons why I believe this trend should give us cause for concern, but here are my main two:

First, if an agency is invited to submit a bespoke response to an open-ended RFI, competing with an unknown number of other agencies, this may create a barrier to entry to the most suitable candidates. But even when there is no barrier to entry, it's nonetheless a pretty arrogant start to the relationship with the winning agency. If I were tendering for an airport to be designed and I wanted Foster + Partners to develop proposals for me, why would I make them perform a dog and pony show for me first? I know they're the best, surely my tender process and potential relationship with them would get off to a better start if I respected that.

Second, there is a hierarchy of needs in procurement (see *figure 24*, chapter seven) to be satisfied when sourcing a new agency. Each client will have their own needs and will ensure that available agencies are, for example, the appropriate size, stability, longevity, reach and so forth, before requiring them to compete in the field of creativity. The point is that it serves nobody's purpose to find a fantastically creative agency only to discover later that they're not suitable according to more fundamental criteria. That's why the hierarchy of needs is a hierarchy and not a list. The elaborate examples of RFI submissions described above are illustrative of how our attention can be diverted from the real purpose behind a well-executed RFI.

The proper application of an RFI questionnaire allows for a much higher number of eligible agencies to be approached and considered. So, in a market as complex as we know the creative ad agency market is, and where client conflicts are abundant, it is clearly very important to be as intelligent as you can in your selection process. We need to narrow the field by sourcing strategy, not discretionary and expensive showcasing.

Most agencies won't tell clients, let alone intermediaries, that this trend is damaging – understandably they don't want to bite the hands that feed them. Agencies look much more favourably on clients that behave responsibly. Therefore, it's up to clients and their intermediaries to do the right thing.

The optimal sourcing of marketing services agencies requires a blend of the smartest of marketing procurement practices and an in-depth understanding of marketing needs and of agencies.

The odds of winning an account are poorer for an agency at the beginning of a sourcing process when the number of agencies is highest. Therefore, their investment at this stage of the process should be lowest. As the field narrows, and the number of agencies falls, so the odds of the remaining agencies improve. As the agencies' odds improve and more effort is required, so does the prospective client's expectations of time, effort and money expended by each agency (see *figure 26*).

Figure 26

Agencies' Investment in the Pitch Process

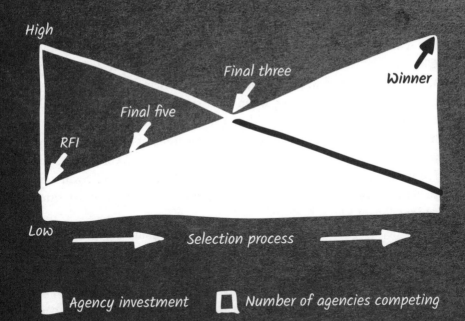

Using a model of risk and investment like this protects agencies from themselves to some degree. It is not only in the brand's interests to prioritize agencies according to the hierarchy of needs, but it also increases the pitch's appeal and better motivates the agencies and their people.

But some agencies are the problem here, too. Many agencies will enjoy any opportunity to show off by 'going the extra mile' and 'demonstrating their passion'. Quite hypocritically, some will be the same agencies that complain about RFIs getting out of hand. But unless there's some sort of industry-wide agreement to get this under control, the "If you can't beat 'em, join 'em!" attitude will foolishly prevail and, as I said earlier, it's hard to discipline starving dogs at dinner time.

THE ROLE OF PROCUREMENT

As a business discipline, procurement is much more objective and analytical than marketing when it comes to sourcing suppliers; it is far less reliant on personal connections, 'chemistry' and personal referrals. Often marketers can compromise on results during the longlist and shortlist processes, but procurement can help them stick to their strategy and principles. However, when done sloppily, procurement can deter agencies from being involved in a selection process. For example, I have heard of multiple instances when procurement departments have inappropriately repurposed RFI forms used for cleaning contractors and HR firms, critically harming their brands' credibility. Agencies will view such invitations to tender in a jaundiced light compared to a well-written and intelligent RFI.

So, depending on the brand's business problem and the *modus operandi* of the procurement department, procurement may or may not have value to add. In any event, before embarking on the sourcing and pitch process, it is essential that procurement is clear and appropriately motivated by the nature of the brand's business problem – the kind of advertising monkey they are helping to buy. All the good work of a pitch process can be compromised or destroyed if the procurement department is buying for an Orangutan and marketing needs a Gorilla. However, if procurement is aligned with marketing behind the interests of the brand, then they can be very useful as part of the process. If you can agree that procurement will be accountable to the same key performance indicators as marketing for the management of marketing investment and its return on that investment, then these conflicts of interest vanish.

"It is hard to imagine a more stupid or more dangerous way of making decisions than by putting those decisions in the hands of people who pay no price for being wrong."

Thomas Sowell
American economist, social theorist

THE PITCH PROCESS

There's no shortage of guidelines about how to run a pitch; they are produced and updated by industry bodies regularly. Most pitches for big-budget clients are for brands that already enjoy a significant market share, and that are either in growth markets or markets where they have an opportunity to grow. Therefore, I shall assume the characterization of the brand's need is a Gorilla for the purposes of illustrating a different approach. When it comes to the financial aspect of a pitch, I'll show you three different scenarios for three different monkeys.

We will look at the financial aspect of pitching in some detail, but before that, there are three clear stages in running a pitch process:

1) Preparation
2) Engagement of agencies
3) Evaluation, appointment and commencment of work.

1. **Preparation**
   Sound and thorough preparation is essential to running a productive pitch process.

   1.1) Preparations begin with the characterization of the brand's business need using The Monkey House – the brand's market position and the market's capacity to grow (see chapter two).

   1.2) Identify ALL internal stakeholders in the pitch process; define their roles and responsibilities.

   1.3) Ensure there is stakeholder alignment behind the brand need – the monkey – in terms of risk and its implications for creativity.

1.4) Assess whether the brand's current remuneration model and ways of working with the incumbent agency are consistent with the business problem.[44] Use The Monkey House framework as a diagnostic tool.

1.5) Change ways of working and ways of paying as necessary to make them suited to getting a Gorilla, or whatever advertising monkey you need. Can you afford to allow the agency greater control in the process of campaign development? Can the means of remuneration be changed to allow the agency variable profitability according to their efficiency? Can you incentivize better? Highly valuable and highly attractive accounts attract Core talent (see *figure 9*, chapter three).

1.6) If you are unable to financially compete with the longlist of agencies' other clients, you must assess if you are sufficiently 'attractive' as a client to engage talent or whether you should consider smaller agencies in which you would be a more valued client.

1.7) Design your pitch process such that it will attract the right talent for the brand's business problem. Include details of your campaign development process and ways of working. Bear in mind these may need to significantly adapt for Spider Monkeys and Gorillas, for which you will need to consider how you can make the agency's best talent *want* to work on your business.

1.8) Develop a clear brief for the scope of work you will want the winning agency to deliver: what it includes, what it doesn't include, and scope of work for the first year. (If you don't have a scope of work, can you estimate it based on the last year's scope?)

1.9) Develop an induction presentation for the agencies, a background of the problem, its current circumstances, current and predicted competitive threats. Any other challenges to the brand – legislative (e.g., sugar tax), distribution, technology, etc. Let them know how you see the competitive and business landscape already.

1.10) Write a comprehensive and compelling pitch document. Demonstrate that you understand the magnitude of the gamble agencies are undertaking by participating. Be grateful for their interest and express your excitement. Explain clearly what the judging criteria will be and how they will be weighted. Give specific timing of the process and stick to it.

A common mistake made by brands is to behave like princesses holding court to their suitors. Such behaviour is often encouraged by the agencies themselves behaving like humble suitors, but some humility from the brand team – some acknowledgement of their reliance on the agency for a transformative idea that can change the fortune of their business – is highly motivating, not just because it's true, but because most others will still behave like princesses.

2. Agency engagement

How you engage with the agencies will influence whether they accept your brief, the priority they will give it, the people they will assign to it and the quality of their final pitch.

2.1) Brief the agencies together. To my mind this should be non-negotiable, even if you are including an incumbent agency. Separate briefings take more time and arouse suspicion between the agencies of an uneven playing field. The more open the process is, the fairer the process will be perceived and the more motivated the agencies will be.

2.2) Offer one or two progress meetings after the briefings, when agencies can choose whether or not to share strategy and/or creative work in progress. Do not count the progress meetings as part of the overall assessment of each agency, and if the result is a closer-run competition, then so much the better.[45]

2.3) Allocate pitch presentation meetings fairly – random allocation or first-come first-served on predetermined dates is usually the fairest. Make sure all the stakeholders from your organization will be in EVERY meeting. No exceptions.

2.4) Be available to answer agency questions throughout the pitch process. Assign one person on your team to manage all questions and requests fairly. Each agency must have equal access and attention.

2.5) Arrange for the pitches to be held in the agencies' offices or at a location of their choice (within reason), in case they want to add a little drama. Insist on fairly brutal enforcement of timing in the meetings.

2.6) Tell all the agencies by when they will hear the results, tell them how they will be told and by whom, and make sure you can reach the right agency person to convey your decision.

If an agency team feels (rightly or wrongly) that the cards are stacked against them, then it will affect their performance. If, as sometimes can happen, the agencies attempt dirty tricks on each other by announcing to the press that one or two have been knocked out, take corrective action immediately. Don't allow rumours or inaccurate reporting to fester.

3. Evaluation, appointment and commencement

3.1) Evaluate each agency individually against the pre-agreed criteria. Avoid reaching scores by consensus so the agency selection process doesn't fall foul of groupthink.

3.2) Inform the winning agency and ensure you have an agreement in principle first, in order to ensure that they will accept their appointment before informing the others.

3.3) Inform the losing agencies, openly, honestly and sympathetically. Losing agencies will have lost a significant stake – respect their investment.

3.4) Offer to provide debriefs for the losing agencies *and make good the promise.*

3.5) Provide the winning agency with a proper induction and onboarding programme. Don't expect them to 'hit the ground running' without investing significant effort to help make that happen.

3.6) Discuss and agree how, and how often, you will review your processes and behaviours to improve each other's performance. Agree on grievance procedures for both sides.

The financial part of the pitch process is an area where agencies have been highly critical of brands, and where brands have often done themselves a great disservice. Let's explore how the financial aspect of an agency's proposals could be done differently according to all three of the characterized needs – Spider Monkey, Gorilla and Orangutan – to illustrate why it is frequently done so badly.

Figure 27 illustrates the different kinds of approaches that can be employed for the financial proposal within a pitch, depending on the nature of the brand's business problem and the corresponding buying strategy (see chapter five). Each time the buying strategy reflects the relative buying power of the brand, and the variability of return of the brand.

Figure 27

Pitch Financial Proposals According to Client Business Problems

	 Spider Monkey	 Gorilla	 Orangutan
Buying strategy	Critical	Strategic	Leverage
Shared interest	Marketing and procurement teams incentivized on same KPIs as agency.	Marketing team incentivized to justify maximum agency bonus as proof of marketing's ability to extract maximum value from agency.	Shared incentives based on market share performance (which may see maintenance prioritized over growth) and brand profitability.
Financials	Client to indicate what fee investment is available for the scope of work and incentivize agency investment with generous PRB or similar.	Client should indicate fee investment in agency and scope of work. Agency to propose resource allocations, talent, PRB criteria and weightings. Client to provide templates to ensure like-for-like comparisons of roles and talent based on experience.	Agency to align proposals to brand profitability, providing resource plans. Incentivize agency to work with client on efficiencies. PRB weightings according to brand profitability. (Roster consolidation and globalization.)
Budget	Divulge total marketing communications budget – however meagre it might seem.	Inform agency of total marketing communications budget and breakdowns by channels, 'upstream' and 'downstream' production if possible. Specify how much you intend to invest in their services.	Ask for fee proposals and have agencies compete on money and resource. Employ strategies to avoid low-balling between agencies.
Incentive (PRB)	High – based on high growth, and in the absence of high fees, to pay for full service. Depends on the business opportunity and need; the upside could be unlimited.	Medium – significant enough to maintain supplier preference. Depends on size of revenue between 10-20% of total annual fees.	Medium – but assessed according to innovations to reduce marketing support, maintenance of share and profitability of the brand.
Proportion of proposal assessment	10%	20%	40%

In each of the above scenarios, where the pitch process is altered consistent with the business problem, the interests of all parties are also aligned, which is the key to producing productive, high-trust relationships.

Marketers can sometimes feel the urge to stray from their own pitch process – for example, if the RFI shortlist process knocks out an agency they were interested in. Whatever the reason, if a marketer has a favourite, they should be honest about it in the first place.

If a favoured agency wins in a rigged match, then the harm done to the other agencies is indefensible by any ethical measure, and only somewhat mitigated if the client is paying for losing agencies' pitch costs. It's only in the public sector that an organization is obliged to run a tender process at all, let alone a fair one, so if you know which agency you want to win and they satisfy your sourcing criteria, do a deal and appoint them. If they don't meet your needs, get over the disappointment and leave them out.

Equally, if the brand team's wishes are ignored and it is forced back into a fair process, then this may harm the relationship with the winning agency before it has even begun. The winning agency will want to be wanted. Both scenarios are damaging for the brand, so if you need to pitch, then pitch fairly – and if you can't do that, then see if you can get the agency you want without the expensive ceremony of a pitch, but don't try to have it both ways.

A NOTE ABOUT 'WILD CARDS'

Some brands and some intermediaries like to include what they describe as a 'wild card' in their pitching process. A wild card agency is one that doesn't meet the same criteria for the shortlist as the others. It might have its roots in another communications discipline or be a young agency with a rebellious culture and reputation, or perhaps it's significantly smaller or larger than the others. Clients and intermediaries who include wild cards do so because they are not clear about what they want (so they should go back to the drawing board) or because the wild card agency is exactly what they want – and therefore they shouldn't be running a pitch with a deck stacked against the others.

> *Brands and intermediaries including 'wild cards' in pitches don't know what they want and should revert to their hierarchy of needs.*

The brand's budget, the advertising monkey it needs and its overall risk strategy determine what kind of agency it should be looking for. Not only does the inclusion of a wild card waste one or a number of agencies' time, if a wild card is added to the last round of a pitch, it increases your team's workload by 25-30%. This is because they have to manage an additional agency, along with their enquiries and their development meetings, and the brand team will have to review another whole proposal. For all of these reasons, I have never accepted a pitch brief that included a wild card agency and I would never run a pitch for clients that demanded the inclusion of one.

*Pitches must be run with
the sole purpose of attracting
and motivating the talent
the brand's business
problem needs.*

SUMMARY

- The market for creative advertising agencies is both vast and complex. Brands need sound sourcing strategies as well as robust, appropriate pitch processes.
- There are hard measures that can aid the shortlisting process and softer, less tangible ones. A strategic use of both is necessary.
- Hard measures such as size, reach, specialization and integration are best to start the process. There are benefits and risks associated with each. Lower cost propositions usually represent an increase in risk somewhere along the line, so *caveat emptor*!
- Agencies with conflict clients are rising due to web-based businesses increasing consumer choice and big brands expanding into new categories of products and services. Brands should have an open mind about how conflict can be managed in order to allow optimal access to the agency market.
- Procurement can bring a great deal of sourcing experience and integrity to a selection process, from which brands can benefit greatly. But ensure that procurement and marketing have aligned interests and accountability.
- Sourcing strategies and pitch processes can be designed to identify the right kind of agencies and, within them, attract and motivate the right kind of agency talent for the advertising monkey your brand needs.
- Mapping agencies by size and employer brand strength can be a useful way to differentiate a complex and crowded market.
- Keep the required agency investment levels as low as possible at the start of the process, when their odds of winning are worst, and increase expectations of their investment as the field narrows. Avoid costly RFI beauty parades.
- Design the pitch process and the financial part of the pitch according to the advertising monkey your brand needs. If you need multiple different monkeys, you may be wise to consider different approaches for each or a consolidated process focused on a Gorilla problem so that access to talent isn't compromised.
- Design your process, stick to it and don't be tempted by wild cards.

[34] Billings represents the estimated collective marketing spend of the agency's clients, which is contingent on their creative agency. For example, if the creative agency provides advertising for TV, print, radio and outdoor campaigns with a media spend of £30m, their billings for that client are £30m.

[35] Revenue is the total amount of fees paid to an agency – or its gross profit before tax and after pass-through costs have been deducted.

[36] Though increasingly, interactive is merging into all other communications disciplines.

[37] We should note here that if the role of advertising is not critical to your business, then the relative importance of assurance of supply could be lessened considerably.

[38] IPA New Business Report 2009, "Creative agencies with a gross income of £15m or more estimate that the full pitch process accounts for 99 man days at a minimum resource cost of £178,000, while an additional £31,500 is spent on out-of-pocket expenses."

[39] If the agency has beautiful offices but located in Basildon, they may struggle to recruit.

[40] It is not uncommon for agencies to attempt to join a shortlist, pitch in partnership with a shortlisted agency or sneak back in when knocked out.

[41] As trivial as this may sound, accommodating people's needs on an individual basis inspired huge amounts of loyalty and discretionary effort. It is not uncommon for clients to run pitches over peak holiday times and expect agencies to demonstrate their 'passion and commitment'. Such practices are invariably naïve and counterproductive.

[42] While I believe that benchmarking data can be highly questionable, as a publicly-owned organization, the Post Office has a responsibility to ensure that the rates it pays are competitive.

[43] It should be noted that the relative risk attached to this approach, particularly with time-critical campaigns, is perhaps not suitable for all clients and in no way should it be considered best practice.

[44] If the remuneration and attractiveness of the brand are inconsistent with its needs and therefore prompt the wrong supplier preference, it may be worth assessing whether a pitch is necessary or if the need to pitch could be resolved by changing the nature of the remuneration and the working relationship with the incumbent agency.

[45] The outcome will also reflect much better a collaborative process more akin to a real working relationship.

CHAPTER EIGHT

REMUNERATION AND INCENTIVES

"The notion that there is a client-agency partnership is rubbish.
When one person has the chequebook and the other does not, then
there is no partnership. Unless the agency is prepared to share the risk,
then there is bound to be an element of subservience."

Jeremy Bullmore
Former Chairman, JWT, and Member of the WPP Advisory Board

THE CURRENT REMUNERATION PARADIGM

The majority of current client payment practices seek to reduce the fees they pay to their agencies while increasing their agencies' accountability and performance for their clients' return on investment.

Agency fees are mostly determined through a ceremonial process of negotiation over resources, overhead and scopes of work, only occasionally including specifications of ways of working.

Almost invariably the procurement people conducting the negotiations of agency fees are incentivized to reduce them, but they are rarely held accountable for the impact on the agency's resultant value and its consequent impact on marketing ROI.

Benchmarking agency fees is often flawed; more attention should be paid to the variables making up the data sets and the integrity of the sample sizes.

All of these common practices are consistent with Leverage buying strategies (see chapter four), that are consistent only with buying Orangutans. They are therefore inappropriate to the majority of deals being done with well established creative agencies.

In addition, agencies are prone to do silly deals, because their commercial integrity as organizations needs improvement and owing to their generally inadequate negotion skills.

Consequently, a vast number of clients are suffering diminished supplier preference and therefore diminished value and diminished return on investment compared to what they could achieve with appropriate buying strategies to suit their business problem.

THE MONKEY HOUSE REMUNERATION PARADIGM

The different ways of paying for agency services should be carefully designed according to the specific needs of the client and the advertising monkeys their brand or brands need – there isn't one 'right way' and any single definition of 'best practice' cannot accommodate these different needs appropriately or effectively.

The proper application of buying strategies, according to the brand's buying power and the needs of the brand, will yield greater agency value. The different means of creative agency remuneration and their financial incentives need to be consistent with the different brand needs of Orangutans, Gorillas and Spider Monkeys.

The most prevalent current remuneration practices are mostly consistent with buying Orangutans. Agency remuneration for Gorillas should allow the agency's better performance to improve the profitability of their fees, i.e., on a day-to-day basis, not just through their performance-related bonuses.

Remuneration for Spider Monkeys needs either to be in a smaller agency, whereby it will become a Core account to the agency, or the brand must create an agency relationship and performance-related bonus system whereby the agency is inclined to make an investment that is significantly greater than their fee allows.

Between the big brands and the big agencies, debates have persisted over the way agencies should be paid: media commissions, equivalent media commission paid by the hour, blended rates versus rate cards, commission as a percentage of sales, licensing of intellectual property, project fees, reconcilable and irreconcilable cost-plus fees, overhead contributions, etc. The first thing we have to recognize is that 'the money is the money'. It is rare that the client hasn't any idea how much they actually need to pay nor any idea how much money they have available to pay their agency, so most of the discussion is around how they determine the final number. Most of the time, it is a fairly ceremonial negotiation process.

It is also rare that a deal isn't done between a client and agency because they couldn't agree on the money, so amid all this noise I believe the most useful questions are:

- Between the highest and lowest possible fee a brand can pay its agency, how much should it pay according to the kind of advertising monkey it needs?
- How should this fee (including incentives) be paid so that it is consistent with the kind of advertising monkey the brand needs?

Almost 100% of creative agency remuneration processes for the top 50 creative advertising agencies in the UK comprises fees being paid to the agency for the hours expended on a client's business. The larger the fee, the more likely that it will be reconciled regularly against time sheets. The smaller the fee, the less accountable the agency will be for the actual time spent and the more that the estimation of hours is simply a way of determining a fee.

We examined some of the practical problems with this means of remuneration in chapter five, but for those who would like to understand further the challenges of matching time and value, particularly when it comes to issues such as artistry or innovation, we'll take a closer look here, starting with the relationship between time and value.

WHAT'S THE VALUE OF AN HOUR OR A DAY?

On 16 August 2011, a story was relayed in *Smithsonian*[46] magazine that perfectly illustrates the difference between effort and utility. The tale was of Charles Steinmetz, also known as the wizard of Schenectady, where General Electric was founded. Steinmetz could analyse values in alternating current circuits using complex mathematical equations. His discoveries made him one of the most important and valuable people in electricity for years to come. According to Smithsonian.com, one story of Steinmetz's wizardry appeared in the letters page of *Life* Magazine as late as 1965.

In the letter, Jack Scott wrote of his father's experience of Steinmetz at Ford's River Rouge factory. Ford's electrical engineers were having a problem with a huge generator so Henry Ford called the wizard of Schenectady. When Steinmetz got there, he requested only a pencil, a notebook and a camp bed. After two consecutive days and nights, when he had been listening carefully to the generator and making calculations in his notepad, Steinmetz climbed a ladder and made a mark in chalk on its side. He then instructed Ford's engineers, who were somewhat cynical about his methods, to take off a plate where he had made the mark and to replace 16 windings inside. The engineers duly did as they were bid and the generator worked perfectly.

Naturally, Ford was delighted with the outcome. Then he received an invoice from General Electric for $10,000.

While Ford recognized the wizard's success, he recoiled at the price and asked for it to be broken down. According to Scott, Steinmetz responded to Ford's request personally. Steinmetz told Ford that the cost of making the chalk mark was $1, but that knowing where to make the mark was $9,999. Ford paid in full.

Although this example would be better described as a retrospective Critical purchasing strategy on the part of Ford, it is another great example of the importance of utility over time spent. Steinmetz could have taken a week or a month and nobody would have been any the wiser, but during that time the generator would not have been generating anything.

It is not so simple as to say that time doesn't equal value in marketing services; the best we can do is to say that time doesn't *necessarily* equal value. But, for example, if speed to market is important for a brand, how can purely time-based remuneration be sensible? As much as nine women can't have a baby in one month, when an advertiser needs speed it isn't always enough simply to throw resources at the problem. There is a vast difference between a high-value effortful hour and one that isn't. The key question is, should all clients pay their agencies using an inputs-based (time) remuneration system with all the variability of their different business problems, time pressures and so on, or should they pay for the outputs they specifically require?

Furthermore, there is the variability of agency talent to consider. For example: a good friend of mine, a creative director at one of London's leading creative agencies, would routinely see difficult briefs circulate through his department, going from one team to the next. Each time either the creatives couldn't crack the brief (because they couldn't or because they didn't want to), or the client rejected the work, and the brief went back to the drawing board. Finally, it would come to him and his art director partner. After being passed around the department for three or four weeks, he would get two or three days to work on it. This was a brief that had already proved too difficult for most other teams in the department. But nine times out of ten, this team would crack it, either the first time or with minor reworks. This team made significantly more work than any other team in the agency. And the work was good. You can only imagine how good it might have been if the briefs had come to them first. Time does not equal effort; you cannot assume that if you're paying for an hour that the person was working hard in that hour. Neither effort nor time equal value. Talent equals value.

> *Time doesn't guarantee either effort or value. Only motivated talent produces value.*

But we must also be careful not to fall into a trap here – particularly with regards to the role of creatives. Once an idea has been developed, there's a lot more work to be done to make that idea into advertising that will be appropriate, relevant and persuasive to its intended audience. The craft of executing advertising can be a necessarily time-consuming exercise. After ideas have been approved, the creative team is involved in every detail of execution, from research stimulus to a finished film, including: art direction, casting, wardrobe, selecting photographers, or illustrators or directors, choosing voiceover artists or celebrities, choosing music tracks or briefing original composition, briefing artwork, design and typography – plus overseeing the quality of all of these while coordinating with art buyers, TV and radio producers, traffic managers, let alone account management – until the whole thing is finished.

Brands' briefs in agencies are highly variable in the amount of time they take. Retail accounts have work done to a strict deadline because they are highly time sensitive and/or price sensitive.

Many fast-moving consumer goods (FMCG or CPG) accounts can take far longer to develop and produce creative work.[47]

The process of developing strategy and creative can be like picking a lock or it can require seemingly Sisyphean effort. Great ideas can pop out at a moment's notice or can take forever to find and then refine – the Cadbury Gorilla is a great example. As I said in chapter five, it's not unlike prospecting for oil – sometimes you might get rich quick.

When we consider some value contributions that marketing services can make, for example, in the field of behavioural economics, a single, simple yet pivotal idea can make a massive difference to a client's fortunes. Such ideas are worth vastly more than the time it took to generate or execute them. If you had had the idea to scrap a 'Register' button on your retailer client's website and instead invite site visitors to buy without registering, and you saw that retailer's revenue increase by $300 million in one year, would you value the time it took to think of it and make that change or would you value the phenomenal increase in revenue?[48]

> *An agency's utility can be far more significant than the effort they expend to create it.*

Once again, responsibility and control need to reside in the same place (see chapter four). For example, if a brand dictates the fee to be invested in developing the idea, but which the agency objects to, then the brand should share responsibility for the idea's quality. But if the agency has a say in the budget, then they should take greater responsibility for the idea's value. Similarly, if the agency dictates the fee, then they should have total responsibility for it – and dig into their own pocket if their forecast was too low. This is not to suggest clients should pay agencies whatever they ask for, but it is to suggest that there is a necessary dialogue to reach a fee based on agency outputs.

For every upside of a profitable and efficient brief, there is usually a downside of other briefs that take much more time and effort than their fees allow. Crucially, this variability in efficiency, this unpredictability of time and effort required to yield a good strategy or creative idea, has to be the agency's responsibility to manage. If all the agency's clients are clawing back investment for the efficient yields and refusing to pay for the inefficient ones, the agency's business suffers and we're back to the downward spiral of value overall.

There should be a collective responsibility among an agency's clients, whereby each pays responsibly, and the agency should enforce this responsibility, but because of the reasons we explored in the previous chapter – perceived oversupply in the market, high competition – agencies are often quick to compromise in return for securing any available revenue rather than potentially losing a client. Brands therefore have to assume this responsibility in much the same way as we assume collective responsibility for anything else – like the environment, or law and order. Put simply, a financially healthy agency is more stable. It can invest in better people and produce greater value. But each client needs to contribute in a way consistent with their supplier preference status. In addition to having responsibility for their resources, agencies should also have the discretion to service an account that is massively inefficient but improves the employer brand. Indirectly, these accounts – although they are few in any agency – are being paid for by the others, but the agency's other accounts, likewise indirectly, are benefiting from the agency's improved reputation and employer brand status.

Brands that know they have both critical mass financially and are attractive enough to agency talent can leverage their financial negotiations. They will be confident that they will not damage their Core supplier preference status to become Bread and Butter, but I would argue that it is still unwise to do so. By way of example, according to an article in *Ad Age*,[49] on 31 May 2016 it was announced that in the US, McDonalds was reviewing its creative agencies but that it would require the winning agency to work at cost. Although McDonalds was reportedly happy to pay the agency's profit based on the agency's performance (e.g., brand and advertising measures) – all to be negotiated with the appointed agency – there wouldn't be any 'automatic' profit for the agency.

Two challenges arise from this model. The first is surmountable, insofar as the winning agency must have suitable control over the development of their recommendations if their profitability is dependent on it;

otherwise, the agency's profit margin is contingent on their *client's* ability to develop effective work rather than their own ability to conceive of it and produce it. The second challenge is that other brands that believe they should be afforded the same kind of deal then successfully negotiate similar terms with their agencies. However, they don't end up getting the talent they need and don't get the great advertising because they weren't attractive enough. There are only a handful of mega-brands that can pull off a deal like this, but I have heard such initiatives presented to procurement groups as a new best practice. It isn't. In most instances it's exactly what Gerry Preece and Russel Wohlwerth describe in *Buying Less for Less.* And, although agencies that accept these deals may take comfort from knowing that their clients will get what they pay for, their management should perhaps ask themselves how their other clients might feel if they knew they were sharing their agency with a client that doesn't contribute directly to its profitability and thereby its overall wellbeing.

In the case of McDonalds, such is their size and scale that Omnicom, which won the account, established a dedicated agency to handle their business, which avoids such concerns from other clients. But few brands could do this effectively without compromising their access to talent and therefore value.[50]

The final reason I'll offer to dispense with charging by the hour, and this might be an unpopular point of view, is that I believe it is impossible to collect accurate data for hours spent. (Short of standing over an agency's personnel at the end of every single day and forbidding them from leaving the office until their time sheets are completed.) The very best you will get is a well-intentioned guess at any given point in time. For clients' accounts with full-time staff the task is a little easier, but still opaque. Time sheets in agencies are often completed based on what people *should* have been doing rather that what they've actually been doing. But as long as the account is serviced and the work gets done well, what difference does it make?

Many brands' procurement departments also fall into the trap of trying to compare different agencies' hourly rates and overhead – to drill down into their costs, rates and profits. To my mind this both misses the point (i.e., it has nothing to do with value) and it makes the fatal error of believing that one agency's account manager or junior creative team is comparable to another agency's account manager or junior creative team.

Likewise, overhead and how it is calculated can vary enormously and make up a substantial part of any hourly rate, but cheaper isn't necessarily better.

BENCHMARKING

It is almost a universal truth that human beings judge financial value by comparison: how much is this versus that? Price comparisons allow us to rationalize our buying decisions to ourselves and to others, reassuring us that we're not being ripped off. But price comparison as a means of forming our opinions of value for money is far from watertight. To start with, it assumes that there is always sufficient price competition. Also, benchmarking assumes that product or service a is the same as product or service b.

In the procurement world, price comparison is pervasive and deemed an essential tool. Comparative pricing should be able to prove that the goods or services procurement have bought represent good value for money. But there are a number of reasons why using benchmarks to negotiate lower fees may be damaging value:

1) How accurate and useful is the data to start with?

   For example, if you take the benchmark data provided by one UK industry body, the variance of rate by role, or even within the quartiles of each role, is enormous. In the top quartile, an account director's rate can vary by more than 60%. If you're buying account directors, which rate should you be paying?

2) What's the sample size?

   The response rate for the same report was less than 20% of advertisers polled – there were more than 300 nonrespondents. How representative of the total sample were the respondents? Where were their agencies located? What size were they? Were all these significant factors sufficiently comparable?

3) How do we make sure we're comparing apples with apples?

   What is an account director? Or what makes an art director a 'junior art director' rather than just an art director? There are no standardized qualifications, competence or measures of experience that determine junior from senior or one title from another.

Although this explains the variance to some degree, it renders the comparison meaningless.

4) How well did the agencies negotiate their rates?
The benchmark data may include rates that have been aggressively negotiated and rates that have been poorly negotiated. So, the benchmark could include rates that make an agency run an account unprofitably, just covering their fixed and variable costs.

5) How consistent are agencies' calculations?
When it comes to the comparison of overhead between different agencies, we need to be aware that agencies' circumstances can vary wildly and the means by which they calculate their overhead can vary just as much. Do the agencies' overhead include c-suite staff costs or are they counted as billable staff who are directly chargeable to their clients? Does the overhead calculation include contributions to international management teams as part of their overhead? Are there pension funds to be maintained?

———————

The argument (put by most of the people with whom I have had this debate) for using time as a proxy for value and benchmarks as a means of checking value for money is that there isn't anything else by which they can measure inputs. But, by the same logic, we might choose to evaluate which fine artist we commission for a portrait by benchmarking the amount of paint they say they'll need, just because we think we can draw an accurate comparison.

In summary, I believe benchmarking is at best a very blunt instrument and often unfit for purpose; in fact, it can harm the value an agency might provide because benchmark-negotiated rates mean that a client's supplier preference has been compromised. Even though procurement folk are often the first to protest that they know that cheapest isn't always best, they are reticent to stop buying cheapest because it proves the worth of their role with the money 'saved' and justifies their end-of-year bonuses (see Upton Sinclair in chapter five).

Furthermore, it is very difficult to persuade people to stop doing what they've been doing for years – even with all the logic and good reason you might wish for.

"I know that most men, including those at ease with problems of the greatest complexity, can seldom accept even the simplest and most obvious truth if it be such as would oblige them to admit the falsity of conclusions which they have delighted in explaining to colleagues, which they have proudly taught to others, and which they have woven, thread by thread, into the fabric of their lives."

Leo Tolstoy, 1828-1910
Russian Author

Hourly rates are not a substitute for talent or effort, and thereby value. An hourly rate will not tell you which team members you are getting, or how hard they work and whether or not they know what they're doing. One thing is for certain: if you're buying a Gorilla and you're in any serious doubt, it's probably wise to spend more, not less.

Reassuringly expensive is much better than dangerously cheap.

HOW DOES THIS AFFECT THE DETERMINATION OF AGENCY FEES?

In other words, if benchmarking is only a blunt instrument, how should brands decide how much they want to invest in their agencies and negotiate deals that are consistent with achieving optimal value from them? In short, the answer is that brands need to decide what they want to invest.

In the days of agency commission, the amount a client invested in its agency was decided for it by the percentage; later the commission rates became negotiable, but agencies were still essentially paid a lump sum for a scope of work. But the commission model would struggle to be reinstated today, because the media landscape for which it was originally established (before the fragmentation of broadcast and print media) and the scope of work the agency was required to deliver (which now includes online, in its various forms, and content development) have changed beyond all recognition.

Most brands and most agencies will be aware of the 'good, quick, cheap' model – however, it is still too easily forgotten. For those unfamiliar with it, see *figure 28*.

Figure 28

Good, Quick, Cheap

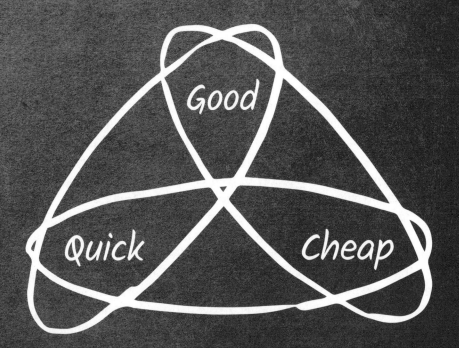

The premise is simple: you can choose two. You can have good and quick, but it will not be cheap; you can have quick and cheap, but it will not be good; and you can have good and cheap, but it will not be quick. Why?

Good and quick – if you want to ensure that you'll get high value fast, you diminish your risk by paying for the best available talent, and for more of them to do the work.

Quick and cheap – the immediacy of the brand's need and the available budget are more important than quality.

Cheap and good – you don't have the money for speed, but you're reliant on quality, so you allow the agency more time to fit in your needs around their other priorities.

(These three crudely align to the needs of Gorillas, Orangutans and Spider Monkeys, respectively, but not enough to warrant further correlation.)

The most common current paradigm for establishing agency fees involves a process of ceremonial haggling rather than strategy. The process comprises multiple rounds of meetings in which the client and agency pore over the agency's resource plans, which are reworked and rehashed each time. Procurement presents the agency with benchmark targets, the agency protests the complexity of their client's briefs – and most of the time, all this effort and energy put into negotiation is fruitless.

Between a client's walk-away point (i.e., agency fees are too high) and the agency's walk-away point (i.e., the fees are too low) there is either an overlap – which creates a zone of possible agreement – or there isn't.

If there is no overlap, then no amount of negotiation will achieve anything, but 99 times out of 100 there is a deal to be had. Therefore, the question is: What is the optimal amount to pay? If it's too little, then even if supplier preference hasn't deterred the best talent, there's insufficient time, even with good people, to prospect for the best strategy and ideas. If the fees are too much, then money is wasted on a diminishing return of value from the agency. So, within that zone, the choice of how much to pay requires a strategy; it should not be determined by which side has the more skilled negotiator, and should certainly not be influenced by one side having a personal incentive to reduce their investment so they can qualify for a personal bonus.

Having said all that, the calculation of what an agency might want for a scope of work can be a useful input to the information pool from which a marketer should make the value judgment of how much they want to invest. And the processes for making these value judgments will vary depending on the nature of the business problem the marketer wants to solve.

Fees for Gorillas should not compromise on the agency's value and can, more than likely, afford significant investment because they are a market leader. Spider Monkeys cannot compromise agency value either, but instead have to make themselves an attractive prospect to work with in order to compensate for what they lack in funds. Orangutans have less to fear from competitive activity and may therefore be more prepared to compromise the agency's maximum possible value in favour of a more cautious strategy for ROI – for example, they may not need a whole new campaign, just a rework of an existing one and a new pack shot.

To decide on a figure for a fee, there are various resources to draw upon:

1) What does the agency think? Provide the agency with a scope and specific objectives for the work. It makes no difference if you're establishing a budget for an annual retainer or a project: ask the agency what they need to get the job done – based on the business problem you are asking them to solve.

2) How much money have you got? You should have divided up your budget into rough budget headers of your different needs, so how much is there for the agency fee?

3) What do you think other brands spend? We have to be careful to ensure we compare like-for-like here. Although we have already explored some shortcomings of benchmarking, if a brand has no idea what it should spend, then benchmarks may be a useful, but blunt, instrument.

4) What do you think you need to invest? What is the objective you're trying to achieve? Is it particularly difficult? If so, should you invest more? Is it relatively straightforward? A bit like last year? If so, what did you pay then?

5) If the scope of work relates to media space, what would the equivalent commission level have been if we invested x amount? You could consider splitting the scale of commission rates to agencies to three sectors for Orangutans, Gorillas and Spider Monkeys. You could even include production investment in much the same way, thus:

Figure 29

Budget Breakdowns

Business problem	Agency fee	PRB	Production budget
Spider Monkey 	Variable according to brand need. Retainer or project fee.	High in lieu of reduced fee.	Variable according to need.
Gorilla 	9-12% of media spend. Retainer.	-10% to +15% of total fee based on advertising effectiveness.	15-20% of media spend.
Orangutan 	6-9% of media spend. Retainer.	-10% to +10% of total based on brand profitability.	10-15% of media spend.

6) Have you changed agencies? If so, why? Were you dissatisfied with the last one? Was it because you paid them too little? Did you overpay and become a lucrative Bread and Butter client who should have been Core? Will money make the difference to the relationship?

With these factors in mind – and in particular if your business need is a Gorilla – you must decide what you want to invest. This figure becomes the starting point for agency negotiations. And the way you and the agency shape the contract, the scope of work, the ways of working, the resources – all the things that impact the agency's value – become the items for negotiation. But, at the same time, they must remain consistent with the advertising monkey that you need (see *figure 29*). Most large agency contracts will include a performance-related bonus (PRB). The PRB must be budgeted for by the client, and the client must have a desire to pay it, because paying the PRB means the agency will have delivered their maximum possible value according to their client's need.[51]

In my experience, many clients have tried to limit their PRB pay-out, even when they have openly stated that the agency's performance was the best they have ever experienced. Such practices are inconsistent with a Strategic buying strategy and actually end up damaging the relationship.

KEY COMPONENTS TO A PRODUCTIVE CONTRACT

If the client/agency relationship has been well established, with shared interests and clarity of purpose before work commences, then once work has commenced, the contract should be nothing more than a safety net, something to which either party can refer in order to clarify any doubt or to resolve a dispute. But if the contract is regularly used as a weapon with which to beat one another, then there is a deeper-seated problem. Both client and agency teams should be spending as much time and energy as possible on the creative, constructive behaviours that develop great strategies and communications campaigns, i.e., contributing value. Defensive, protective and even sometimes aggressive behaviours like referring to contracts, scopes, time sheets, resource plans, etc., largely constitute time wasted: time which still has to be paid for but which doesn't actually produce anything of value – it doesn't deliver a return.

SCOPE OF WORK

The scope of work (SOW) is a document that is as detailed a schedule as possible of the actual work that the agency will be required to do over a period of time, usually one year. The SOW should include the channels that are likely to be employed by the brand, budgets for media and production, and the timing of campaigns as accurately as it is possible for them to be estimated or forecast.

If a brand has little or no idea what the full scope will be, it is still best to proceed even without one – and brands should do their utmost to make a safe guess. Often the past can be a likely indicator of the future, so a guess is a decent starting point. If it turns out to be different, it is rarely so significantly different that brands would need to radically change the amount they are investing in their agency. It is far better to agree to a starting point than not, and if it is vaguer than the client and the agency would both like, agree on how to adjust it and when. Agree on the assumptions and agree how you will fairly reconcile the differences if your assumptions are wrong.

Agencies may also need to be a little more patient with what are usually protracted contract renegotiations. Often agencies fail to recognize that the client's business forecasting and budgeting periods can overlap with the agency's need to forecast its own revenues. Marketers' budgets need to be approved by their leadership, too, and often they don't get confirmed until after the calendar year contract with their agency has expired.

WAYS OF WORKING

In addition to the scope, it is important to agree 'how' you will develop campaigns together. In particular, at the beginning of a relationship and often during established relationships, the client and the agency can have completely different ideas of what actually needs to be done and who will do what. Ways of working, client and agency behaviours, clear processes and fairness all contribute to the relative attractiveness of one account versus another in an agency. In chapter nine we will look more closely at how the process of campaign development can be broken down into manageable, logical chunks from which clearer roles and responsibilities can be better defined.

STAFFING PLAN

The staffing plan shows how the agency intends to resource a client's account with client facing and non-client facing staff – though it does not include back-office administrative staff, such as finance and HR. The plan can be variable in its specificity; demanding clients may want more specific commitments to individuals and less demanding clients will want reassurance that there are sufficient resources allocated to deliver against their needs. If higher calibre talent than the client deserves is contractually negotiated for an account, odds are the agency will either move them anyway or the talent will choose to leave the agency when a better opportunity comes along.

It's perfectly legitimate and sensible for a client to want reassurances that the agency is allocating appropriate resources to their needs, but wiser clients stop far short of trying to control, demand or dictate agency resources; instead they create relationships that attract and retain the resources they need.

PAYMENT TERMS

The contract must specify normal payment terms and make provision for anomalies that can arise in the course of doing business together. From initiatives put forward by an increasingly aggressive procurement community, there is a growing trend to extend payment terms more and more as part of annual contract negotiations.

When tough payment terms are agreed, it is likely they will diminish the agency's supplier preference and hence attract lower calibre or demotivate existing talent. Additionally, if an agency is desperate enough to accept such extended payment terms, it does not necessarily bode well for the condition of its business. Extending payment terms and becoming a burden to an agency's cash flow is a Leverage buying practice and will achieve the opposite of what a client should be looking for from their agency, sometimes even with Orangutan needs.

Payment terms for third-party costs also need to be dealt with in the contract, in particular for high-level investments such as TV production. There is much more that can be written about the complexities of production companies and content-creation companies, more than I can cover here. So instead, in summary, I would say that clients must remain conscious of their buying strategy and stick to the principles of that strategy for agency fees and third-party costs.

MINIMUM INCOME GUARANTEES

A minimum income guarantee is designed to provide the agency with some compensation for its fixed and variable costs in the event that the brand has to radically reduce or even stop its advertising activity. Minimum income guarantees usually apply to larger accounts and, in particular, those that require high levels of dedicated agency personnel.

NOTICE PERIOD

Notice periods are again variable and should depend on the brand's buying strategy. Brands needing a Spider Monkey, i.e., with limited buying power, will not be able to negotiate long notice periods as easily as those needing Gorillas or Orangutans might. Brands should bear in mind that their agency will be much more quickly replaced than they will be as a client, so fair notice periods will be reciprocal.

PERFORMANCE-RELATED BONUSES

PRBs and the related measurement of the agency's performance KPIs need to be designed according to the business problem, not simply cut and pasted from the last contract.

First, agency KPIs that most influence their PRB should be consistent with the agency's value contribution, not the brand's business performance (responsibility and control again). Yes, business performance or sales can be a part of it, but if the advertising has a specific objective, then the objective(s) should be the most important KPI. It is also important to be careful if your investment in media, i.e., the exposure of that advertising is variable. If so, the KPI has to be about the persuasiveness of the creative work – it's not your agency's fault if you don't expose the ad enough.

Secondly, agencies are garbage-in, garbage-out businesses, i.e., terrible clients rarely get great work. So if you include a relationship measurement, it must be contingent on the client achieving a reasonable score from the agency, as well as vice versa. Any such measurements should be done by an independent company, of which there are many – including my own, of course.

Thirdly, the agency, not the client, must be responsible for what it does with the bonus. Some clients try to insist that the bonus is applied directly to the people working on their account. While I can understand the desire to do this, it is another example of clients extending their control. The client doesn't necessarily know what the agency's financial priorities are.

Fourthly, marketing and procurement should share the PRB objectives with their agency. Marketing influences the work, and procurement influences the agency's resources, so together they influence the ROI. Therefore, the objectives of all parties should be the same.

> *Marketing and procurement should share the PRB objectives with their agency.*

Finally, consider a blend of a number of KPIs: advertising effectiveness, relationship measures, brand sales and so on, ensuring that the emphasis fits the business problem. You can see this in *figure 30*.

The contract clauses above can be applied according to the kind of advertising monkey the brand needs and its corresponding buying strategy.

Figure 30

The Monkey House and Agency Contracts

Business problem			
Buying strategy	Critical	Strategic	Leverage
Conflict policy	Little buying power will make a tough conflict policy trickier to negotiate.	Can be tough but should be specific to category, trying not to stifle agency's opportunities for growth.	Consider using a tougher conflict policy as a negotiation point for lower fees.
Scope of work	According to affordability.	As specific as possible with fair provision for reworks as may be necessary.	Specific but with emphasis on efficient use of copy and creative assets.
Ways of working	Low control, highly efficient. Reliant on agency discretionary effort.	Specific and must apportion responsibility with control fairly through each stage of the campaign development process.	Specific with emphasis on efficiency. High client responsibility for efficient stakeholder management to keep development costs and fees low.
Resource plan	Rarely applicable. Unlikely to require any full-time allocations, and moot due to reliance on agency investment.	Agreed on fairly as part of the negotiation process. No need to specify key personnel because it should attract the right talent priority.	Negotiated as part of fee agreement. Specifying key personnel where possible to ensure efficiency of continuity.
Payment terms	Usually 30 days. May require pro forma.	Usually 30 days and 50% to 100% pro forma for significant third-party costs.	Longer negotiated terms for client cash flow or shorter terms to negotiate reduced fees.
Minimum income guarantee	Usually not a large enough account to warrant it.	Fair minimum income guarantee necessary. Should also include provision for increased investment.	Negotiate lowest possible to allow greatest opportunity for cost-free divestment from brand.
Notice period	Little buying power to negotiate more than standard 3-month reciprocal notice period.	Minimum 6-month reciprocal notice period.	Longer negotiated terms for client cash flow or shorter terms to negotiate reduced fees.
PRB KPIs	High PRB based on growth of brand's sales to encourage greater agency investment up front.	High PRB based on advertising performance, sales and relationship. Aligned with marketing targets. Marketing and procurement to share PRBs and be incentivized to award bonus.	Moderate PRB, aligned with brand profitability, efficient use of marketing expenditure and maintenance of market share. KPIs shared with marketing.

I believe that one of the key challenges here is for clients to recognize that agencies need different terms for different business problems. However, agencies must also realize that clients' differing needs and appetites for risk and return mean that the control they exercise over their agencies, contractual and/or procedural, can be strategically legitimate.

SUMMARY

- Start with the business problem you need to solve, then employ the corresponding buying strategy and design appropriate remuneration terms.
- Time is not an accurate measure of either effort or value. Agencies must be directly responsible for their businesses, in particular the aggregation and management of efficient and inefficient briefs and clients.
- Benchmarking agency rates and comparing agency prices are practices riddled with fallibility. One agency's account director is another agency's account manager.
- Agencies are also responsible for their talent. Named agency staff in contracts will only secure talent that the agency would have allocated anyway. If a client somehow punches above its weight and gets better talent than it deserves, either the client or the agency will usually struggle to retain them.
- Brands need to decide how much they want to invest in agency fees – it's a strategic decision. Brands can use multiple sources and calculations but, ultimately, it is a value judgment that should be based on the business problem needing to be solved.
- Good, quick and cheap – you can only have two. An agency contract is a backstop to which client and agency can refer if necessary; if it has become a stick for either party to beat the other with, there is a bigger issue to be resolved.
- Agency contractual terms should be variable according to the business problem needing to be resolved. Marketing, procurement and agencies should share the KPIs that trigger the performance-related bonus.
- Marketers should be incentivized to demonstrate that they have elicited maximum value from their agencies.
- The client/agency relationship is the sum of all these parts; getting your contractual and financial terms of engagement right is the entire commercial side of your 'nurture'.

[46] Gilbert King. Smithsonian.com, 16 August 2011.

[47] However, when new creative work is effective, advertisers should consider the revenue lost by the campaign not running sooner.

[48] This is not an exaggeration; Google 'the $300 million button' to find out more.

[49] http://adage.com/article/print-edition/mcdonald-s-demands-working-cost/304218/

[50] http://uk.businessinsider.com/ddb-ceo-wendy-clark-mcdonalds-2016-9?r=US&IR=T

[51] On multiple occasions, I have experienced clients marking down the agency in its performance assessment for various questionable reasons, but primarily to limit their pay-out. In one instance, my agency had become the global standard of agency excellence on a financial services account and it was awarded 4 points out of a possible 5 on all performance criteria purely because the client 'doesn't give fives'.

CHAPTER NINE

DESIGNING NEW WAYS OF WORKING

"It is not enough to do your best, you must know what to do and then do your best."

W Edwards Deming, 1900-1993
American management consultant

THE WAYS-OF-WORKING PARADIGM

The processes and behaviours that advertisers employ with their agencies in the development of campaigns determine the level of control they exert over them. Frequently, high-control relationships inhibit the quality and value of the advertising (see chapter four).

Whereas agencies that behave badly will usually be fired, brands that behave badly to their agencies will usually only deter and demotivate the agency's talent, thereby compromising the agency's value. Occasionally they will be fired by their agency.

Advertisers with more than one brand often employ the same campaign development processes for all their brands, regardless of their differing market and business circumstances.

Advertisers and their agencies often each have different ideas of what the process should be to develop an advertising campaign. These differences about process often emerge at a crucial point in campaign development, creating conflict and crisis at times of highest pressure.

Clients' widespread distrust of agencies is based on the belief that agencies pursue creativity over effectiveness. Consequently, over time, clients' demands for agencies' ideas to be proven effective before they are employed in the marketplace has increased.

Research of creative work, in particular quantitative research, can sometimes be unreliable or limiting. When used as a pass/fail device, false negatives are difficult to disprove. Foreknowledge of the tests often encourages agencies to develop formulaic advertising that they know is more likely to 'pass' such pre-tests, but which is less innovative as a result.

Whereas such risk-averse creative development processes are often appropriate for Orangutans, they are usually considered as 'best practice' for Gorillas, too.

THE MONKEY HOUSE WAYS OF WORKING PARADIGM

The first step in creating a productive working relationship is to recognize the brand's needs according to The Monkey House.

Clients and agencies must then design and agree on their campaign development processes according to the needs and circumstances of the brand. These processes need not be reinvented each time, but can be guided by the needs to nurture Spider Monkeys versus Gorillas versus Orangutans.

Each stage of the campaign development process identifies which party has what degree of responsibility and what degree of control. It is important that these steps and processes are agreed in advance because bad decisions can be made under the time pressure of campaign development.

Both parties must recognize and respect each other's core competencies. Both parties must be ready to change and adapt their processes as necessary, as anomalies to their agreed processes inevitably emerge.

As the market or business circumstances of brands change, so do their objectives and therefore so must their campaign investments, processes and relationships to risk/creativity.

At all times the interests of marketing, procurement and agencies must stay aligned, such that they can more easily trust one another and so one party's efforts do not hamper another's.

Client/agency relationships should be maintained by regular and mutual appraisal, which is both independent and inclusive of all people involved in value creation in the relationship.

Before we proceed, I think it is important to restate that my frequent use of the word 'process' relates exclusively to the inevitable stages in the development of a campaign from the very start to the finish – not to the way in which a communications strategy or a creative idea is formed within the agency. The former may or may not be a collaboration; the latter rarely is. Formula never created an original creative idea; likewise, formulaic or ritualized collaborations don't create great ideas. In a recent interview at *The Guardian's* Changing Media Summit, Sir John Hegarty said:

"The danger in collaboration is it leads to consensus, and consensus leads to normality ..."

John Hegarty
Founder, Bartle Bogle Hegarty

Some copywriters, some art directors and some creative teams may have their own processes to develop creative ideas, but this is something that goes on inside an advertising agency, whereas in HTBAG we are only concerned with the interaction between client and agency.

So, the processes I describe are only designed to determine 'who does what', not 'how who does what'. Vitally, the processes also must be clear about 'who doesn't do what' because 'not doing' is an equally important part of an effective campaign development process. Not doing by one party allows the most talented person in the process the freedom to do their very best.

Not doing is not easy. It is much like the art of effective delegation. Great delegators brief for outcomes; great clients brief their advertising agencies for outcomes, but there are many differences between these two. Delegation usually requires a delegator – a person with proven competence – to supervise the delegate, who usually has unproven competence. But clients can't do what their agencies do; therefore, they depend on their agencies and have to have faith in their competence. In delegation, the levels of supervision can be determined by the supervisor – from light touch to control freak – and the skill of the delegator is getting that level right. In a client/agency relationship, the level of the client's involvement is often determined by the agency. The client has influence over the agency and can ask to be more involved, but it can't force a talented agency team to do anything. The client can coerce its agency, threaten it with firing, but that is only likely to deter and demotivate talent.

For the sake of shorthand, let's call this skill of not doing 'negative capability' – a term coined by Keats in his description of Shakespeare's seeming ability to live with uncertainties, mysteries and doubts. This is much like a marketer who has to live with the uncertainty of what the agency's work will look like, when it will be ready, whether it will work, whether they will like it or not. It's a difficult but very important skill – regardless of the business problem that the brand wants the agency to solve.

When we look at the case studies – Sony Bravia, Cadbury, Direct Line, Snickers and more – the successful development of these highly creative, highly effective advertising campaigns demonstrates various things in common:

1) The marketing client has an unshakeable commitment to the creative work and the agencies' recommendations of how it should be executed – in which they do not interfere (negative capability). They defend the work to the hilt within their own organizations.
2) The integrity of the creative work is more important than whether or not it has met all 'normal' creative research KPIs (or even been researched at all).
3) Both client and agency respect each others' responsibilities and core competencies and allow them control of what they do consistent with that responsibility (negative capability).

These principles can be found as far back as the early 60s in the DDB/Avis advertising philosophy. By 1947, Bill Bernbach was a creative director at Grey Advertising in New York and was frustrated by the formulaic approach the industry was taking to advertising. There was plenty of science knocking about – and it could explain how to develop the most effective advertising[52] – but it frustrated Bernbach. In a letter to his company directors, Bernbach wrote:

"There are a lot of great technicians in advertising. And unfortunately they talk the best game. They know all the rules. They can tell you that people in an ad will get you greater readership. They can tell you that a sentence should be this short or that long. They can tell you that body copy should be broken up for easier reading. They can give you fact after fact after fact. They are the scientists of advertising. But there's one little rub. Advertising is fundamentally persuasion and persuasion happens to be not a science, but an art."

Bill Bernbach, 15 May 1947
Founder, Doyle Dane Bernbach

Bernbach was the first to put copywriters and art directors together to develop their ideas as teams but, most importantly, he concentrated on advertising's ability to engage, not whether the idea had been researched by a well-worn methodology.

"Rules are what the artist breaks; the memorable never emerged from a formula."

Bill Bernbach, 1911-1982
Founder, Doyle Dane Bernbach

There were other agencies making waves at the time. However, there are few people in the advertising industry who would deny that Bernbach was a pioneer of creativity who produced unconventional, highly creative and very effective advertising.

Clients of DDB New York allowed Bernbach to flout the conventions of the day and the result was groundbreaking ads for the likes of VW and Alka-Seltzer. Avis was one of the flagship accounts that epitomized this revolution. It is a story that most people in the advertising business should know, if not through the legends of the industry in bar conversations, then through Adam Morgan's excellent book *Eating the Big Fish*[53]– its name inspired by the Avis creative work.

At the time of DDB's appointment, Avis was in trouble. The business was losing money year after year and the market leader, Hertz, was outspending Avis in media by 5 to 1. They needed a radical approach that could overcome their low share-of-voice; to that end the client and agency agreed on a philosophy (see *figure 31*).

Figure 31

Avis Advertising Philosophy

1) Avis will never know as much about advertising as DDB and DDB will never know as much about the rent-a-car business as Avis.

2) The purpose of the advertising is to persuade the frequent business renter (whether on a business trip, a vacation trip or renting an extra car at home) to try Avis.

3) A serious attempt will be made to create advertising with five times the effectiveness (see #2 above) of the competition's advertising.

4) To this end, Avis will approve or disapprove, not try to improve, ads which are submitted. Any changes suggested by Avis must be grounded on a material operating defect (a wrong uniform, for example).

5) To this end, DDB will only submit for approval those ads which they as an agency recommend. They will not "see what Avis thinks of this one."

6) Media selection should be the primary responsibility of DDB. However, DDB is expected to take the initiative to get guidance from Avis in weighting of markets or special situations, particularly in those areas where cold numbers do not indicate the real picture. Media judgments are open to discussion. The conviction should prevail. Compromises should be avoided.

7) All ads will be Fordable, and the agency will secure approval in writing from Ford on each ad.

The ads that were born of this philosophy were bold, brave, creative, simple and phenomenally effective. But, according to Morgan in his fol-low-up book *The Pirate Inside*[54], the most extraordinary thing about the Avis advertising philosophy was that it was the work of a man called Robert Townsend, not Bernbach. Following the acquisition of Avis by the bank Lazard Frères, the new Avis president, Townsend, spoke to Bernbach about their business challenge and following those conversa-tions Townsend wrote the philosophy. One can only infer that he wrote it to make clear to his own people what kind of risks they needed to take and what kind of creative bravery would change their position. Through this philosophy, the president of Avis instructed his team to relinquish control over to their new agency at the most critical time in Avis's his-tory. That was in 1962, and a year later Avis reported its first profit in 13 years, which it then doubled the following year.

The need for clarity of process and the need for clients' negative capability appears almost paradoxical. The paradox is resolved when we recognize that the process is describing the stages of the development of a campaign and who has responsibility for them, not what needs to be done in the process. The difference is between the 'nurture' in which the campaign is being developed and the 'nature' of the campaign being created.

The development of any campaign follows five key general stages applicable to any monkey (*figure 32*):

1) **Information**

The provision and interpretation of all pertinent data, information and research relevant to the campaign. Information includes all sales data, market segmentation, consumer research, market re-search, insight research, proposition research, usage and attitude studies, and so forth.

2) **Strategy**

The consolidation of the information into a campaign strate-gy that specifies the business objective, the marketing objective, the target audience, their barrier to purchase or equivalent, the proposition to overcome that barrier, supporting claims about the product/service and campaign budget breakdown. In short, the campaign brief.

3) Creative

The expression and presentation of the core creative idea in one or multiple media channels (TV, press, posters, online, etc.) persuading the target audience to change their behaviour to achieve the communication objective of the brand. This may also include researching the creative idea.

4) Execution

The realization of the creative idea into finished advertising executions and materials (finished TV commercials, radio ad recordings, press ads, etc.) by photographers, TV directors, illustrators, designers, typographers – all under the agency's creative direction.

5) Measurement

The measurement of the campaign's effectiveness according to the objective set out in the brief. Outputs of measurement then contribute to the Information stage of the next campaign.

(In this illustration I'm still limiting the process cycle to creative agencies, but it applies to other disciplines, too, e.g., media: information, strategy, planning, buying, measurement.)

It is important to recognize that different brands' categories will have different steps within the stages and different priorities for the completion of each stage (e.g., retail brands will differ from fine fragrances). However, each stage will still apply to some degree or another. The nature of the business problem – the kind of advertising monkey a brand needs – determines the necessary differences at each stage.

Figure 32

The Meikle Matrix and the Creative Cycle

Brand need...	 Spider Monkey	 Gorilla	 Orangutan
Greatest control lIes With ...	Agency	Agency	Client
Meikle Matrix Agency Response	Genius	Flow	Compliance
Meikle Matrix Agency Output	Innovation	Excellence	Conservatism
Stage One: Information	Economic use of bespoke research. Greater use of intuition, higher risk.	Thorough use of market and consumer research, full disclosure of all sales and research data to agency.	Efficient use of research to eliminate risk, confirm existing assumptions.
Stage Two: Strategy	High-level input and guidance from agency.	Highly collaborative development of briefs between client and agency.	More prescriptive, likely to be a development of existing strategy to known audience.
Stage Three: Creative	May be controversial – polarize the market. Little or no research. Presented to highest-level client decision-maker.	Highly creative, distinctive. Research for guidance and non-prescriptive. Access to high-level clients as necessary.	Builds on existing campaign idea. Researched to disaster-check. Access to high-level clients is unnecessary.
Stage Four: Execution	Highly creative, distinctive, innovative.	Highly creative. Uncompromising production values, distinctive, innovative.	Budgeted production according to specific needs of the brand.
Stage Five: Measurement	Economical measurement, sales oriented.	Sophisticated measurement of sales, brand awareness and perceptions.	Economical health checks of key measures.

If we take the three characterized needs according to The Monkey House, and these correspond to three quadrants of the Meikle Matrix, we can begin to see what clients and agencies can actually do differently in each section.

You will notice that I have only included Genius and Innovation as agency responses and outputs for a Spider Monkey and, likewise, only Conservatism as an output for an Orangutan. This is based on the assumption that for a Spider Monkey, the agency is sufficiently motivated to do its best work in service of their clients' needs rather than the agency's own self-interest, and that the Compliance quadrant of the Meikle Matrix is the right strategy for the brand.

Within each of these stages, there is a huge amount of detail in processes, protocols and ways of working that should be defined in advance. By way of example, if we were just to look at the execution stage, we should be able to ask and answer all of these questions differently, according to the advertising monkey the brand needs:

- Has a budget been set and agreed upon?
- How many TV directors should be costed and presented to the client?
- Who are the client stakeholders who need to approve the final executions?
- How many photographers should be costed and presented?
- Which client has final approval over photographers?
- Which client and agency people will attend a photographic shoot?
- Which client and agency people will attend a TV shoot?
- What role, if any, does procurement have in the production process?
- Who coordinates with other client agencies for use of original creative assets?
- What role does the lead agency have over other agencies' use of those assets?

The list can be almost endless, but how the client and the agency agree to answer these questions determines the level of control of the client over the agency, and therefore makes a difference to the final work.

Control over the process between the client and the agency is a continuum. It is only at the extreme ends of the continuum that it is clear as to who has total control, but there's a grey area in the middle. It doesn't have to consist of an endless list of questions, but the agreement on a number of principles will make that allocation of responsibility and control a whole lot easier.

That is the beauty of the Avis advertising philosophy. When Townsend had written in the guidance that pre-approval of cars from Ford would be arranged by DDB, or that "any changes suggested by Avis must be grounded on a material operating defect (a wrong uniform, for example)," he hadn't anticipated ads like this (see *figure 33*):

Figure 33

Eating Big Fish Ad

When you're only No.2, you try harder. Or else.

Avis can't afford to relax.

Little fish have to keep moving all of the time. The big ones never stop picking on them.

Avis knows all about the problems of little fish.

We're only No.2 in rent a cars. We'd be swallowed up if we didn't try harder. There's no rest for us.

We're always emptying ashtrays. Making sure gas tanks are full before we rent our cars. Seeing that the batteries are full of life. Checking our windshield wipers.

And the cars we rent out can't be anything less than lively new super-torque Fords.

And since we're not the big fish, you won't feel like a sardine when you come to our counter.

We're not jammed with customers.

No uniforms to check, no cars to be pre-approved by Ford, just a head-line, a pencil drawing and some type. By agreeing to the principles through which each party had appropriate responsibility and control over their own fields of expertise, Townsend brilliantly released the full potential of DDB to meet Avis's business objective. Which is why the first line of their advertising philosophy is so important: 1) Avis will never know as much about advertising as DDB and DDB will never know as much about the rent-a-car business as Avis.

So, we can look at the five stages in terms of how the locus of control and responsibility changes for each stage in principle. From this we can extrapolate the details of the process steps according to the needs of each individual brand, the category in which they operate, their market circumstances, etc. (see *figure 34*).

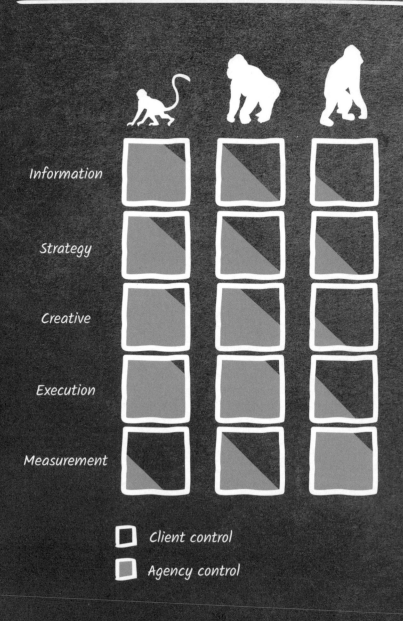

Figure 34

The Monkey House and the Locus of Control in Process

It is for this reason that I always recommend a thorough onboarding process at the start of a client/agency relationship. This is much more than sharing team charts, telephone numbers and company mission statements; it's getting right into the detail of how the two parties will come together and cooperate to solve brand problems. Yes, team-building stuff is important, but the teams have to know what they're doing, too.

Also, teams change, people change, circumstances, strategies and briefs change, so it is vital to continuously review and improve. The relationship and the processes have to be reviewed and adapted regularly.

The most common and most expensive mistakes in the campaign development process are: poor briefing, poor stakeholder management and the misuse/overuse of research. These three are also the most frustrating and demotivating to the agency people working on an account. It's worth spending a little time on each.

BRIEFS AND BRIEFING

The brief for a creative advertising campaign is the focal point in the process, where the communications strategy is summarized into one, ideally concise, document. The brief is mother to the 'nature' element of the campaign.

The brief is the contract of work that the client wants the agency to fulfil; as such, it is a client document, which should be written by the client and agreed to by the agency. If the agency doesn't agree to it, then they may suggest how it can be changed or modified, or how parts such as the proposition are expressed differently. But, before creative work is begun, it should be agreed to and signed by representatives of the client and the agency. However, too frequently this does not happen.

Many brands routinely brief their agencies over the phone or ask the agency to write their own briefs. Some clients routinely use the agency's creative concepts to research different strategies. When briefs are written by some clients, they can be so poorly written that agencies have to rewrite what they think their clients meant. However, the fault here is with the agency's capitulation as much as it is with the client's failure to build their competence in brief writing. Clearly, it would be a preposterous scenario if I briefed a builder to build me a house and when he asked what kind of house, I respond with, "Just build one and I'll see if I like it." But this is painfully similar to what happens in creative briefings. Yes, the client and agency can and should work together on the strategy; yes, there might be a number of drafts and iterations that might be frustrating to the client, but the client must sign off on their brief before the agency starts any creative work – just like you would agree to an architect's plans before building a house. And the highest stakeholder who will have to approve the final creative work should sign off the client's brief – which is marketing's licence to spend a significant amount of money in the form of agency resources – and which provides an elegant segue into our next subject ...

STAKEHOLDER MANAGEMENT

Although poor stakeholder management is a common complaint for agencies, it is important to register what is at stake for the brand. The decision to proceed with an advertising idea is pivotal in the investment of a huge amount of capital. Not only does it represent the brand's investment in the agency's fees, in the production of the advertising and in the media the brand is buying for the campaign, but it also represents one of the key determinants of the ROI on which the brand's business depends. With this in mind, agencies should not be surprised and should not protest that a whole bunch of senior client people will need to see and buy into an idea.

At the same time as writing this in the brand's defence, the same logic about the magnitude of the brand's investment would also suggest that brands should have clear, formalized and intelligent stakeholder engagement processes from the very start. A simple RACI model should do the trick.[55] Once again, it would be unconscionable to ask a builder to build a house only to tell him afterwards that he has to do it again – at his cost – because your boss wanted a bungalow, not a townhouse.

Marketing must stand firm on this issue, too – if they are given the responsibility for the delivery of a return on marketing investment, they have to have control consistent with that responsibility. At the very least, marketing must know who they need final approval from for a campaign, and have access to them throughout the development process. But problems often occur even within marketing, and this is an area where marketers have to get better.

Too often brand managers and marketing managers brief their agencies; then their agencies produce the work; then the brand managers and marketing managers change it; then they take it to their marketing directors; and the marketing directors change it; and then they take the campaign to their CMO; the CMO then changes it and takes it to the board – who have three more additional changes. Agencies call this 'death by a thousand cuts'. The more elements there are to a campaign and the more levels of hierarchy there are within the brand's organization, the costlier and the more demotivating the process of stakeholder management becomes. Marketers would benefit from applying the principles of the Meikle Matrix internally, too. Importantly, different advertising monkeys respond to stakeholder management differently. Orangutans are usually affable enough and understand the risk aversion of their role; however, the performance of Gorillas and Spider Monkeys will be significantly compromised this way.

CASE STUDY: OGILVY AND IBM

The movement of advertising accounts from one agency to another are both frequent and newsworthy to audiences in the advertising and marketing business, but very rarely are they relevant to a broader audience. When IBM announced it would move its account from more than 40 agencies around the world into one agency, Ogilvy & Mather, it was covered in *The New York Times* on 25 May 1994. Worth between $400 and $500 million, this was a phenomenal win for Ogilvy & Mather.

Ogilvy was, and still is, a formidable organization – one which has been built and designed to handle vast, complex, global pieces of business. But the breadth of IBM's product offerings, multiplied by the volume of marketing materials each product required, multiplied by the number of stakeholder levels each piece of marketing material had to go through, was almost incalculable. The marketing process was grinding to a halt, costing IBM a fortune and driving Ogilvy's people to distraction. Each time marketing material was presented to a client for approval, they would have a point of view about it and change it. The agency would go back to their office, rework their proposal, take it back to the client for approval, then take it to the next level of approval where it would routinely be changed again.

Ogilvy's solution was simple and elegant; IBM and O&M agreed to one rule for the approval process: "You can't say 'no' unless you can say 'yes'." This meant that a marketer could not reject a piece of work or insist on changes to it unless they had the final authority to approve it. It did not render the whole marketing hierarchy redundant: at any stage, more junior marketers could offer advice and give their thoughts on a piece of work, then it would be up to the agency to decide whether to accept the advice and change the work or not.

The result saved countless dollars and headaches.

Brands must bear in mind that the issue of stakeholder management isn't just about the money. When ideas get killed or become so misshapen that they bear no resemblance to the original proposal, it is heartbreaking for the agency people who developed the work. Even the most resilient agency people will lose the will to live if stakeholders are badly managed and their efforts are treated like cannon fodder. Brands like this quickly gain a reputation in an agency and the talent, particularly the creative talent, will try to avoid them.

But brands that manage their stakeholders well attract and inspire the best talent an agency has to offer.

"Any fool can write a bad advertisement, but it takes
a genius to keep his hands off a good one."

David Ogilvy, 1911–1999
Founder, Ogilvy & Mather

USE AND MISUSE OF RESEARCH

This excerpt on the subject of creative research from Luke Sullivan's wonderful book, *Hey, Whipple, Squeeze This*,[56] gives some insight into the impact of run-of-the-mill creative research on the life of an agency's creative director.

"Here's how advertising works. You toil for weeks to come up with a perfect solution to your client's problem. Then your campaign is taken to an anonymous building on the outskirts of town and shown to a focus group – people who've been stopped on the street the previous week, identified as target customers, and paid a small amount of money for their opinion.

After a long day working at their jobs, these tired pedestrians arrive at the research facility and are led into a small room without windows or hope. In this barren, forlorn little box, they are shown your work in its embryonic, half-formed state, while you and the client watch through a two-way mirror.

Here's the amazing part. These people all turn out to be advertising experts with piercing insights on why every ad shown to them should be force-fed into the nearest shredder fast enough to choke the chopping blades."

Sullivan's view is shared by many in agencies' creative departments. Once again, when we consider the scale of investment behind a campaign, it is reasonable to expect that brands will take steps to mitigate the risk of an ineffective campaign, but sometimes brands need to take a leap of faith. The challenge for research is that consumers viewing and judging advertising have two handicaps in addition to Sullivan's observation that they are not experts. The first is that their judgment is limited to their own frame of reference i.e., that of ads that they already know and that they like, what they have experienced. As Bill Bernbach put it:

"There is no such thing as a good or bad ad in isolation.
What is good at one moment is bad at another.
Research can trap you into the past."

Bill Bernbach, 1911–1982
Founder, Doyle Dane Bernbach

The second problem is that research subjects are being asked to think actively about what they consume passively. Their resultant response is best described as a ceremonial display of rationality. Some of the more progressive research companies have recognized that you can't 'logic' consumers into action and developed their methodologies accordingly. The good researchers seek to understand and influence more than test and qualify; they know when good ads should be left alone.

"A few lessons from Elvis, Jacko and Johnny Cash. What's interesting is that Elvis and Michael Jackson, two people both with personal physicians, died so young. In truth, most of the time people are better off being medically left alone, most of the time. Those creating advertising tend to assume that more research, more tissue sessions, more inputs, more opinions will make the outcome better. Yet, as with medicine, beyond a certain level they are more likely to be damaging than beneficial. The result of this tampering is that simplicity gets lost. Clarity gets muddied. Most likely of all, a certain charm gets killed off. For the hardest thing sometimes isn't to do something good. It's to leave well alone. To get it simple and have the courage to keep it simple."[57]

Rory Sutherland
Vice Chairman, Ogilvy London

Classic consumer comments (that are not always appropriately filtered out either by research moderators or the brands commissioning the research) include: "Don't make the consumer look like an idiot," which would have killed Hamlet's famous photo booth ad. Or, "We need to see (or see more of) the product," which would have ruined Sony Bravia's balls ad. Cadbury's gorilla was a research disaster but an advertising phenomenon.

Many qualitative and quantitative research methods are blunt instruments, and not well used as decision-making tools. Depending on the brand's business problem and therefore its risk appetite/aversion, research can be applied differently (see *figure 32*).

"Striving to better, oft we mar what's well."

King Lear, Act I, Scene 4.
William Shakespeare, 1564 – 1616

Advertising ideas can be researched to greater or lesser degrees of scrutiny, or research can be avoided altogether for the right idea. But it is vital for the client and the agency to have agreed in advance what a brand's strategy is for the use of research; this will better motivate the agency and get a better result. Even if the strategy is a massively risk-averse use for research for an Orangutan, it is better to state this first so that the right agency talent will more likely write the most appropriate work sooner. Likewise, agree if you need research to manage internal client stakeholders, and then use it for that purpose – just make sure that the use of research isn't ceremonial, but in support of a solution to the brand's business problem, i.e., to get the advertising monkey it needs.

Onboarding a new agency or simply conducting process-design workshops with an incumbent agency are both opportunities to straighten out all these things and, in so doing, create happier, more motivated, more productive and more efficient ways of working. When two teams of people are working to a deadline and try to resolve their differences at a point of unforeseen conflict, the time pressure is not conducive to good decision-making. Generally, people stop being open minded and become less inclined to accommodate others' interests. The negotiation between them is more often a zero-sum game in favour of the brand – because the client always holds the chequebook.

STAYING CLOSE TO THE CLIENT'S BUSINESS

As my aforementioned friend and colleague, Paul Burns, observed, you can also chart a path of how close a typical creative agency is to its client's business – it probably looks a bit like this (see *figure 35*):

Figure 35

Agency's Knowledge of Client Business

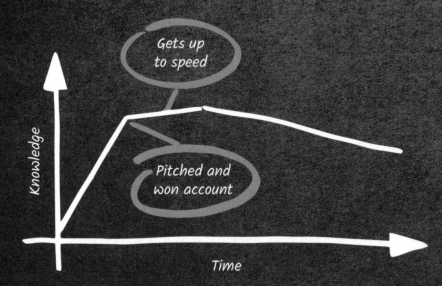

Gets up to speed

Pitched and won account

Knowledge

Time

When briefed for a pitch for a client, there is rarely a stone left unturned by the agency in pursuit of understanding all things related to that brand's business, their market, their consumers, their potential customers and their competitors. But once the account has been won and the agency's time and energy are focused on the delivery of ad campaigns for them, the knowledge starts to fade. Staff on the account change, market conditions change, and the agency's overall knowledge and understanding of their client's business start to ebb.

> *Once an account has been won, the agency's knowledge of the client's business often starts to fade.*

To counter this otherwise common decline in an agency's knowledge of its client's business, a client/agency relationship also benefits from an annual client business review. This is something that I believe should be part of the agency's annual scope of work and willingly paid for by the client. It should comprise a presentation of up to two hours in which the agency presents to the most senior clients an agenda that includes, for each brand that the agency is responsible for:

- Market growth – year-on-year
- Market shares – volume
- Market shares – value
- Competitive analysis – creative and media
- Interpretation of the above and competitive brands' activity
- Category trends
- Cultural/consumer trends that might affect the category
- Presentation of the agency's strategy and creative work since the last review
- Analysis of campaign performance since last review
- Forward planning.

Just as with The Monkey House, this continued focus on the client business helps to ensure that all activity the agency undertakes for the client is consistent with their business needs. Some clients believe that agencies should invest their time in this kind of background contextual work. Again, this demonstrates the sort of attitude that is not conducive to the best client/agency relationships, particularly for Gorillas. Such clients should try explaining to their private healthcare advisor that they won't pay for all their medicals, only the doctor's first examination.

Once the client/agency relationship is either course-corrected or appropriately onboarded, it takes a continued effort and commitment to maintain it. The most effective client/agency relationships are mutually respectful, candid and fair – but planned interventions are needed to keep them that way. One of the challenges of both agency management and senior marketers is to know what's happening on the front line. Many agencies now run a client satisfaction questionnaire that gives them verbatim feedback from their client's front line, but other than a disaster check, this doesn't really provide a useful diagnosis of the relationship. A relationship assessment needs to understand how well the two teams are sticking to their process, but also the relationship needs to be measured in terms of the client/agency behaviour. It ain't only what you do, it's the way that you do it.

People are different and people under pressure are different again – and the way people behave can be just as important as the process they're using when it comes to establishing an effective client/agency team. Throughout my career I have experienced a pretty broad range of client behaviour, from the divine to the downright abusive and even deceitful. Likewise, both from my time in agencies and in my current capacity as a consultant to marketing and agencies, I have seen agency people lie, evade responsibility, and manipulate – and I have witnessed both aggression and passive aggression on both sides. The good news is that these instances are rare; the bad news is that between these extremes there's a continuum of behaviours that need to be managed. Most bad behaviour happens on the front line and with more junior staff – and when they're under pressure.

Threatening to fire the agency is the most common complaint from agencies. Brands get frustrated as agencies resist their client's control and so resort to, "If you won't do what I ask there are plenty of agencies that will" type of behaviour. Similarly, clients will sometimes use another roster agency as a threat, or brief a project to another agency as a warning. The problems with these behaviours are twofold: first, when the brand prevails by using these tactics, it is assuming that it was right in its judgment and that there wasn't a better way – a lack of integrative thinking which is common under pressure. The second is that because the agency capitulates, the brand believes that its behaviour has been an effective tactic and it is therefore encouraged to use it again; the agency is training its client to use bad behaviour. What the brand doesn't see is the damage done to its reputation inside the agency. It doesn't see that its attractiveness as an account has been compromised and that its ability to attract and motivate agency talent has been harmed. A client can have an attractive brand, clear processes, efficient and good stakeholder management and an appetite for innovation but, if its behaviour is bad, talent might actively avoid it nonetheless.

> *Nobody wants to go to work to be abused by his or her client and, after a while, they won't.*

Agencies must be accountable for their behaviour, too. Although most agency people act in a manner consistent with a service industry, occasionally individuals emerge who are capable of appalling behaviour. The most common complaints from their clients involve: not listening, not listening and not listening. When a client isn't being heard by its agency, it's about as frustrating as can be imagined. Not only should agencies make sure they are listening, but they need to be 'actively' listening to their clients to better understand the pressures they might be under.

Brinkmanship is another common complaint about agencies: they take so long that a client has little or no option than to accede to the will of its agency. Such tactics by the agency are likely only ever to be short term because either the client will demand a change of people or a change of agency. It is a complex area here, too. Brands need to be careful, because sometimes things are not what they seem, particularly when it comes to account management. For example, an agency might have a creative department with a disproportionate amount of power, which is dismissive of client comments or concerns over creative work such that it appears that the brand's account director isn't listening, whereas in fact it is the creative director who simply ignores the account director's requests. Now, I have known some crazy client comments and questions over creative work, but any agency worth their salt should be able to calmly respond to every comment or concern rather than ignore them. This is not to say they should accommodate them all; indeed it is the agency's role to speak truth to power when talking to its client – as much as a doctor must tell hard truths to his or her patient. But it should also be able to explain why it either cannot or will not do as it is asked.

For these reasons, performance assessments need to cover both processes and behaviours. An assessment needs to gather inputs from all the brand people involved with the agency and all the agency people involved with the brand, and both parties need to be accountable to each other. Assessments also need to produce action plans, the implementation of which needs to be included as another performance measure. Clients and agencies with rigid beliefs about ways of working need to be consigned to yesteryear. Media, technology and, consequently, consumer behaviour, are all changing so fast, there's no place for stubbornness.

"They ran their heads very hard against wrong ideas, and persisted in trying to fit the circumstances to the ideas instead of trying to extract ideas from the circumstances."

Great Expectations, Chapter 16
Charles Dickens, 1812–1870

WHEN THINGS GO WRONG

The multiplicity of events, materials and people that have to come together to make an ad campaign is mind-boggling, so mistakes are going to happen. But the measure of a person and the measure of an organization can be made by how they manage a mistake. Furthermore, the measure of an effective and productive client/agency relationship is one that manages mistakes well. Some clients are known to be intolerant of any kind of mistake and will even try to ensure that agency people are fired for their mistakes. Agencies rarely capitulate to such demanding clients; at the very most they will remove somebody from an account, unless the error was so egregious that they would have needed to fire them anyway. Such clients are few, thankfully, but they will quickly get the reputation of tyrants and the best agency talent will avoid them.

Errors can be procedural, contractual, large and small. Entire campaigns can fail – even through no fault of their own, but due to an unforeseeable future. For example, publicity stunts and events that would have enjoyed free publicity through news channels may go unnoticed if their launch coincides with a huge and unanticipated news event on the same day (as a common strategy for Spider Monkeys, this is one aspect of their increased risk). They say 'success has many fathers and failure is a bastard', but to keep getting the best from your agency, both clients and agencies need to commiserate their failures the way they celebrate their successes – together, as one team.

> ## Brands and agencies must avoid blame-storming if ads or campaigns fail.

Brands and agencies must avoid blame-storming if ads or campaigns fail. Deal with the mistake first, learn from it and, if appropriate, take measures to avoid it happening again (if that can be done). Yes, there should be accountability for mistakes, but bear in mind whether there was negligence or if it was an accident; was there a material consequence of the mistake in terms of campaign performance or did it just make things harder to fix? And the brand and the agency need to avoid managing one another's people, respect each other's reporting lines and use them.

These things may sound obvious, but I have seen them so many times that it's as well to point them out. Developing ad campaigns is not easy – in fact, it's really, really hard. This difficulty is exacerbated if people are working in a hostile or vulnerable or frightening environment.

> *Better clients get better people, get better relationships, get better work, get greater value.*

SUMMARY

- A key skill for marketers is to allow their agency the freedom and latitude to develop its work to the best of its ability. They improve agency value if they create motivating conditions, brief for outcomes and interfere as little as possible. We call this skill 'negative capability'.
- Outstanding creative work, for Gorillas and Spider Monkeys in particular, needs the unshakeable commitment of the brand to chaperone the creative work through its own stakeholders.
- The client/agency process needs to be clear about where the locus of control is at each stage of a campaign's development. These controls can vary by design to better suit Spider Monkeys, Gorillas and Orangutans.
- The most common procedural failings of brands are in briefing, stakeholder management and the use of creative research. Where brands' processes are poor, there is an impact on agency talent and motivation.
- Qualitative and quantitative research methodologies can be useful, but they can also limit or even damage ROI depending on how they are used. Most quantitative research can more expertly measure the effectiveness of risk-averse creative strategies.

- New client/agency relationships should use onboarding sessions to iron out differences in processes and controls before they arise in practice.
- Annual client business reviews should be prepared by the agency and paid for by the client so that the agency remains as close to the client's business as it was at the time of its pitch.
- The client and the agency need to be held accountable to one another for their behaviour, as well as their adherence to agreed processes.
- In the interest of continuous improvement, both client and agency have to be ready to adapt and change their agreed processes according to the changing media and technology landscapes.
- If things go wrong, stop. Go back to the beginning and ensure that there is alignment behind the business problem, the strategy, the goal and the process. Check that you have the people, the resources and the appropriate controls for each party to produce the best result. Allow each party to manage the performance of its own people.

[52] The most effective that advertising could be according to the ways it had been done to date, obviously not the most effective it could have possibly been done, as Bernbach went on to demonstrate.

[53] Wiley, 1999.

[54] Wiley, 1999.

[55] https://en.wikipedia.org/wiki/Responsibility_assignment_matrix

[56] Wiley, 2015

[57] http://www.campaignlive.co.uk/article/973481/close-up-best-rory-sutherlands-blogs-2009

PART

THREE

INTRODUCTION

Before we look at the implications for change in marketing, procurement and agencies, it's worth stepping back to look at the holistic implications of changing to The Monkey House as an approach to marketing communications. The Monkey House's singular purpose is the creation of greater value for brand advertisers – those companies that invest in marketing communications in one or many forms – whatever their definition of value might be. But corporate cultures differ enormously, as do their performance objectives, and their marketing competence can be anywhere between consumer and marketing centricity in one company and poor marketing literacy in another. Some organizations, though I doubt they are many, will be driven entirely by their profitable delivery of products that need Orangutans. They will not be looking for transformative creative work from the best advertising talent that the world has to offer; this is not a problem, and The Monkey House is there to help them do that. But my suspicion is that most readers will either be looking for a fresh approach to improve their marketing return on investment and want to buy a Gorilla, or they might have a portfolio of brands or businesses with various different problems that need to be solved and they may want to consider The Monkey House as a means of navigating through the differing needs of those brands or businesses.

But the problem is that common marketing and procurement practices are often inappropriate for extracting the value they need from agencies. This is a holistic problem insofar as it implicates changes necessary for marketing, procurement and agencies. The prevalent condition of mistrust and divergent interests between these three was not designed, it emerged over time. As one party has changed its approach, the other two have reacted, and this has happened over and over again until we have reached something described as 'normal'. This means that if one party suddenly changes its approach, the other two won't automatically snap back to match that change and create the missing value all of a sudden. If your existing marketing, procurement and agencies triangle is tied up in the inefficient knots of mistrust, and defensive, protective, aggressive behaviours, it will require a great deal of thought and vision to bring about a high-trust, productive, value-driven triangle.

*"For every complex problem there is an answer
that is clear, simple, and wrong."*

HL Mencken, 1880–1956
American journalist and satirist

The solution to the problem isn't easy; it is likely to require a change of management strategy for the c-suite of the brand's organization. If the brand's leadership of its procurement and marketing functions has hitherto been conscious of the conflicts and compromises their relationship entails, or if the organization cannot recognize its own risk-averse culture to adopt The Monkey House, then there are two possible approaches to persuade them. The first is to tackle the need for change head on, and the second is to apply for licence to demonstrate what might be won by doing things differently. Either way, there's a conversation and agreement to be had at the top.

Then the brand needs to start with a diagnostic exercise of where it is, what it needs from The Monkey House and what it needs to change in each of the three matrices. Part of the assessment may be ensuring that the right people are in place, and part of it will include assessing whether the right agency is in place (but bear in mind your brand and procurement teams may have been indirectly responsible for previous poor performance). Once these are sorted out, you can start the process to implement change.

It is worth remembering here that The Monkey House is still only concerned with 'nurture', i.e., the environment within which the advertising is being created, not the 'nature' of the advertising itself. If your diagnostic exercise has discovered that your nurture has been inappropriate for your brand(s), it would be unsurprising if the nature of your strategy and your creative work had been wrong as well.

Nature and nurture are interdependent. A great product or campaign brief (nature) will surely suffer in a poor nurture environment, and will be more likely to succeed in a good one. Likewise, a poor nurturing environment is less likely to produce the germ of a great idea (nature). But a good nurturing environment is far more likely to produce a good idea and see it through to its greatest potential value contribution.

But to manage just the nurture aspects of The Monkey House, you need to create a logical path for change and create the circumstances required for that change to stick:

- What is the pressure to change? What will happen if you don't?
- What capacity do you need to change? Has your team got it or do you need to build it?
- Share a vision of success. Describe how your new portfolio strategy looks and how The Monkey House works within it.
- Break down the change process into simple and specific measurable steps.
- Identify a sponsor or be the sponsor for the change, the go-to person who will remind the team of their purpose, resolve conflicts fairly and lead in tackling the problems as they inevitably arise.

After much thought and debate, I have concluded that the champions of change must be marketing.

Currently there is little in procurement's interest to change the way they work, and agencies have insufficient power in the buyer/seller relationship. So, the next three chapters are here to offer some thoughts on how to go about achieving the kind of multilateral change you might need in each corner of the triangle, starting with those who need also to be the catalyst.

CHAPTER TEN

IMPLICATIONS FOR MARKETERS

"The secret of change is to focus all your energy not on fighting the old, but on building the new."

Dan Millman
American author and lecturer

THE MARKETING PARADIGM

Many companies continue to try saving their way into growth – driving efficiencies in marketing departments (downsizing) and trying to lower marketing expenditure.

Marketers are being asked to deliver more for less without increasing risk – and it cannot be done.

The pressure to deliver more for less, the denial of the freedom to experiment or to fail, implies a belief that there is an inherent danger in innovation, but without innovation and its implicit risks, growth through Spider Monkeys and Gorillas is impossible.

Instead, marketers and procurement are gravitating to a mean of what they call 'best practice' so the value they seek is eluding them. The corresponding ROI is unremarkable.

Procurement has an increasing influence over marketing investments and expenditure, although marketing is still held singularly accountable for ROI – responsibility without control.

When marketing and procurement believe they have achieved more for less, usually they simply haven't been able to identify the increased risk. Sometimes they get away with it, sometimes they don't.

THE MONKEY HOUSE MARKETING PARADIGM

Marketing has the responsibility to initiate all the changes necessary to adopt The Monkey House and, in so doing, increase the value return they need according to whatever different business needs they might have: Spider Monkeys, Gorillas and/or Orangutans.

Marketing will also initiate the alignment of objectives between marketing, procurement and agencies, so that each party is focused on delivering the same definition of value for the brand.

Marketing will resist the rising influence of procurement and the growing pressure from their boards to deliver more for less. Marketing will accept 'more for less' only with a licence to increase risk – and if the business problem merits it.

Marketing will insist that procurement improve their marketing category knowledge and skills, encouraging their involvement in marketing. This will be as long as:

- Procurement shares marketing KPIs
- Value KPIs are applied to investments (strategy, creative, original execution)
- Savings targets will only be applied to costs where absolute quality measures can be applied and savings do not have a direct or indirect impact on other marketing investments.

Marketing will have sensible conversations about risk with their business leadership for Spider Monkeys and Gorillas, remembering $a \times b = c$ (see *figure 6*, chapter two).

Marketing seems forever under the cosh from their business (which demands a greater ROI) and from procurement (which restricts marketing's efforts by reducing investment and increasingly controlling expenditure). While not everyone will have the very worst of both of these worlds, to some this is a day-to-day reality. Additionally, few marketing departments are growing in headcount, although the workload and the channels that they need to manage are expanding.

The overriding problem is this: there is a finite lifespan to any strategy to improve business performance based on reducing investments and marketing expenditures year after year. Yes, if you're running a business or brand based on Orangutans, you might find the constant push for savings serves you well, but if your business needs a Gorilla, then something has to give.

The implications of adopting The Monkey House for marketers vary enormously. The Monkey House can either fine-tune an already high-performing, well-oiled marketing machine or it can initiate root-and-branch transformation of the marketing function. It varies too, depending on the business problem you have to solve. In any event, of the three corners of the triangle – marketing, procurement and agencies – marketing has the greatest power of all and with that the greatest responsibility to effect change.

> *Marketing has the greatest power of all and with that the greatest responsibility to effect change.*

So, assuming you're ready for the challenge, there are broad implications of what it means to adopt The Monkey House and then there's the approach to managing change itself. The broad implications for actions include:

1) Tackle the conversation about risk and reach an agreement.
   We've examined the nature of risk and investment throughout this book, but now we have to talk about its implications. First, we must remember that risk is relative to perception – the patient perceives risk differently from the surgeon. Second, we need to confront the fact that we cannot improve returns on investment unless we increase investment or increase risk. This is not to say that advertising is the only answer – by no means. You can increase your investment in new product development, you can invest in new markets or a push for improved distribution – but all of these

represent risk, just different kinds of risk. If you want to improve your advertising effectiveness, you need to get an agreement about greater investment or greater control – first for you and then for your agency – that represents risk to your management.

Remember the $a \times b = c$ model, (see *figure 6*, chapter two). Most importantly, play the war games of what your competitors' opportunity would look like if you choose not to lead on all fronts.

"A ship is safe in harbor, but that's not what ships are for."

William GT Shedd, 1820–1894
American theologian

2) Be honest with yourself and others about the opportunity for your brands.

When in consultation with a client once, I was talking to a marketing manager when their marketing planner interrupted to say that their sales of a certain product were down and that they would likely miss their target. "What's the market doing?" I asked innocently. They both laughed out loud. It turned out they hadn't bought market data for a few years and that frankly it didn't matter. This wasn't an amateur organization; it was a national brand with a 10-figure revenue. It was certainly the case that the situation was dire for them but, in these circumstances, we need to be honest with ourselves about the magnitude of the problem by knowing where our starting point is. We have to also be honest with ourselves about the relative importance of our brands and their roles in our businesses. I have met many marketing directors with grand plans and great speeches about the breakthrough work they need, only to discover that it wasn't the case at all. So, we start with the characterization of the business situation:

- Is the market in growth or decline?
- Does the customer base respond to advertising?
- Is our product good enough that we should advertise it?

3) Assess whether you have the right people working on your brand.

Regardless of what your agency tells you, and according to your business problem, what do you think your supplier preference is (see chapter three)? If your behaviours and processes have become entrenched and your reputation well established, it may be difficult to get your agency's talent to think differently about you as a client, although I have both done it and seen it done. Attempting to change your reputation would usually be preferable to running a pitch and starting all over again. Ultimately you must answer: Do you have the right people in the agency? Are they properly motivated? Would you know it if you didn't?

This is the crucial point of the diagnostic. If the answers are no, then it is likely some significant changes will need to be undertaken. If the answer is yes, then the question is whether there is room for improvement with the use of The Monkey House.

Part of the problem here, too, is that you may have never experienced what the most talented agency people can do on your business, so you don't have a comparison by which to judge. But you could do far worse than to strive to be your agency's best, most loved, most treasured, most zealously-defended client if you're in the market for Gorillas. If you're not sure this is the right strategy, ask yourself if you would be happy being the opposite sort of client.

4) Be ready to change your processes if the business problem requires it.

Assuming that wholesale change is the requirement, ask yourself: Am I ready to take that on? Might I need help? Am I ready to buy in the help I need? Have I got the licence, the commitment and the budget to do this properly? This is more than a question of whether or not you have the core skills to effect change management in your department. It is more of a question about whether you have the nerve to make the changes and then stick to them through immediate and inevitable short-term discomfort and until you can assess the outcomes.

"The best people and organizations have the attitude of wisdom:
The courage to act on what they know right now and the humility
to change course when they find better evidence."[58]

Bob Sutton
Professor, Stanford University

5) Challenge procurement and, if necessary, challenge their leadership.
Marketing has the overall responsibility for marketing ROI. It is therefore unconscionable that procurement – a different department with different leadership, objectives and incentives – could have such a great influence over marketing budgeting and expenditure, as to directly impact the value of marketing investment. Procurement, more often than not, has control without responsibility – hence, a lot of the time I spent encouraging the procurement community to think differently fell on deaf ears. In fairness, if I were in procurement, I'm not sure I would voluntarily make myself more accountable for my work. So, it's up to marketing to insist on that change.

It may be that procurement doesn't have a great deal of power over marketing, but if procurement folk are sent in after the fact to get better deals with agencies (as is often the case), they are most likely damaging supplier preference and thereby talent and value.

Familiarize yourself enough with procurement, the models we have explored in this book, its current performance measures and objectives, and directly challenge its people where they are inconsistent with the needs of your brand(s).

6) Take back the budgeting reins.
Over the years, marketing has become too responsive in the way it sets budgets. Instead of making value judgments according to its priorities, marketing enters into a process of arbitration as it tries to allocate budgets to the multiple demands of an increasing agency roster of specialists, additional media channels, media, promotions, etc.

Zero-based budgeting, starting with your marketing activity priorities, is likely to get you a better result than to spread around the budget to do a bit of everything.

"There is nothing quite so useless as doing with great efficiency
something that should not be done at all."

Peter F Drucker, 1909–2005
American management consultant and author

7) Increase your awareness of your agencies' perspective.

You may not get a candid answer from your agency's CEO or their Client Services Director, but you will get a much better idea from the whole agency team that works on your business. There are plenty of relationship management products on the market that are suitable for client/agency relationships. I recommend using a tool that ensures every individual who works on your account has their say and rates you as a client – unsupervised by their colleagues. Use the outputs to inform a process of continuous improvement for your relationship in both the things you do and the behaviours you employ when you do them.

Additionally, you have to be honest about money: Are you efficient with your agency resources? Is your process of remuneration fair and consistent with your business problem and the monkey you need? If not, what will it take to fix it and how will you know you have fixed it?

8) When they get it right, be prepared to bet the farm on the agency's work.

As I have stated before, my broader observation that made me want to write this book is that many brands are acting like they're buying Orangutans when they should be buying Gorillas. It may be that your brand was one of those, but that you have changed your remuneration process, your ways of working and your behaviours. It may be that the agency is now producing better, more innovative, more transformational ideas – but you still have to bring them to life.

Cadbury, Sony, Mars, Sainsbury's, Direct Line – behind every breakthrough campaign that has overdelivered on anticipated ROI and delivered outstanding results there has been marketing leadership that was prepared to stick its neck out.

*"Businesses have to choose between being Ubered or doing
the Ubering – one way or the other, every category
is being transformed somewhere."*

Magnus Djaba
Global President, Saatchi & Saatchi

Growth needs innovation, innovation is uncomfortable and will be resisted, and it therefore needs a champion.

9) Make yourselves accountable for your agency's performance.
Agencies are largely garbage-in, garbage-out businesses. Marketers, therefore, have some responsibility for agency performance. As we have investigated, agencies will respond better to good clients than to bad ones. So, make yourselves accountable for your agency's performance. Make your agency's performance assessment one of your KPIs for a bonus. Then your interests will be aligned.

10) Don't use your agency fees or project fees as a safety valve for your budgeting problems.
Once you have determined the investment you need to make, you have to protect it. Some brands already have a streamed investment system for agency work, such as red, amber and green for different project fees according to the complexity of the brief or the originality of the idea required (new idea versus new execution of the same idea versus adaptation, for example). However, they often end up arguing over whether the investment level is red or amber in order to save some budget. The market conditions, competitive circumstances and your business should dictate what kind of monkey you need and then, consistent with that, you should be making investments in your agency and protecting those investments.

————————

You can't plough a field by turning it over in your mind.

In about 2001 or 2002, I attended a half-day workshop with the senior management of Ogilvy & Mather London. There must have been at least 20 of us. We had a great afternoon, really exploring our boundaries and realizing our potential. By the end of the afternoon, the room – already filled with the highest-paid help in the agency across all departments – was full of people so motivated, so full of self-belief, that they all felt unstoppable. The guy running the course, Andy Middleton, asked us at the end of the day something like:

"Have you had a good afternoon?"
"YEEEES!" came the resounding reply shouted from the lips of every-body present.
"Is there anything you can't do?"
"NOOOO!" we all replied in unison.

Andy paused. Then quietly he asked:

"Then what will you actually do differently tomorrow?"

[Silence]

It took an uncomfortable time for us to think about what we could do with our newfound self-belief and freedom. We were visibly shaken by the question. But once the first ideas started coming, then more and more came. Human beings are creatures of habit, but at some point there is a realization that we have to stop doing what we've always done – if we want something different, then we have to do something different and that means changing ourselves first.

To start you off with your action plan, use the list of conditions for successful change management in the introduction to part three and cre-ate a list from those requirements.

There will be resistance to change – there always is, and it is likely that there will be plenty of it. So, get a sponsor. Either for a specific brand or across the business, find somebody with the authority to let you make the changes you want to make and who will back you up in times of internal conflict.

HOW WILL YOU KNOW IF IT HAS WORKED?

You won't have an alternative history to show you how much better you have done than you would have had you not changed to The Monkey House. But that's the very reason we've ended up in the mess we're in. Those in global organizations have the opportunity to trial new ways of working in one or a few countries, and they can create parallel histories to test new ideas. National brands don't have that luxury.

It might be the case that you're paying your agency well and you're regularly working at your relationship, you've aligned your interests around your business problem and you're taking some responsibility for your agency's performance – but you're still not noticing a difference. Then either you have a different problem to the one you think you have, or your perception in the agency is so deeply entrenched that you need a dramatic intervention to reset the relationship. This may mean that you need a new agency. Or it may mean that the work they're proposing is better than you realize. Because when all parties are acting in their collective interest and in their own best interest, there's nothing left within the brand's control to compromise the results. You simply have to go for it.

"Our doubts are traitors
And make us lose the good we oft might win
For fearing to attempt."

Measure for Measure, Act One, Scene IV
William Shakespeare, 1564–1616

HITTING THE WALL.

If you hit the wall of senior management stubbornness, don't give up, keep at it. First, because persistence can be an effective negotiation strategy, and secondly, because there's more than one way to skin a cat.

If your proposals for change are not being accommodated, go for some smaller wins first. If you're an international brand, can you try a new way in just one country? If you're a national brand, can you test something regionally? What aspects of change and ways of working can you change without permission?

I was once told by an account director who worked on a successful male grooming brand that the multinational company behind it insisted on quantitatively testing all copy before a new campaign could go on air. The marketing director complied with the protocol but, every time the research company came to debrief the marketing team and the agency, instead of making changes to the work according to the research company's recommendations, the marketing director would thank them for their insights and say he'd bear them in mind for the next ad. I don't know whether he did or not, but the ads were all resounding successes and the agency was hugely motivated.

WHAT OF THE 'NATURE'?

For marketers, as for agencies, once you have the right nurture in which to produce your campaigns, you may still have to tackle getting the right nature. It is in the marketing department where these two factors overlap. It is no use getting the licence to implement new processes, new means of remuneration and so on if you still have rules and regulations affecting the nature of what you are doing.

Likewise, there is little point in giving your agency licence to create something new and different for your brand if your senior management kill it at the last minute or impose old rules on new ideas.

"It is not necessary to change. Survival is not mandatory."

W Edwards Deming, 1900–1993
American management consultant

There are plenty of other great works to look to if your business problem is that of a market leader or a challenger brand – indeed, Adam Morgan's *Eating the Big Fish* is an excellent place to start.

Unfortunately, the reality is that the burden of all this change is mostly on marketing. You'll get out only according to what you put in.

There's little more to say but to suggest you write yourself a plan and stick to it. And, as my American grandfather used to say:

"The first step's a bitch ... and always keep your knees bent."

Robert Williams, 1913–1986
Williams Amsterdam Dairy, Schenectady, New York

SUMMARY

- The pressure endured by many marketing departments to deliver more for less is unsustainable in the long run. In particular, brands that need a Gorilla or a Spider Monkey have to be treated appropriately and differently to brands that need an Orangutan.
- Business leadership needs to be challenged by marketing to understand the nature of risk in marketing. There is as great an inherent risk in playing safe as there is in doing things differently if you operate in an actively competitive field.
- The onus is on marketing to initiate, manage and chaperone change to adopt The Monkey House; marketing has the most to gain and the greatest influence.
- Marketing and procurement must work differently together. Marketing must embrace the benefits of the procurement discipline and procurement must recognize most marketing expenditure as investment, not cost, and therefore needs different talents, skills and strategies.
- Marketing must also take the initiative to determine their budgets – their levels of investments – based on the strategic needs of their brands, not media channel wish lists and ceremonial negotiations. Try zero-based budgeting.
- The best agency talent is available to any client if they deliberately change processes, behaviours and remuneration to access it. But this takes unending commitment, humility and a readiness to change.

- Most marketing leaders will need a senior management sponsor to help when they hit bumps along the road to change. Get one, share the vision and commit.
- And don't forget, this is just to prepare the right nurture for great strategies and ideas to flourish – the nature of what marketers and agencies do together must also be ready to innovate.

58 Bob Sutton, "15 Things I believe". http://bobsutton.typepad.com

CHAPTER ELEVEN

IMPLICATIONS FOR PROCUREMENT

"I realized that I was sitting on a rocket with six thousand components,
every one built by the lowest bidder."

John Glenn, (attrib)
Former astronaut and US senator

THE PROCUREMENT PARADIGM

Levels of understanding and sophistication around the procurement of marketing vary hugely from one organization to another, but few integrate the marketing procurement function into marketing very well.

Precedent and management continue to encourage 'cost' savings for marketing expenditure, driving down investment levels and thereby either also driving down return or unwittingly increasing risk. Savings targets and incentives are prioritized over the correct application of buying strategies.

There is little or no accountability in marketing procurement for the effectiveness, suitability or value of the goods and services it procures for marketing.

Marketing is differentiated as a category to varying degrees, largely dependent on the size of the brand's organization: from the sophisticated differentiation of sub-categories of marketing to the bundling of marketing with any number of unrelated buying needs.

THE MONKEY HOUSE PROCUREMENT PARADIGM

Procurement, and the skills, models and processes it has developed as a business function over the years, has an important role in developing effective marketing, but should be properly integrated within marketing departments.

Changes need to be made to some procurement practices and models to ensure that investments are properly differentiated from costs.

Procurement can be incentivized by cost savings in marketing categories only where a Leverage buying strategy is appropriate, such as downstream production, print and promotional goods.[59]

In all investment areas of marketing spend, procurement should be measured by the same key performance indicators as marketing.

Objectivity, rationality and strategy will be valuable qualities procurement will bring into the marketing world. They will ensure that investments are being managed appropriately by marketing and their suppliers and, as necessary, ensure that third parties are being treated fairly or well, consistent with Strategic or Critical buying strategies and other rules of The Monkey House.

My son attends a primary school a couple of miles from Bodicote, the village where we live, so it's not the most convenient. But, since the day my wife and I first met the Head Teacher, Bev Boswell, we were entirely confident that this would be the right place for him.

The school is not in a particularly affluent neighbourhood, and when I asked about the diversity of children in the school, Bev replied:

> "We've got all sorts here; we've got kids with parents who are internet millionaires and kids with dads in prison, but that's life isn't it?"

When Bev accepted the role at the school about two years previously, the school inspectorate, Ofsted, had deemed that the school required immediate improvement – what they call 'special measures'. Bev was told that, all being well, in perhaps two years' time she will have raised standards to such a level that the school would be classified as 'satisfactory', which is the next grade up. This was partly because it takes some time for the current students to turn over so that the attainment of new students will improve results for the school overall to warrant an upgrading. Within six months the school had passed 'satisfactory' and was classified as 'good' – such a quick jump is unheard of.

I sit on the board of governors as vice chairman, so I observe quite closely how the school operates. And I once asked Bev what it was like when she arrived. She replied:

> *"I walked in the door and there were about ten children stood right up close to the wall, facing it, being disciplined. I said, 'THAT'S not happening any more, for starters'."*

What has this story got to do with marketing procurement? Two things. First, change starts at the top, so we will first look at implications for the Chief Procurement Officer (CPO) or the Finance Director (FD), whoever is responsible for the procurement function. The second is the difference between costs and investments. Bear with me …

Schoolchildren withdraw into themselves, experiment less, share less, do less – if they are afraid. That was one of the areas where the school had been going wrong. It wasn't an environment of encouragement, creativity and fun; it was a place of control and constraint with the threat of punishment looming overhead. It's the same with any living thing – shout at a dog and it won't do tricks; encourage it, call to it, offer it a reward and it will. As much as a threatened animal might comply with commands, it will always be looking for a way to escape. The same is true with people, be they marketers or agency staff. In both instances, if you want to get greater value from them, you have to give them some freedom. Freedom to think, freedom to do things differently, freedom to invent – even freedom to fail.

> *Shout at a dog and it won't do tricks; encourage it, call to it, offer it a reward and it will.*

From experience, I can confidently state that there can be more in common between agency people and schoolchildren than agency folk might like to admit. Great creative ideas come from nurture, encouragement, freedom and inspiration. This is what the buyer needs to facilitate. But people don't change that much. So, if your marketing procurement people are unable to make a shift to this kind of nurture when managing agencies, then they ought to stay in other categories.

PROCUREMENT LEADERSHIP

"The test of a first-rate intelligence is the ability to hold two opposed ideas in mind at the same time and still retain the ability to function."

F Scott Fitzgerald, 1896–1940
American novelist

Therein lies the greatest challenge, because the two opposing thoughts for CPOs are:

"Our role is to spend money wisely and to serve our company's financial interests over those of our suppliers," and, "I want my marketing agencies to prosper and consider us their most treasured client."[60] What makes their contradiction slightly less painful is their unifying purpose in the long-term interests of the company. The modi operandi to achieve them are, however, completely different. The challenge for the leadership is one of having the capacity to change oneself. Most of the people I have met in marketing procurement either openly or secretly relish winning the zero-sum game. They enjoy achieving better deals and finding money where it could be 'saved'. It is a big change to transition part of your world into managing investments, i.e., causes for which you want to spend money.

"Most people in marketing procurement have been looking through the wrong end of the telescope since there have been people in marketing procurement. The kind of change that needs to take place is root and branch, but it has to start at the very top."

Gerry Preece
Senior Consultant, External View Consulting and former Global Director of Marketing and Media Procurement, Procter & Gamble

So, if you are a CPO who can make that change and accommodate these completely different supplier philosophies, then great. But if you fear that's not you, then marketing procurement needs a different reporting line. If marketing procurement starts to report through the CMO, then there will probably be a need for some training and education on the way in which procurement – in its revised capacity – will help marketing efforts.

If you're a CEO or an FD and you don't want to make this change, we should perhaps explore why. The most common answer is that business leadership believes they have deliberately constructed a creative tension between marketing and procurement by having things the way they are. Essentially this leaves the fate of company investments in marketing to the winner of a contest of wills, which in my opinion is not a smart way to run a company. The business problem dictates the need for investment or not, creativity or not, innovation or not. This is a far better way to determine what a business should do and how much it should invest than who wins a competition of wills and internal politics between marketing and procurement.

PEOPLE AND BUYING STRATEGIES: MATCHING TALENT TO TASK FOR PROCUREMENT

The quote attributed to John Glenn, above, is a well-worn gag in the procurement community at large. And when I first heard it I thought it was funny, too. Then, for no reason I can think of, I started to think more and more about this quote because it just didn't make sense to me. Then I realized why: the spacecraft's components. If the components were bought from the lowest bidder, then there would have been a series of quality tests on each component first, because Leverage buying requires ensuring quality measures. So, these components would have been variably tested at extreme heat and extreme cold, tested under high pressure and in vacuums, stress tested, hit with rocks, had space dust shot at them at high velocity – and if they passed all these tests then the procurement guy could buy on price.

However, if John Glenn had said (if indeed he said any of these things at all):

> *"I realized that I was sitting on a rocket*
> *DESIGNED by the lowest bidder."*

… then he would have really had cause for concern. Products can be tested; the design is one solution to a problem with unlimited solutions. But my belief is that procurement find this funny because there are so few who actually execute Strategic buying strategies.

Intuitively, it is a fair assumption that 'competitors' and 'collaborators' are two different types of people, suited to different strategies, when it comes to negotiating deals. On the one hand, a competitor will want to make sure that they 'win' or do not 'lose', so that they don't get taken for a ride, cheated, and that everything is fair. On the other hand, a collaborator will be more inclined to make sure that the objective is being met, that the players are all aligned and motivated and that nobody harbours any cynicism about what you are trying to do and how you are trying to do it.

Products and services requiring Strategic buying strategies need to be handled by people who are inclined and able to manage these sorts of deals – collaborators. If marketing procurement is part of the larger portfolio of a category manager, it is essential that the category manager is able to buy strategically. If not, then Strategic buys should be left to marketing and the procurement role limited to Leverage buys.

If marketing represents a category in itself, then consider how the different disciplines and different needs might be grouped most consistently with their appropriate buying strategies, rather than the marketing discipline. In other words, costs such as printed materials, downstream production, promotional goods (all likely Leverage buying strategies) would be handled by one person, and Strategic or Critical buys – such as creative agency services, media planning, upstream production, design, consultancy, research and so on – would be handled by another.

They would have different incentives and different performance measures appropriate to the difference between costs and investments. In many organizations, this may already be the case; if so, then it's only a question of incentivizing and executing the appropriate buying strategy for the brands' business problems.

Strategic buyers need to be savvy collaborators. I add 'savvy' because Strategic buying doesn't mean capitulating to the wants of your agencies. It means having a clear idea about how much you want to invest in a project, what you want the outcomes to be (both tangibly and in terms of a return on investment) and ensuring that those you are investing in are clear and happy with those terms. As ever in the client/agency relationship, with a Strategic buy the client is still in control. Natural-born competitors might find it difficult to negotiate these kinds of deals.

Leverage buying strategies are much better suited to naturally competitive characters; indeed, a Leverage buy is largely the procurement expression of a zero-sum game in favour of the buyer, whereas a Critical buying strategy is a zero-sum game in favour of the seller. From my experience with a broad number of procurement professionals, there are few with the collaborative skills to manage the procurement of agency services; generally, they default to a belief that agencies are ripping them off, and so on. In fairness to them, their point of view is well supported by the profligate behaviours of agencies in the past and is still sometimes supported by agencies in two ways:

- Doing silly deals, accepting contracts for contribution only
- Very occasionally agencies have been known to rip off their clients.

But this has created flawed reasoning in many marketing procurement people I have encountered: "If this ad agency dropped their rates by 50%, then all agencies should be able to drop their rates by 50%." Or even, "If this company was shown to have ripped off its client and this company is an ad agency, then all ad agencies rip off their clients." This backwards logic risks compromising agency value, and thereby ROI.

INCREASING VALUE IN STRATEGIC INVESTMENTS

The analytical skills of the procurement discipline have much that they can bring to marketing. As I mentioned in chapter three, stakeholder management is forever one of the top complaints of agencies, so the introduction of improved processes, discipline and accountability in an area like this means agency effort is spent on the creation and the craft of advertising rather than rounds and rounds of unnecessary amendments. By the same efforts, accounts that are more efficient when clients are more decisive motivate agency staff more and attract better agency talent.

Another area where procurement can be useful is by helping their own agencies to buy better. For example, there is plenty that the procurement discipline could do to assist agencies in the way they buy upstream and downstream production. Once again, if agencies consequently bought upstream production better, it would represent improved value for money, and if they bought downstream production more economically, then the savings could be reinvested in marketing efforts.

When buying Orangutans, procurement will need to consider and decide how the agency can be best incentivized to perform against a business problem that wants to make the maximum profit for the minimum investment. For example, perhaps they should be incentivized according to the brand's gross profit?

Some of these areas will be relatively unchartered by the procurement discipline, so I would urge you to recruit the right people according to these needs. You should give them the right incentives according to the business problems to which they need to contribute solutions, and allow them responsibility and control to aid the marketing effort as best they can.

SUMMARY

- Saving money from an investment is easy, you just choose to invest less. Therefore, procurement leadership has to choose to deal with investments differently, to change their performance measures and be accountable for their role in managing marketing.

- Buying strategies for marketing expenditures with variable returns on their investments must be aligned with the needs of the brand.

- Such a change requires the determination and commitment of the leading stakeholder for procurement – either a CPO or an FD.

- For large advertisers, marketing procurement would benefit from being integrated into marketing departments.

- Procurement has to assume some responsibility for marketing ROI if it is to influence or control marketing investments.

- CPOs in large, marketing-centric organizations may need to be simultaneously holding two conflicting ideas of what procurement is and what it needs to be, and then designing a procurement team to deliver against it.

- Different kinds of procurement talent with different skill sets will be needed for the differing buying strategies of different categories of marketing spend.

- Procurement can bring huge benefits to the marketing function, but for most business problems this will be in different ways than in the past. Stakeholder management, supplier relationship management, sourcing, roster design and much more – all can benefit from the objective and strategic input of the procurement discipline.

[59] Although I have only touched on media, as the biggest area for investment, it is usually the focal point of interest for procurement. Media planning and media buying must be separated in terms of buying strategy. The former solves problems with unlimited possible solutions, and therefore needs a Critical or a Strategic buying strategy. Media buying is essentially subcontracted specialist procurement. The media agency does the leverage buying for the clients.

[60] Again, I am assuming the brand need is a Gorilla here. This statement would vary if the need were for Spider Monkeys and Orangutans: "I want my agency to believe in our business and invest in our mutual success," and "I want my agency to prioritize our business for our size and scale."

CHAPTER TWELVE

IMPLICATIONS FOR AGENCIES

"It is not the most intellectual of the species that survives; it is not the strongest that survives; but the species that survives is the one that is able best to adapt and adjust to the changing environment in which it finds itself."

Charles Darwin, 1809–1882
English naturalist

THE AGENCY PARADIGM

Creative agencies are trapped in the commodity business of selling hours to their clients. Consequently, their opportunities to improve their bottom line are limited to:

- Billing a higher percentage of the hours they actually spend on client business[61]
- Winning more clients
- Increasing the scope of work or range of services they provide to existing clients.

Agencies are being made more accountable for the performance of their advertising, while their clients' investment in agency fees is being reduced and the client's control over the agency and the work they do is also increasing.

Competition for talent that wants to work in the creative industries is becoming tougher due to the growth of new tech and creative unicorn[62] businesses.

Commercial and negotiation skills are highly variable, both in account leadership and agency leadership, as is the financial literacy of many advertising agency leaders.

The explosion of media channels has made account management shift their attention to project management, often at the expense of focus on their clients' business problems.

Few agencies actively manage their client relationships beyond very simple client satisfaction surveys and their client's own efforts at relationship management. These are usually annual agency performance assessments rather than performance or relationship improvement programmes.

Agencies often lack relevant, tangible differentiation in what is otherwise an oversupplied market without that differentiation. Agencies' current differentiation is too focused on 'how' they develop advertising and the advertising they have developed, rather than 'what' they are and the 'talent' they've got to do it.

Millions of pounds in third-party costs and staff hours are wasted by agencies on new business pitches, which are often overdemanding and inefficient with the participating agencies' resources.

THE MONKEY HOUSE AGENCY PARADIGM

Creative agencies will have a portfolio of remuneration methods from their clients based on their clients' variable business needs – the different advertising monkeys they buy.

For Gorillas and Spider Monkeys in particular, agencies will have responsibility for their output and greater control over the investment levels required to produce them. Agencies will not be accountable to their clients for the time or effort they expended.

Agency leadership and account management will become commercially literate and skilled commercial negotiators.

Account management will have to get closer to their clients' businesses through the application of The Monkey House, the business rationale for the resultant campaigns and the delivery of annual client business reviews.

Agencies' improved financial performance will allow them to invest in their businesses and people, and improve their stability, negotiation positions and employer brand strength.

Clients will receive greater value, regardless of the advertising monkey they need, and will stay with their agencies longer.

I decided to write *How to Buy a Gorilla* because I saw an opportunity for brands to improve their business performance and their competitive advantage by deriving greater value from their agencies – not because the agency world needed an advocate to fight for them.

The fact that the methods of working and types of remuneration I recommend – for brands that need Gorillas, in particular – are good for agencies is incidental; they are purely in pursuit of the talent that can deliver the value. I have no particular axe to grind, but having run an agency myself, I know how I have responded to clients' differing practices and I have seen how talent responds. You will have read my arguments about why it is in the brands' interest for their agencies to succeed – to be better employer brands, attracting better talent and delivering greater value. But agencies have been complaining for years about the treatment they receive at the hands of brands and their procurement departments and little has improved – if anything, their circumstances have generally worsened.

Change won't happen overnight. I'm not expecting most brands to suddenly abandon their processes and ways of working and adopt The Monkey House; instead, as you've seen in the preceding two chapters, there is much for them to do, too. And, as the cheque writers, clients will always have the greater degree of control in the client/agency relationship, so wholesale change will rely on the client's initiative. But even small changes in each corner of the marketing, procurement, agency triangle will be an improvement – and in the absence of their clients taking The Monkey House plunge, agencies can make a start on making things better. As I mentioned in the introduction, I have been relying on generalizations here, so some or many of the points discussed will likely not apply to every agency, but many will apply to some agencies and some will apply to many agencies. In any event, I think there is consensus that the way things are currently isn't sustainable – so some kind of change is inevitable.

So, in the absence of a client taking the initiative, if the agency wants to start to improve its relationships with the brand teams it works for, it can start to propose changes that will, one step at a time, make things better.

The first step for agencies is to refocus on the brand's business problem. The negotiation of any procedural or remuneration changes will stem from that based on The Monkey House.

ACCOUNT MANAGEMENT LEADERSHIP

Since the explosion of media channels on and offline, there has been a shift in the strengths of account management's competencies. This ranges from understanding the client's business and their basic marketing processes and strategies, to the management of integrated projects across many more channels and in more formats than ever before. In 2015, a research firm, Hall and Partners, was commissioned by the IPA to assess the state of the client/agency relationship. The report, entitled 'From Mad Men to Sad Men', wasn't flattering of the advertising business per se, but their research of marketers' opinions about how agencies were failing them echoed my instincts: agencies are only driven by creative, can't build business cases, are out of touch with the business problem and are not looking at the big picture.

There was a time when 'excellence' in account management meant that an account director and his brand's marketing director could theoretically swap roles at a moment's notice – except that the account director would struggle with the brand's supply chain and the marketing director would struggle with the account director's creative department – such was the closeness of their relationship. But the number of times I have asked account directors what their brand's market share is or what their client's markets are doing and been met with a shrug of the shoulders is unnerving, to say the least. Not unlike doctors writing prescriptions when they haven't even examined their patients.

But it's not altogether surprising that this is the case. Procurement has squeezed agency revenues through tough negotiations of their resource plans, so something was bound to give. Staying on top of their client's business performance would be in the service-level agreement of most agencies, but it would be the least conspicuous to drop when something has to be sacrificed because resources are scarce – at least at first it might go unnoticed. And it was assumed that the marketer would take on the role of being on top of the business problem. But to adapt and to regain the trust of their clients, agencies will have to relearn these skills in account management and negotiate better to have their clients pay for them.

LEADERSHIP

I think it would be fair to say that there is an alarming lack of financial literacy among account management and agency leadership. Finance and the vulgar issue of money have been left to FDs to sweep up. It is no coincidence then that the more financially literate and proficient agency leaders have enjoyed greater success. The common misquote "if you build it, they will come," from the movie *Field of Dreams,* is considered a business model that largely worked when the convention of paying your agency 15% of media, plus this and plus that, meant it would be hard to fail financially. The concentration on value delivery has frequently been at the expense of profitability – agencies would just make something happen and worry about the reconciliation later. In fairness to agencies, it is a frequent complaint of brands that have agencies that are more commercially astute that they are constantly asking for more money when other things need to be done – agencies are often in between a rock and a hard place.

Today, profitability cannot be taken for granted, and while I agree wholeheartedly that the provision of value is the route to financial success, too few agency leaders understand the basics of business finance. It is not just a legitimate and necessary business interest for an agency to be profitable, but how else can an agency's clients rely on it to be there when they need it? The decisions made by non-financially astute agency leaders have financial implications – it doesn't require a great leap to understand that finance has to be better integrated into the agency process and that has to establish a commercial agenda.

Once the commercial agenda is better established, then responsibility for its wellbeing needs to be cascaded through account management and through the next generation of agency leadership. Likewise, better and timelier internal management information for account leadership is necessary so that commercial challenges can be caught and addressed earlier, rather than the current model of bringing out a begging bowl when an account proves unprofitable on analysis a year later.

Agencies love simplicity in all things and this will need to be compromised, too. Unless agencies are happy to remain in commoditized businesses of providing service hours to their client, then they should encourage a more complex diversity of different remuneration platforms with variable profitability according to their prioritization of clients, the clients' different needs and their choice to invest in them or not – i.e., the consequences of differing buying strategies and remuneration models.

CLIENT SERVICE

Though it is not a universal truth, most accounts in most agencies are not run as single commercial business units. As I mentioned above, poor management information is one of the main reasons for this, but it is also because creative agency account leadership has not been brought up this way. The digital agency world is, by necessity, significantly different; in most digital agencies, account leaders are constantly aware of the resources they're using and the profitability of their accounts. Law firms and other professional services organizations are far better at tracking client performance and profitability, and they tend to give far less away – if anything at all. Agencies tend to strive to please, to the extent that a lot of work is done that was never in the scope of work. This is not to say that all agency people are 'yes men' – far from it, but they usually do want to please their client such that they do a lot of work for nothing. If agencies want to improve their financial performance, they will need to get better at saying 'no' at all levels.

Perhaps controversially, account management's influence over other departments may also need to increase. And if they are to be more responsible for an account's profitability, the resources it needs must still be recorded in order to do that, so management information needs to improve, even if they stop charging by the hour. Creative departments may either need to agree on a specified amount of time they'll spend on briefs, or creative departments will need to be managed as agency overhead and their cost distributed proportionately across all accounts. Resources will need to be consciously allocated according to the nature of the client business problem. The challenge here is to maintain a balance between the autonomy of the creative department to do its best work and the control of account management consistent with the responsibility it has. Agencies with cultures of account management leadership over creative have rarely startled the world with great ideas.

CLIENT SATISFACTION

Most creative agencies use some form of referral rating – an attempted equivalent to The Net Promoter Score (NPS) that was devised by customer loyalty guru Fred Reichheld. The scheme, whereby clients are asked whether they would recommend a product or service to their friends or colleagues, provides a satisfaction number that agencies track over time. It's usually applied by agencies as a disaster check – when they see an account's score start to decline, then they take corrective action. However, the genius behind Reichheld's idea was to incentivize frontline customer service providers to achieve high NPS scores and then roll out the initiatives that achieved those higher scores to the rest of their organization. It's an incentivized process of continuous improvement.

Creative agencies' accounts usually work in silos except when they are reviewed at a department head level and at a senior management level – but those reviewing account performance and client satisfaction often overlook the details of the day-to-day operations. If the account's circumstances are dire, then management will either intervene, change the personnel allocated to it, or both. But there's an opportunity to share better ways of working, principles and features of account service much like universities conduct internal course reviews. Peer-to-peer appraisals in much more detail could be a regular part of how a quality control process could steadily apply the same principles of continuous improvement. Just the knowledge that your peers will be reviewing your work will improve it.

COMMERCIALITY

Echoing account management's need to say 'no' to mounting out-of-scope client requests, client/agency contracts need to be tightened up substantially. Although the UK is far ahead of the US, where there are still some 'all-you-can-eat' agreements, service-level agreements remain pretty vague.

Nonetheless, there is no shortage of clients using creative work to determine their communications strategy and agencies undertaking almost unlimited reworks of creative ideas because of poor client stakeholder management. If clients and agencies nail down their ways of working – and specifically, the number of rounds of amendments, conditions for reworks and so forth – clients will have to be more efficient to adequately manage their own budgets. Such a change is not straightforward; it will require a cultural change in agency account management to enable account managers to say 'no' without harming their client/agency relationships.

Agency asset utilization is another area for improvement. It is worth taking a moment to define the term: the creative advertising business is currently remunerated in more than 90% of instances according to the hours spent on an account; therefore, let's take one agency asset as a person with billable hours from which the agency can derive revenue. An agency pays most billable roles (assets) a flat salary; overtime is mostly unpaid in account management, planning or creative. If an asset is completely utilized, this means they have worked on billable business for an entire working day – billing eight hours would equate to 100% asset utilization. If their working day is longer than the eight hours for which they are paid and the extra hours are also billable, we could describe them as super-utilized – they are deriving revenue for more than the hours for which they are being paid. Many larger accounts' contracts will essentially 'buy' agency people – assets – i.e., they will pay for 100% of an individual's time. When a client does this, it is against the law for the agency to charge that client for any hours in addition to those for which the employee is contracted; i.e., if overtime is free for the agency, then it is free for their client, too.

> *When agency staff is 100% allocated to their clients, highly profitable overtime hours are given away.*

There are very, very few full-time people in revenue-generating roles in agencies who work no more than a 40-hour week. If agencies allocated staff on their accounts to a maximum of say 80% or 90%, it would allow them to charge their additional hours to other accounts. And because their time is billable up to the first 7.5 or 8 hours per day, and this covers their variable cost and their contribution to fixed costs, it means that these additional hours, these overtime hours, are highly profitable. But when staff is 100% allocated to their clients, then these highly profitable overtime hours are given away. When agencies are often failing to re-cover more than 80% of legitimate hours expended on a business, why would they give away the benefits of any super-utilization?

Agencies are as individual as the brands they service, not least by size and scale. While one agency may be of a size where it feels it can dispense with time sheets altogether and concentrate only on total staff costs and overheads versus revenue, others of greater size and complexity may rely on records of hours, so not all of my suggestions will apply.

NEGOTIATION

The high-pressure, fast-paced environment of a creative agency is entirely inconsistent with the kind of environment needed to succeed in commercial negotiations. One of the keys to successful commercial negotiations is preparation, and agencies are, more often than not, woefully unprepared when it comes to negotiating with their clients. Again, the larger, longer-established agencies are far, far better and not remotely gung-ho, but the mid-range of the top 50 creative agencies have little or poor data, little and limited knowledge or use of negotiation strategies, techniques and tactics. Agencies need to invest more time in training and in preparation for negotiation to better protect themselves from making deals they should be rejecting.

After poor preparation, one of the next biggest mistakes is the assumption that the client will be as interested as the agency in agreeing to a win-win deal. I would hope that The Monkey House will help some agencies agree to better deals, because many deals for Gorillas currently have Leverage buying strategies, i.e., a win-lose deal. Most of the time, agencies are simply trying to survive negotiations, particularly when they're negotiating with procurement.

RECONSIDER DIFFERENTIATION

Procurement people are here to stay, and if they can just get their procurement strategies sorted out, so they should. Agencies need to learn to talk procurement's language and understand why procurement might be asking the kind of questions of an agency that they are. A small, recently formed agency – regardless of how brilliant its founder might be – may represent too high a risk for a massive piece of business to be awarded to it – so stop asking. It's entirely reasonable for procurement to want to understand how large its business will be relative to other accounts and relative to the whole agency's revenue so that a) they don't pose a risk to the agency if they move the business, and b) so you don't pose a risk to them by becoming compliant to a brand that represents a vast piece of income. In the selection process, too often agencies believe "it's all about the ads love." It isn't; its about business, too, and sometimes no matter how good your reel is, you're just not the right agency.

When you are the right kind of agency and you want to compete, consider differentiation in terms that connect directly to value creation. Case studies are useful but so is the strength of your employer brand. See *figure 25,* chapter seven and try to see the world from the client's point of view, particularly procurement's.

Of all of these things, refocusing on the business problem throughout the agency is by far the most important. It is a lot easier for a client to trust his or her agency when everything it does is grounded in the solution of their client's business problem, either directly or indirectly. If I had my time again running an agency, every presentation of creative work would require a logical chain of thought:

- What is the client's business problem we're trying to solve?
- What is the role for marketing?
- What is the role for advertising?
- What is the advertising strategy?
- What is the creative idea?
- How will the creative idea contribute to the solution of the business problem?

If you can make this chain of logic lead to the right monkey for the client, why wouldn't they buy?

And of all these areas for agency improvement, I believe differentiation is the most important. If agencies are well differentiated by the things their clients want most, then their ability to strike more equitable deals is vastly improved. Never was there a better example of the cobbler's children syndrome.

SUMMARY

- The benefits an agency might enjoy from The Monkey House are incidental – it is not The Monkey House's purpose to improve agency businesses.
- Many clients will not adopt The Monkey House anyway, so agencies still have to improve their commercial performance, irrespective of whether or not their clients want to improve their remuneration terms.
- Agencies can nonetheless begin a process to change and improve their client relationships by applying the principles of The Monkey House step-by-step and relentlessly focusing their efforts on their clients' business problems.
- Account management leadership needs to refocus on the solution of their client's business problems. Multi-channel fulfilment and reduced resources have likely taken agency eyes off the client's business ball. This is a frequent client complaint, but there's no reason why clients shouldn't be expected to pay for it.
- Agency leadership that is not from a financial background needs to improve financial literacy and commercial acumen. The days of the "build it and they will come" attitude, focusing purely on creative work and pitch conversion, are gone.
- Agency account management, likewise, has to become more commercially savvy and accountable. Negotiation skills need improvement at most levels, consistent with increased commercial accountability.
- Client satisfaction needs to go beyond disaster checking and into active plans for continuous improvement.
- Differentiation is still a woolly area. Agencies can differentiate their value through talent, as well as through the case studies of their advertising success stories. Better employer brand gets better talent gets better work gets better client results.

---

[61] Agencies call the charging of billable hours 'time recovery'; 80% is a 'good' level of recovery, but many agencies only achieve significantly less than this.

[62] Unicorn is a relatively new term: mostly new-tech businesses that are valued in excess of $1 billion.

POSTSCRIPT

For the purposes of introducing The Monkey House in this book, I deliberately limited it to what would be conventionally called above-the-line advertising. The reality is that there are very few agencies now that are engaged in such a limited and specific scope of work any more. The explosion of media channels and 21st century technology mean those agencies' scopes of work are usually as unique as fingerprints.

There is limitless complexity in the differing needs of brands, their circumstances, their competitors, their budgets, their categories, their markets and the mix of communication channels that they might employ. But the answer to dealing with such a level of complexity has been simplification to the point of compromising the fulfilment of brands' needs. The solution to complex problems is not to compromise, it's to strategize.

> *The solution to complex problems is not to compromise, it's to strategize.*

As a set of models and principles – a strategic framework, if you will – The Monkey House is designed to navigate that complexity. It can, however, work for all marketing communications disciplines that solve problems with unlimited solutions – that is their singular uniting feature. You can use The Monkey House for media planning, media buying, PR, direct marketing, digital, social, content development – anything at all. Once you are familiar with the principles and the models, it is almost impossible to imagine how The Monkey House couldn't be better than the old way of doing everything the same way.

The fundamental insight that created The Monkey House and the extensive nature of the solution are intrinsically linked. At the outset, I demonstrated how marketing, procurement and agencies frequently (if not almost always) have at best divergent and at worst mutually exclusive interests, creating a Mexican standoff between the three parties responsible for managing significant investments upon which huge returns rely.

One of these three parties cannot fix this standoff alone (although they can perhaps make gradual unilateral improvements). The problem exists because each party has developed and adapted their processes, behaviours and priorities according to the other two. The only effective way out of a Mexican standoff is multilateral disarmament. The Monkey House is a logical path to that, flipping a negative equilibrium of mistrust between marketing, procurement and agencies into a positive one. Such a change won't necessarily be easy, but the alternative is for brands to rely on fate to deliver them a Gorilla when they need one – and they are too few and far between. I've worked on more than one or two briefs for a Gorilla that turned out to be poor Orangutans, and I've tried to sell more than a couple of Gorillas that never saw the light of day. These were transformative ideas that I remain convinced were right for the brands. In each of these circumstances, a clear, shared understanding of brand's need, priorities and processes would have helped enormously and I genuinely believe that marketers who can spend a little more time on the 'nurture' as well as the 'nature' will reap significant business benefits.

———————

While making an introduction to a discussion panel at the 2011 annual conference of the American Association of Advertising Agencies in Austin, Texas, Brian Perkins, then the Vice President of Corporate Affairs at Johnson & Johnson, said: "I'm a very firm believer in the old adage that clients get the work they deserve."

This maxim was written by David Ogilvy nearly 50 years earlier,[63] around the time of what became the renaissance of advertising, which saw the giants of Madison Avenue transform both the nature of their advertising and the fortunes of many of their clients. Ogilvy also observed: "Some [clients] behave so badly that no agency could produce effective advertising for them."

At the time, most clients invested in their agencies' services similarly in terms of a proportion of their media investment, so both of Ogilvy's observations were based purely on the 'behaviour' of clients. These days, the world of advertising and marketing communications generally is much more complex, and the levels and the means of agency remuneration vary wildly, but because of the way agency talent responds to clients we now know why his famous aphorism has stood the test of time.

Advertising and marketing is an intrinsically human business – not only is the very nature of these businesses about appealing to and persuading people using the most emotive means possible, but also the people who work in these industries. The people who are drawn to marketing and advertising have to be emotional, fallible and persuadable – and more than most, in order to understand the human condition and to do what they do well. So, the way clients and agencies work together needs to reflect that more organic, human nature.

The way relationships between clients and agencies have evolved has forgotten this human aspect to a great degree. Ceremonial rationality and protocols have gradually crept in where there had been a more personal and human balance to the relationships between marketers and their agency people, albeit in a simpler world as it was then.

Procurement departments have become a necessary and valuable addition to this mix, but they need to accept a strategic and cultural adjustment to this more mercurial and unpredictable business world, where you still get what you pay for. But this expression is an aphorism rather than a contract.

There are great products out there, with great brands aching to grow with the optimal application of marketing strategy and investment. The talent that's required in agencies, in marketing departments and in procurement that is capable of achieving these transformations all exist, many of them chomping at the bit for the chance to show what they can do. The barriers to success can be deconstructed and the path to greater success can be charted if, between marketing, procurement and agencies, we can align our interests, trust each other's capabilities and, above all, recognize that there isn't a way of avoiding a degree of risk in any investment. There is perhaps a fine line between bravery and stupidity, but with the right talent this line becomes much clearer.

"The men who are going to be in business tomorrow are the men who understand that the future, as always, belongs to the brave."

Bill Bernbach, 1911–1982
Founder, Doyle Dane Bernbach

---

[63] *Confessions of an Advertising Man*, David Ogilvy, Scriber, New York, 1963

ACKNOWLEDGMENTS

Some business ideas are spontaneous and brilliant, while some ideas have a more complicated birth; suffice to say, *How to Buy a Gorilla* was the latter. It began as a germ of an idea that was nurtured into life over a long period, but I doubt it would have been realized at all without the regular encouragement of Nick Ford, Rory Sutherland and my good friend Antonis Kocheilas, to whom I am indebted for their interest, their intellectual contributions and, not least, their patience. Huge thanks, too, goes to Mark Earls, who encouraged me to rebuild the idea and extend my interest in primates, leading to the adoption of Spider Monkeys and Orangutans (not a sentence I could have foreseen myself writing).

For providing insights into what had before been the entirely opaque world of professional procurement, I have to thank Phil Massey. While I would not profess to be a procurement practitioner, I would not have been able to develop this work without learning some of their language, models and business culture. Staying with procurement, I am grateful, too, to Gerry Preece for his great enthusiasm, contribution and his belief in *How to Buy a Gorilla*.

For their courage to adopt the early form of The Monkey House framework into a pitch process and a training programme, respectively, I have to thank Pete Markey, formerly of the Post Office, and Ian Pearman and Katie Stanley of AMV/BBDO for their faith in me and my ideas.

There is a significant debt of thanks owing to my readers and reviewers who have not already been mentioned: Tom Lewis, Mark Evans, Blair Enns, David Abrahams, Tom Knox, Tim Williams, Graham Kemp, Tim Lindsay, Ron Baker, Scott Knox, Gemma Greaves, Debrah Harding and John Kearon.

Thanks also must go to the following people for their direct and indirect assistance, contributions, interest and general support: Bridget Angear, Heidi Atwar, Jenny Biggam, Malachi Bogdanov, Bev Boswell, Alison Bowditch, Paul Burns, Ronan Cloud, Mark Cooper, Marcus Corah, Adrian Croney, Magnus Djaba, Jamie Elliott, Michael Farmer, Alex Fraser, Helen Foulder, Stewart Fox-Mills, Keith Gulliver, Roger Ingham, Neil Jenner, John Kay, Belinda Kent-Lemon, Tom Kinnaird, Aimee Luther, Janet Markwick, Bob Mason, Craig Mawdsley, Andrew Meikle,

Jokhim Meikle, Andy Middleton, Gabriella Neudecker, Piers Newson-Smith, Steve Pollack, Nicola Sams, Leonid Shutov, Simon Steel, Jonathan Stirling, Luke Sullivan, Katy Talikowska and Russel Wohlwerth. And finally, thanks to Mike Welsford and Rachel Tsai for suggesting I write a book in the first place.

Sadly, I am unable to express my thanks to my late friend, Michael Frankenberg, with whom I had the pleasure to work exploring the qualities of trust in organizations, albeit for a cruelly short time.

Words are inadequate to describe the contribution to this book made by my late father, Robert Burns Meikle. Without a business bone in his body, he tirelessly read, reread and edited early drafts of the manuscript in an effort matched only by his overwhelming enthusiasm for the journey I had undertaken. As he once said to me: "Thank you sometimes doesn't seem enough. That's what you say to somebody who holds the door open for you." He was, and forever will continue to be, an inspiration.

I must, of course, thank my ever-patient wife, Olga, who has bravely tolerated the stresses and strains of being married to a first-time author, probably not an experience many could recommend; and my son Daniel, for his patience as I appeared imprisoned in my study instead of playing with him in the garden.

Lastly, I have to thank Juan Cabral for writing Cadbury's ad and, of course, Phil Rumbol – for knowing how to buy a Gorilla.
(SFX: badum-tish.)

ABOUT THE AUTHOR

David Meikle is a business and marketing consultant, a natural innovator and a problem solver. He has held senior positions at Grey and O&M in London, and was Group Managing Director of Ogilvy Russia. In 2009, David founded the marketing consultancy, Salt, delivering marketing transformation, pitch management, process design and training. David rebranded his business The How to Buy a Gorilla Company after his book in 2017.

David lives in Bodicote in Oxfordshire with his wife, Olga; his son, Daniel; a Russian Welsh terrier, Knopa; a whippet called Molly and a couple of chickens.